PROFESSIONALIZING
LEADERSHIP

OTHER BOOKS BY BARBARA KELLERMAN

Hard Times: Leadership in America (2014)

The End of Leadership (2012)

Leadership: Essential Selections on Power, Authority, and Influence (Editor, 2010)

Followership: How Followers Are Creating Change and Changing Leaders (2008).

Women and Leadership: State of Play and Strategies for Change (Coeditor with Deborah Rhode, 2007)

Bad Leadership: What It Is, Why It Happens, How It Matters (2004)

Reinventing Leadership: Making the Connection between Politics and Business (1999)

The President as World Leader (Coauthor with Ryan Barilleux, 1991)

Leadership and Negotiation in the Middle East (Coeditor with Jeffrey Rubin, 1988)

Political Leadership: A Source Book (Editor, 1986)

Women Leaders in American Politics (Coeditor with James David Barber, 1986)

The Political Presidency: Practice of Leadership (1984)

Leadership: Multidisciplinary Perspectives (Editor, 1984)

All the Presidents Kin: Their Political Roles (1981)

Making Decisions (Coauthor with Percy Hill et al., 1979)

BARBARA KELLERMAN

PROFESSIONALIZING
LEADERSHIP

OXFORD
UNIVERSITY PRESS

OXFORD

UNIVERSITY PRESS

Oxford University Press is a department of the University of Oxford. It furthers
the University's objective of excellence in research, scholarship, and education
by publishing worldwide. Oxford is a registered trade mark of Oxford University
Press in the UK and certain other countries.

Published in the United States of America by Oxford University Press
198 Madison Avenue, New York, NY 10016, United States of America.

CIP data is on file at the Library of Congress
ISBN 978–0–19–069578–1

1 3 5 7 9 8 6 4 2

Printed by Sheridan Books, Inc., United States of America

For Friends

Carol

Dave

David

David

Deborah

Jerry

Rachel

Randy

Susan

Timmie

Todd

Tony

CONTENTS

ACKNOWLEDGMENTS

My thanks to Dana Born, Mary Cheryl Hargrove, and Craig Stack for providing me with material to which I would not otherwise have had access. And to Alex Costa, Catherine Kearns, and Jeanne Marasca for their unflagging support throughout the writing process.

Great gratitude to Eni Dervishi, who is as special as she is smart. And to Rachel Bratt and Deborah Rhode—as splendid colleagues as they are friends.

PROFESSIONALIZING
LEADERSHIP

Introduction

Learning Leading—Lame Undertaking

When *The End of Leadership* was published in 2012, I was almost alone. The leadership industry was already evoking some bitching and moaning, but the objections were minimal. By and large the industry remained unscathed, free from the sorts of criticisms that I had put in the book, which maintained that despite the "now countless leadership centers, institutions, programs, courses, seminars, workshops, experiences, trainers, books, blogs, articles, websites, webinars, videos, conferences, consultants, and coaches claiming to teach people—usually for money—how to lead," there was scant evidence that this enormous investment of time and money had paid off. I went so far as to declare that the leadership industry, over its approximately forty-year history, had failed in any major, meaningful, measurable way to improve the human condition.[1]

Since then, I am no longer so alone. Since then I have been joined by a small but fierce cadre of others who point to the yawning gap between what the leadership industry claims to do, and what it does. A survey by the Center for Creative Leadership indicated that half of all leaders and managers are considered "a disappointment, incompetent, a mis-hire or a complete failure."[2] The Corporate Research Forum (CRF) found that less than one-third of respondents rated "their overall ability to develop leaders as 'good' or 'excellent.'" A 2016 article in the *Harvard Business Review* was titled "Why Leadership Development Isn't Developing Leaders."[3] Only 6 percent of respondents in a study by Deloitte rated their leadership pipeline as "very ready," while McKinsey found that in both the United Kingdom and the United States only a minority of senior managers thought "their companies develop global leaders effectively."[4] And, in a book that aggressively takes on the Harvard Business School—the relevant chapter is titled "Can Leaders Be Manufactured?"—author Duff McDonald writes that while few business school faculty would "summon the courage to admit such a thing," most so-called leadership learning "is bullshit."[5]

Assessments of leaders in the public sector are even worse, certainly in the United States. No surprise by now that Americans' trust in government, especially the federal government, is at or near an all-time low. In 2015 the Pew Research Center found that the American public was "deeply cynical about government, politics and the nation's elected leaders in a way that has become quite familiar." Just 19 percent trust government always or most of the time. Only 20 percent think that leaders are doing a good job of running government programs. And fully 55 percent believe that "ordinary Americans" would do a better job of solving national problems than those formally charged with doing so. Given the numbers of programs now targeted at leaders in the public sector, their abysmally low approval ratings are further reasons to question the efficacy of the leadership industry.[6]

In recent years, some academics have signed on with the skeptics. They constitute only a small minority, but I have been joined in the jaundiced camp by an occasional critical colleague, such as Jeffrey Pfeffer, professor of business at Stanford University. Pulling no punches, and in a book titled *Leadership BS*, no less, he wrote that "the leadership industry has failed."[7] In fact, he went further. He argued that not only does the industry not do much good, it does harm. "It's not just that all the efforts to develop better leaders" have failed "appreciably" to improve leadership, Pfeffer maintained, but sometimes they make "things much worse."[8] Three professors of business at Harvard looked at leadership from a different angle—leadership studies as opposed to leadership development—but their perspective was no more positive. They concluded that "the current state of leadership education lacks the intellectual rigor and institutional structure required to advance the field beyond its present (and precariously) nascent stage."[9]

There are other measures as well—other metrics that support the charge that the leadership industry is falling short in the private and public sectors, and in the nonprofit one as well. They include the high number of bad leaders—however "bad" is defined. The high rate of turnover among leaders. The frequency with which CEOs are being challenged—by boards, by shareholders, especially shareholder activists, and by clients and customers among others, all horning in on their power, authority, and influence. (In 2017, the *Wall Street Journal* described activist investors as an "existential threat" to CEOs.)[10] And, arguably, most important, the high rate of dissatisfaction among followers. "Workplaces are mostly horrible," Pfeffer wrote, with high levels of job dissatisfaction and low levels of employee engagement. "Regardless of the time and money spent on leadership, the situation in workplaces, not just in the United States but around the world is dire, with disengaged, disaffected, and dissatisfied employees everywhere."[11] The public has rendered its verdict as well. Never in American history were the two leading presidential candidates so widely disliked and distrusted as in 2016. In July of that year fully two-thirds of survey respondents disapproved heartily and nearly equally of both Hillary Clinton and Donald Trump.

But, in what would seem something of a paradox, this growing clatter of criticism has done zero to slow industry growth. The numbers are hard to pin down, but some estimates are that globally some $50 billion is being spent annually on leadership education, training, and development.[12] (In 2015 some $356 billion globally was spent on "employee training and education"—though the fraction of that spent on *leadership* training and education is difficult to discern.)[13] Moreover, in spite of the high levels of dissatisfaction, building leadership talent remains a priority not only in the public and nonprofit sectors, but in the private sector as well, where CEOs remain willing to make the investment, notwithstanding their doubts about whether the investment will pay off. A 2014 CRF survey found that 46 percent of organizations planned to spend more on leadership development in the three years subsequent, not less. It's the equivalent of investing in a stock that's no better than a long shot.

So, what's the problem? Why is the payoff so likely to be so meager? Why has the leadership industry failed to deliver on its original high-minded promise? This is not to say, of course, that it never delivers, that the industry as it is currently construed has nothing whatsoever to recommend it. Rather it is to point out how far short it falls of any imagined ideal. Rather it is to say that whatever good it does do, it does not do nearly enough. Rather it is to suggest that in the twenty-first century the need for good leadership, and good followership, is so great that we ought to be doing a better job, a much better job, of developing better leaders, and followers, than we do now.

One of the reasons leadership education, training, and development have stayed stuck is, believe it or not, nomenclature—the word itself, "leadership." The fact is that neither scholars nor practitioners have been able to define it with precision and conciseness, certainly not in a way that is widely agreed on. It's a problem. It correctly suggests that all kinds of processes and persons are labeled leadership (or leader) without any carefully considered notion of what leadership (or a leader) actually is.[14] Social psychologist Bernard Bass, an expert on the subject, once remarked that any two-day conference on leadership begins with one day of argumentation about what "leadership" means.[15] One of his peers, Fred Fiedler, similarly observed that "there are almost as many definitions of leadership as there are leadership theories—and there are almost as many theories of leadership as there are psychologists working in the field."[16]

Here's what I mean. Here are ten different definitions of leadership—a random sample among scores of others: (1) leadership is purposive behavior; (2) leadership is persuasive behavior; (3) leadership is the exercise of power; (4) leadership is the exercise of authority; (5) leadership is the exercise of influence; (6) leadership is the art of inducing compliance; (7) leadership is a process; (8) leadership is a relationship; (9) leadership is an activity; (10) leadership is an attribution.

The different descriptions and definitions—precisely what, by the way, do we mean when we say that a leader has "charisma"?—do not exactly lend themselves to warm, fuzzy feelings of cooperation and collaboration among the disparate and distributed leadership experts. Still, the experts do not, of themselves, constitute the highest hurdle to furthering the field. Rather their differences conceal even deeper cleavages in how we think about leadership—and in how we think about how to teach how to lead. Some examples:

The unsettled question of values. With few exceptions leadership experts assume that leadership is *good.* The adjective goes without saying, which is why teaching leadership and learning leadership implies teaching *good* leadership and learning *good* leadership. The idea that teaching and learning leadership might entail teaching and learning something about bad leadership is, if not inconceivable, then certainly not central.

The unsettled question of who is a leader. For thousands of years, the word "leader" has been associated with position, and mostly it still is. Mostly we still use the word to describe someone who is filling a leadership role, holding a position of authority, even if he or she does not engage in activities, or successfully engage in activities, that reflect leadership work. Increasingly, though, leadership is viewed as being independent of role. Increasingly it is being defined as an activity that anyone from anywhere in the group or organization can undertake, and in which anyone can engage. No position, title, or status required.

The unsettled question of what if any is the difference between a leader and a manager. Historically the words were interchangeable or nearly so. But, more recently, the leader's tasks tend to be regarded as quite different from the manager's, the former more formidable, the latter more pedestrian. Warren Bennis, for instance, maintained that the manager administers, while the leader innovates. That the manager is a copy, while the leader is an original. That the manager relies on control, while the leader inspires trust. You get the idea. Bennis's point was that they are not one and the same, and that being a leader is somehow more demanding or higher a calling than being a manager.[17]

The unsettled question of how to teach how to lead. The leadership industry is built on the (unproven) assumption that leadership can be taught—and that it ought to be taught. The points of contention center on how to teach how to lead or, better, on how best to teach how to lead. The various pedagogical approaches are not necessarily mutually exclusive. In fact, one could argue that though they are wildly disparate, they ought comfortably, even profitably, to coexist. But, generally, they do not. Generally, leadership teaching at one institution bears only incidental resemblance to leadership teaching at another institution. And, generally, leadership teachers are, in effect, independent actors. Because there is no widely agreed-on core curriculum, most teachers teach what they want to teach and how they want to teach it. For instance, some leadership teachers employ a cognitive approach, others focus on experiential learning, and still others emphasize skill development. The point is that there is inadequate research on what works best, inadequate discussion of pedagogical collaboration, and inadequate attention to having a template for learning how to lead. Most of the time leadership teachers simply do their own thing. And, most of the time, because they lack the necessary academic credentials, so-called real-world leaders remain largely an untapped resource.

The unsettled question of who should teach how to lead. Were you taught how to lead by a philosopher or by a psychiatrist? If the first, you had one sort of experience; if the second, you had quite another. Were you taught how to lead by a political scientist or a behavioral psychologist? If the first, you had one sort of experience; if the second, you had quite another. Or, perhaps, you were taught how to lead by someone from outside the academy, by, say, an executive coach, or a community organizer, or a scout leader. These would, of course, have been still other sorts of learning experiences. The question, then, is not only whether some pedagogies are better than others. The question is also, who are the pedagogues and what are their credentials? What expertise or experience certifies them, us, as leadership teachers?

Which raises another point. We can presume that the small minority of those who teach leadership studies, who are, that is, academics, are at least modestly qualified as experts and educators. But many if not most academics have no special experience or expertise that qualifies them to teach *how* to lead—as opposed to teaching *about* leadership. They have been educated and trained in leadership studies, not in leadership development. Moreover, large numbers of those professing to provide leadership education, training, and development are located outside the academy. This means that they are not required to jump through even a single professional hoop. The truth is that anyone can claim to be an expert on leadership, and anyone can claim to know how to teach how to lead. No demonstrable experience required. No demonstrable expertise required. No demonstrable credential required.

The unsettled question of whether leadership should focus exclusively or even primarily on leaders. Again, their numbers are small. But some leadership experts (yes, me among them) would argue that you cannot talk about leaders without simultaneously talking about followers. Most everyone in the leadership field would agree with the proposition that leadership is a relationship. And they would agree that this relationship involves at least two people, one leader and one follower. However, most everyone would not agree with the proposition that this dictates that followers merit our collective attention. For a complex constellation of reasons—money among them (there's money to be made, sometimes big money, claiming to teach how to lead; there's no money to be made, or not much, claiming to teach how to follow)—the field has evolved largely to ignore followership while it obsesses about leadership. Which raises three key questions. First, do those of us who teach leadership theory do our students a favor by favoring leaders over followers? Second, do those of us who teach leadership practice do our students a favor by favoring leaders over followers? And third, does it, for that matter, make sense to teach leadership, or followership, devoid of the contexts within which leaders and followers both, perforce, are located?

The unsettled question of whether leadership matters. Of course, most leadership experts think that leadership matters a great deal—it justifies the importance of what we do. But some leadership experts are more skeptical. They find that leadership matters not so much, or maybe only under certain circumstances, or maybe even not at all. My late colleague Richard Hackman, a psychologist, coined the term "leader attribution error" to point to our proclivity, probably partly hardwired, to attribute to leaders whatever it is that happens. Leaders get credit for outcomes that are good—even when there is no evidence that they are directly responsible. And they get blamed for outcomes that are bad—even when there is no evidence that they are directly responsible. We tend to believe in the importance of leaders not so much because we have proof that leaders are important, but because it makes things simpler. The idea that things happen the way they do because of a small number of leading actors helps us to order a universe that would otherwise seem hopelessly, frighteningly disordered.

Unsettled questions such as these are not trivial. They are significant, serious, and sometimes divisive. Moreover, the fact that they remain unanswered, even, in the main, unaddressed, goes a long way toward explaining why the leadership industry now looks much the way it did at its inception, four decades ago. To be sure, the industry today is much, much larger, and much, much more profitable. But it is not in any obvious way better. It is not more coherent, or more rigorous, or more solid and substantive. More damningly, it is not more productive. It is not, to all appearances, any more proficient at educating, training, or developing leaders than it was when the industry was in its infancy. It is not, in short, more *professional.*

Which brings me to the question that inspired this book: why has the leadership industry failed to progress from being one thing to being something clearly and demonstrably different, something clearly and demonstrably better? The reasons are several—though here I will focus only on one. The one of paramount importance. Leadership remains as it was four decades ago—an *occupation.* Leadership has not become over time even a *vocation,* let alone a *profession.* Leadership has stayed stuck.

An "occupation" is an activity; it is something we do. Sometimes it's work, sometimes it's paid work. A "vocation" in contrast always is work—and always is paid work. A vocation is a trade, or a career, that requires applicable knowledge and skills to be acquired, for example, in a vocational school. A "profession" is work as well, work for which people expect to get paid, and generally do. But professions are different from occupations and vocations in at least two critical ways. First, unlike occupations and vocations, professions involve education and training that are elaborate, extensive, and, usually, of long duration. What exactly this education and training should consist of—is education, for example, years in school? or testable knowledge? or experience of the world?—is open to debate. But the exclusivity associated with professionalism implies, among other things, levels of education and training that are high. Second, unlike occupations and vocations, professions suggest a higher calling. Typically, they connote both a call to service and commitment to a code of ethics, which bestow on the profession, and on the professional, a special status. Occupations such as leadership are, in other words, different from, and lesser than, vocations and professions. Occupations demand no special education or expertise. Occupations demand no demonstrable skill or proof of competence. Occupations demand no commitment to a code of any kind or to a higher calling. You want to be a leader? Say you can lead. Or take a course, or attend a seminar, or sign up for an executive program, or participate in a field experience of some kind, and you too can call yourself a leader.

Some leadership educators teach *about* leadership; most leadership educators teach *how* to lead. The overwhelming majority of leadership educators teach or purport to teach how to exercise leadership. Some teach those who already claim to be leaders how to lead better. Others teach those who do not claim to be leaders how to lead, in effect, from scratch. But by and large leadership education, training, and development remain games for amateurs. They bear no resemblance whatsoever to education, training, and development in areas of professional endeavor, such as medicine and law. Moreover, they bear no resemblance whatsoever even to education, training, and development in areas of vocational endeavor, such as hairdressing and truck driving.

Leadership has no body of knowledge, core curriculum, or skill set considered essential. Leadership has no widely agreed-on metric, no clear criteria for qualification. Leadership has no license or credential or accreditation or certification considered by consensus to be legitimate. Leadership has no professional body or association to oversee the conduct of its members—or to guarantee minimum standards. Leadership receives no attention from federal, state, or local officials who tend otherwise to regulate the different professions *and* the different vocations. Finally, unlike a profession, leadership does not necessarily imply service, nor does it have a code of ethics to ennoble or even enhance the enterprise.

We cannot distinguish those who are qualified to lead from those who are not. We have no widely accepted yardstick to measure performance or widely agreed-on metric of success. Nor are there any criteria for admission into any-thing resembling a professional course of study. Medical and law schools require applicants to proceed through an admissions process. Further, medical and law schools require graduates in some way to have proved their professional prow-ess. But there are no leadership schools that do anything proximate. Arguably business schools are the closest analogues, but teaching people how to lead is an uncertain and inconsistent enterprise that is, in any case, only one area of an otherwise crammed and increasingly curtailed curriculum. Moreover, neither business schools nor any other professional school teaches leadership in a way that meets any reasonable professional standard. Which is one of the reasons why learning to lead seems relatively easy, first because it is relatively easy to get into most leadership courses, seminars, workshops, and so on. And second because when the program of study has been completed, the presumption, by self and others, is that much if not most of what it takes to learn how to lead has been learned. No test passed, or license acquired, or credential required as proof of competence, not to speak of the level of competence that would befit a professional.

Instead, learning to lead has become a metaphor, a semaphore, for every-thing from becoming authentic, to developing self-awareness, to gaining self-confidence, to achieving success, to engaging others, to acquiring a skill, to managing people and managing projects, and to creating change. What it has not become is a purposeful pedagogy of theory and practice. What it has not become is a purposeful pedagogy that is logical, sequential, expansive, extensive, and cumulative. What it has not become is a purposeful pedagogy that ensures a minimum standard of competence, not to speak of excellence. What it has not become is a purposeful pedagogy that inculcates even a modest ethical standard. And what it has not become is a purposeful pedagogy that conveys a level of accomplishment that recognizably is professional.

It's past time to stop turning a blind eye. It's past time to be clear-eyed about a pedagogical problem of considerable consequence. For what we have now is a miserable mix. On the one hand are large numbers, very large numbers, of people of all ages and stations, intoxicated by the idea of learning how to lead. On the other hand is an industry in which teaching people how to lead has been seriously shortchanged, bearing no resemblance whatsoever to teach-ing a profession—or even a vocation. Not everyone who leads wisely and well attended any sort of leadership school or participated in any sort of leadership program. In fact, only a tiny minority of those exercising leadership learn to lead in anything resembling a formal setting. Nor am I suggesting that everyone who wants to lead wisely and well should go to a leadership school, or participate in a leadership program. What I am saying though is this: *that individuals and*

institutions that do invest human and fiscal resources in leadership education, train-
ing, and development should get what they pay for.

This is by no means beyond the realm of the possible. In fact, as we will see in the pages that follow, there was a time when learning how to lead was taken as seriously—no, more seriously—than learning how to do anything else. Which means, of course, that there was a time when teaching how to lead was thought tantamount to teaching the world's most crucial and critical profession. Additionally, there are those who *now* teach leadership on the assumption that it is a profession, and who teach it to persons presumed to be, or to become professionals—professional leaders. More specifically, there is a single American institution, the American military, that gets it right in the here and now—or, at least, as right as it reasonably might, given that leadership is not a widget. It is an endeavor, a deeply human endeavor, that is, however, not immune to being taught, or to being learned, wisely and well.

The book is divided into three parts: "Becoming a Leader," "Being a Leader," and "Becoming a Professional." Part I is about learning how to lead in the past, in the present, and in the future. Part II is about why leadership has stayed stuck— remained an occupation, as opposed to becoming a profession. Additionally, Part II is about how leadership can get unstuck—progress toward professional- ism. Finally, Part III is about changing our conception of what leadership learn- ers should learn, of how leadership learners should learn, and of leadership per se. From regarding it as an occupation to respecting it as a profession. Mostly this book is about meaning-making—about the meaning we do make of leader- ship by treating it so casually and carelessly, like an occupation. And about the meaning we might make of leadership by treating it more soberly and seriously, like a profession.

Professionalizing Leadership looks at a leadership culture that is as widespread as deeply entrenched. It looks at an industry that is enormously profitable but entirely unregulated. It looks at a pedagogical practice that falls stunningly short of any imagined ideal. And it looks at what can be done to bestow on leaders a semblance of the gravitas that we associate with professionals.

PART I

BECOMING A LEADER

1

Past

The peculiarity and alacrity of Donald J. Trump's ascendency to the presidency were singular—if only because he was elected to the nation's highest office without any political, military, or government experience or expertise whatsoever. While many American voters were appalled during the campaign by what they perceived to be his ignorance, impulsiveness, and mendaciousness, the link between these qualities and his inexperience either in government or in the military seemed beside the point. Moreover, many other American voters were undeterred. They voted for Trump as if to be the leader of the United States of America and the so-called free world required no special education, no relevant training, no time on any job that was even vaguely related.

The question this book poses is, how could this have happened? Why do we demand that our doctors and lawyers demonstrably be qualified, and for that matter our hairdressers and truck drivers, but make no similar demand on our leaders? Why do we set standards, in most cases clear standards, of experience and expertise for, say, electricians, but not for leaders? Large swaths of the American electorate think that Donald Trump has debased the presidency and demoralized the country. But the questions I raise are not about any single individual. Rather they are about why we think so little of leadership, why we so demean and diminish it, that we presume people can lead by winging it.

We presume that leadership can be exercised without special preparation. We presume that leadership is an occupation—not a profession or even a vocation. We presume that leaders are born, not made, for if we presumed that leaders were made, we would make them. We would rigorously educate them, rigorously train them, and rigorously develop them. But we do not. We do none of these—at least not as a requirement, a prerequisite for leadership. In fact, some leaders are completely uneducated, untrained, and undeveloped, while others get some education, some training, and some effort at development, but not much. Only a very few American leaders—mainly they are in the military—are the beneficiaries of a pedagogical process that is intentionally professional. The rest are subjected to a pedagogy that is swift and superficial—or to no pedagogy at all. It's a conceit that's peculiarly contemporaneous.

The Distant Past: Government

Teaching leadership—teaching people how to lead—is one of the world's oldest professions. It goes back, all the way back, to early recorded history, when leading was considered a calling for men who were the best, the brightest, and the bravest. Thousands of years ago, master leadership teachers such as Confucius and Plato associated becoming a leader with learning, extensive learning, extended learning, learning not just in childhood and adolescence, but in adulthood. And not just in early adulthood, or during certain periods of adulthood, but throughout adulthood. Learning to lead was presumed to mean learning over a lifetime. It was presumed to be a permanent process or, at least, to last so long as the exercise of leadership was expected.

Then as now master leadership teachers were different one from the other. Then as now there was no shared agreement on what constitutes good governance, or on what leaders should learn. Nevertheless, these early master leadership teachers had certain characteristics in common. First, they shared a deep seriousness of purpose, the belief that leadership was among the most significant and urgent of all human endeavors. Second, they shared the belief, evidenced in their literary legacy, that leadership could be learned. Third, they shared the belief that great men, a select few, mattered most, that a very small minority was destined to lead a very large majority—which did not, however, preclude the presumption that the large majority mattered. Fourth, they shared the belief that humankind was not to be trusted, that mere mortals could not be trusted to lead wisely and well or to resist the various insidious temptations of power and authority. Fifth, they shared the belief that their instruction was consequential. Not only was leading important, but teaching leading was important as well. Finally, they shared a belief in their own capacities as leadership teachers. They believed that first by contemplating, and then by communicating what was right and good and true, they themselves could lead by getting others to lead wisely and well.

The first part of this chapter looks at the distant past: at five master leadership teachers—Lao-tzu, Confucius, Plato, Plutarch, and Machiavelli—who lived in various periods from the sixth century BCE to the sixteenth century and whose work endures. Each left a literary legacy that includes a classic of the leadership literature—a masterwork that is timeless and transcendent, that is great not only in content but in style, as aesthetically pleasing as it is seminal and substantial.

The first is Lao-tzu. While we cannot know for certain even that he existed, he is credited with crafting the two-and-a half-millennia-old *Tao-te-Ching*. Translated as "the way" or "the path and its powers," the *Tao-te-Ching* contains or, better, constitutes the religious and philosophical essence of Taoism. It is, other than the Bible, the most widely translated book ever, interpreted through the ages in different ways, for example, as a work of metaphysics, or as a treatise on ethics, or as an exegesis on the human psyche. More than anything else, in any case, the *Tao* is about good governance: about how to lead in ways that lean toward being tranquil and even passive, which is of course at odds with our contemporaneous bias toward leaders who are visibly productive and evidently active. We in the West expect our leaders to be proactive, not, merely, reactive. We expect our leaders to do something, as opposed to doing nothing. Doing nothing is equated with not leading. One of the complaints about President Barack Obama was that he did not lead actively enough or aggressively enough—that he led "from behind." The *Tao-te-Ching* reflects this different, Eastern as opposed to Western, philosophy of life, philosophy of leadership. One line reads, "Practice not-doing and everything will fall into place." Other lines warn against exercising power and authority full throttle. It is better to give others, followers, credit for what is accomplished. "If you over-esteem great men, people become powerless," is one of the *Tao*'s injunctions. Ergo, if you are a leader, be self-effacing; share power with the people. Similarly, "If you don't assume importance, you can never lose it."

Not everyone is enchanted by the Tao's ambiguity, complexity, abstruseness. As one scholar put it, "The concept of leadership that emerges [from the *Tao*] is quite distinctive, if not unique. It is not simply that there is no ruler, but that ruling is the province of rulers who are not rulers, and that ruling is the activity of ruling by not ruling, administering by not administering, controlling by not controlling. How these paradoxes are resolved leads to different understandings of Daoist society."[1] Still, the occasional maddening contradiction notwithstanding, the *Tao* remains important reading for leaders, if not as a practical manual, then as a philosophical treatise.[2] For the *Tao*'s preoccupation with how to lead is evident in many if not most of the book's eighty-one "chapters." Here are two in full—both of which are intended lessons for the man at the helm.

Chapter Nine
Better stop short than fill to the brim.
Oversharpen the blade, and the edge will soon blunt.
Amass a store of gold and jade, and no one can protect it.
Claim wealth and titles, and disaster will follow.
Retire when the work is done.
This is the way of heaven.

Chapter Sixty-Six
Why is the sea king of a hundred streams?
Because it lies below them.
Therefore it is the king of a hundred streams.

If the sage would guide the people, he must serve with humility.
If he would lead them, he must follow behind.
In this way when the sage rules, the people will not feel oppressed.
When he stands before them, they will not be harmed.
The whole world will support him and will not tire of him.

Because he does not compete,
He does not meet competition.

It has been said that Taoism and Confucianism are the two sides of Chinese religion, which brings us to Confucius, whose literary legacy includes a classic of the leadership literature, the *Analects*. Confucius's impact on Chinese history and culture is impossible to overstate. As scholar Simon Leys wrote in his introduction to the *Analects*, "No book in the entire history of the world has exerted, over a longer period of time, a greater influence on a larger number of people than this slim little volume."[3] However, the *Analects* was not, so far as we know, crafted by Confucius, but rather by his disciples, who, like the disciples of Jesus, took it on themselves to ensure that the master and his teachings endured.

While during his lifetime Confucius was neither widely acknowledged nor appreciated, through the millennia he emerged as perhaps the greatest or at least the most influential leadership teacher ever. That is precisely how he saw himself: as an educator, especially, though not exclusively, as a teacher of leaders. It was, Confucius believed, only through study, study over a lifetime, that his students, whatever their ages or stations, could develop their minds and bodies, their characters and capacities, to lead wisely and well.

Confucius followed his own rule. He spent "a lifetime studying in order to understand the world and to better himself, believing that learning was an ongoing process."[4] Confucius was, then, student and teacher simultaneously—his deepest belief was in the virtues of learning lifelong. The teacher was presumed the sage, older and wiser than his pupil, who, for his part, was presumed to have the capacity to change and grow. In time, over a period of many years, the pupil would mature, become a "gentleman," ethical as well as educated, a paragon of virtue not only in theory but in practice.

Unlike Lao-tzu, who seems elusive, Confucius is grounded. What he believed is clear, neither confusing nor contradictory. His world is methodically as well as hierarchically ordered; his instructions to his followers, that is, to leaders, are direct and specific; and his conception of good governance is well articulated and artfully defended. Occasionally there is ambiguity, for example, on the question of who exactly can become a leader. Sometimes Confucius seems to suggest that leadership is a role reserved for a select, elite few; other times he seems to suggest the contrary, that leadership is a role open to those who develop to deserve it. But, in the main, the lessons of the *Analects* are easy to grasp in theory, which does not, of course, mean that they are easy to put into practice. In fact, his standards were almost impossibly high. "For a leader to hold greater power, he must himself be greater in virtue," Confucius wrote.[5] Moreover, his list of requisite leadership qualities is as long as it is daunting: kindness, benevolence, strength, diligence, reverence, responsiveness, reflectiveness, gentleness, sincerity, faithfulness, flexibility, humility, generosity, courteousness, courageousness—I could go on.[6]

But perhaps Confucius's most enduring leadership legacy is less his general approach than his specific lessons. They are many in number. They are wide-ranging and far-reaching. And they are targeted directly at men who are learning how to lead—or at men who are learning how to lead better than they already do.

> "Lead them by political maneuvers, restrain them with punishments: the people will become cunning and shameless. Lead them by virtue, restrain them with ritual: they will develop a sense of shame and a sense of participation."
>
> Duke Ai asked: "What should I do to win the hearts of the people?" Confucius replied: "Raise the straight and set them above the crooked, and you will win the hearts of the people. If you raise the crooked and set them above the straight, the people will deny you their support."
>
> Lord Ji Kang asked: "What should I do in order to make the people respectful, loyal, and zealous?" The Master said: "Approach them with dignity and they will be respectful. Be yourself a good son and a kind father, and they will be loyal. Raise the good and train the incompetent, and they will be zealous."[7]

Plato's *Republic*, only a few hundred years more recent than Confucius's *Analects*, has been called the "first great work of Western political philosophy." It has also been described as a "timeless philosophical masterpiece" and a "matchless" introduction to the "basic issues that confront human beings as citizens."[8] For our purposes the best way to think about *The Republic* is as a "treatise on education," and the best way to think about the Platonic state is as an "educational enterprise."[9] In other words, like the other philosophers and pedagogues to whom I here refer, Plato believed first in the great importance of leadership, and second in the great importance of educating for leadership. That leadership can be learned is a corollary of this second assumption, though according to Plato it can be learned by only a select few who are taught by a select few.

Plato was an idealist, even a mystic or romantic who, given the exigencies of the human condition, sought to create an ideal state ruled by an ideal leader. This ideal leader is a philosopher-king who is perfect or close to it: a ruler who is also a philosopher, or a philosopher who is also a ruler; the one or the other leading wisely and well in a realm of truth and beauty. However, in the prescription is a contradiction. On the one hand, the philosopher-king represents a nearly unattainable ideal. On the other hand, Plato presumes, even predicts, that, lacking such a leader, that is, under any lesser leader, we are lost. In book 5 of *The Republic*, Plato cautions:

> Unless philosophers become kings in our cities, or unless those who are now kings and rulers become true philosophers, so that political power and philosophic intelligence converge, and unless those lesser natures who run after one without the other are excluded from governing, I believe there can be no end to our troubles . . . in our cities or for all mankind. Only then will our theory of the state spring to life and see the light of day, at least to the degree possible.[10]

Plato was aware of how impossibly lofty was his goal. He was not, nevertheless, deterred from trying, at least in theory, to reach it. This raises the question of how Plato thought leadership ought to be taught to maximize the likelihood of good governance. Above all this was instruction reserved for an elite, for an elite cadre of boys and then an even smaller number of special, selected men, who were to be educated, trained, and developed over a lifetime, beginning at an early age. Primary education was to take place between the ages of one and seven, and secondary education between the ages of seven and twenty. Military training was to start in a young man's late teens. There were gymnastics for the body, music for the soul, and art to enable a man to distinguish between the real and unreal. There was to be harmony in all things, equal cultivation of the mind and body.

In early adulthood, distinctions were to be made between those who were, comparatively, ordinary and those (precious few) who were extraordinary, so extraordinary that they were fit to lead. Passing an examination at twenty and then again at thirty set a man apart, prepared him for the study of philosophy between the ages of thirty and thirty-five, and then later, during the fifteen years subsequent, prepared him for practice, for the exigencies of experience. Once every test had been successfully passed, every hurdle had been successfully surmounted, at about age fifty, a man, a singular man, a philosopher-king, was fit to lead. The philosopher-king was the epitome: "He will have grasped the 'Idea of the Good' and the 'Idea of Justice,'" which explains why Plato thought leadership education, training, and development a public function.[11] It also supports political theorist Nannerl O. Keohane, who pointed out that in book 6 of *The Republic*, Plato suggested that all small tasks should be delegated, while the king should "oversee and guide the work of others, relying on the broad perceptions and understandings that are part of the truly kingly art."[12]

Finally, it should be noted that Plato wrote not only about good leadership, but also about bad leadership. In fact, it could be argued that Plato's "tyrant" was the more fully realized counterpart of his elusive philosopher-king. In contrast to the latter, the former was flesh and blood. He was a figure of the here and now—a constant threat not just from without but from within. Plato recognized that "all of us harbor in ourselves unnecessary pleasures and appetites" and that while some of us manage to tame our wilder selves, others of us do not. Others of us succumb to our "wild and brutish part," so that when we are "released from reason and a sense of shame," we do bad things.

Unlike Plato, Plutarch was grounded, a realist, not a romantic. "My design is not to write histories," Plutarch wrote, "but lives," which he did. He bequeathed to posterity both a literary legacy and a leadership pedagogy—biography. The idea was as old as oral tradition, as storytelling, based on the simple assumption that the lives of great leaders make great stories from which great leadership lessons can be learned. Plutarch's classic, *Lives*, is composed of fifty short studies of Greek and Roman statesmen, soldiers, and orators. They are arranged roughly chronologically, and in pairs, better to compare and to contrast Greeks with Romans. Plutarch plainly was less interested in glorious exploits than in minor moments. In his preface to the life of Alexander, he wrote that it was better to be informed about men's "characters and inclinations than the most famous sieges, the greatest armaments, or the bloodiest battles." Plutarch famously likened himself to a painter of portraits, who was more focused on the features of the face than on the rest of the body, for it is the face "in which character is seen."[13]

"The Comparison of Dion and Brutus" is Plutarch at his best. In the writer's equivalent of a few quick strokes, we learn what we need to know about the two men, and about what Plutarch thought important to the exercise of leadership. Above all, Plutarch illustrates how a certain trait, say strict adherence to a high standard, can result in good leadership; but this same trait can also result in bad leadership. For instance, Dion was fiercely determined and highly principled. But along with these traits went, as happens often in such cases, "something of an unbending character and intolerance of other views, and this was ultimately to prove his downfall."[14] In other words, his rigidity cost him.

> Dion then, as was natural, was obnoxious to these men since he indulged in no pleasure or youthful folly. And so they tried to calumniate him, by actually giving to his virtues plausible names of vices, for instance, they called his dignity haughtiness. . . . For not only to a man

who was young and whose ears had been corrupted by flattery was he an unpleasant and irksome associate, but many also who were intimate with him and who loved the simplicity and nobility of his disposition, were apt to find fault with his manner of intercourse with men, on the ground that he dealt with those who sought his aid more rudely and harshly than was needful in public life.[15]

To us though it is Brutus who is familiar—we known him through Shakespeare, whose Brutus is at the center of *Julius Caesar*. (Shakespeare's Brutus is based on Plutarch's portrayal.) Brutus was in many ways like Dion.[16] Both were of exemplary character, but both were also deeply flawed. Plutarch blamed Brutus, shamed Brutus, for slaying Caesar, his mentor. There was no questioning Brutus's motive, which was good and even "high-minded." He "had no other end or aim, from first to last, save only to restore to the Roman people their ancient government." Still, Plutarch's judgment was, ultimately, harsh. "The greatest thing charged on Brutus is that he, being saved by Caesar's kindness . . . did yet lay violent hands upon his preserver."

Plutarch draws no facile conclusions. On the contrary. His lives of leaders are generally so nuanced and complex as to defy simple categorization or quick criticism. Moreover, they are full of failures and threaded with tragedies. What we have in the end, then, is a series of cautionary tales, tales about leaders and the lives they led that are intended to be instructive. Of course, the degree to which leaders can learn from the lives of others remains even now uncertain.

Plutarch and Machiavelli lived some fifteen hundred years apart. But between the former and the latter was a connection. Their aim was the same: to teach how to lead. Further, like Plutarch, Machiavelli believed that leaders, especially when young and inexperienced, should study the lives of great men to learn from their experience and sometimes to emulate them. For example, from the lives of Moses, Cyrus, Romulus, and Theseus, Machiavelli "drew the insight that leaders are most likely to succeed if they do not have to rely greatly on luck."[17] He was, however, sui generis. Machiavelli's sixteenth-century book *The Prince*, which is first and foremost a single, sweeping leadership lesson, is arguably the greatest single treatise on politics ever written. It is, moreover, one of the classics of world literature, continuing to this day to be read worldwide.

What is it about *The Prince* that explains its global appeal and singular endurance? To this question there are at least three answers. First is its universality, specifically in that Machiavelli was a student of the human condition. He was, if you will, as much psychologist as political scientist. So, for all the contextual differences between the sixteenth and twenty-first centuries, the fact that human nature remains the same precludes *The Prince* from being dated. Second is its specificity. Machiavelli gives advice on how precisely to lead, much of it useful now as it was then. Now as then it is useful to be reminded that a prince (a leader) "may secure himself sufficiently if he avoids being hated or despised and keeps the people satisfied with him." (Easier to do when people are reasonably united, as opposed to badly divided.) Now as then it is useful to be advised that a prince "should always take counsel, but when he wants, not when others want it." And now as then it is useful to be instructed that it is "much safer to be feared than loved, if one has to lack one of the two." The third explanation for *The Prince's* continuing appeal is its pragmatism. By taking a pragmatic approach to the preservation of power, Machiavelli broke with his predecessors. His was not a realm of truth and beauty. His was not a realm of otherworldly virtues. His was not a realm of kindness at all costs. On the contrary, his was a realm of realpolitik, in which power was to be preserved by any means necessary.

This is precisely the point of Machiavelli's primer on how to lead. While ostensibly he wrote for an audience of only one—Lorenzo de Medici, who became Duke of Urbino in 1516—he crafted his text so it was more general than specific. For every prince, every leader, must know how to act, how to control and if necessary coerce those beneath him to preserve his position of power. Machiavelli does not even try to conceal his deviation from what came before. He does not even try to conceal his single-minded focus on power, naked power, which is precisely why his book has been described as "a subversive critique of the accepted wisdom on princely virtues."[18] *The Prince* was, after all, the first of its kind. It was the first major treatise on governance that distanced itself deliberately from the Kingdom of God—and from any other kind of moral code or compass. The prince, the leader, was responsible to himself and to his people. He was not responsible to any higher authority.

The word "Machiavellian" is usually thought pejorative, used to describe someone who is manipulative and deceitful. Moreover, *The Prince* seems "to recommend the most notorious methods and aims that had been associated with tyranny since ancient times: deception, the violation of oaths, the assassination of suspect or inconvenient allies . . . even the quest for 'absolute' power."[19] Nor does a hasty reading of *The Prince* do anything to dispel this perception. In fact, given Machiavelli's bleak view of human nature, an authoritarian or even tyrannical approach to governance might be said to make good sense. Of men (humankind), he wrote:

> They are ungrateful, fickle, pretenders and dissemblers, evaders of danger, eager for gain. . . . And that prince who has founded himself entirely on their words, stripped of other preparation, is ruined. . . . For love is held by a chain of obligation, which, because men are wicked, is broken at every opportunity for their own utility, but fear is held by a dread of punishment that never forsakes you.[20]

But while some parts of *The Prince* recommend the monarch be quick with the back of his hand, others make clear that whatever the pain, it should be dispensed swiftly and efficiently. Why? So that as swiftly and efficiently as possible the prince, the leader, can return to ingratiating himself with his subjects—his followers. Put differently, notwithstanding his reputation for being callous, as much as any other great political theorist Machiavelli advises the leader to take account of his followers. Repeatedly he writes about the need for the prince to be held in high regard by his subjects, lest he be hated or despised. "I say that each prince should desire to be held merciful and not cruel," he writes, countermanding the popular impression. In short, contrary to conventional wisdom, Machiavelli's most important lesson is this: it is better by far to be a leader who is decent than dastardly—not because the prince is expected to be kind out of the kindness of his heart, but because the prince is advised to be kind in his own interest. Over the long term, being "merciful" makes it more likely, not less, that the prince's power will be preserved.

My dwelling briefly on Lao-tzu, Confucius, Plato, Plutarch, and Machiavelli should not be misconstrued: they are not the only ancient leadership teachers worthy of note. There are others, such as, for example, Plato's contemporary, the rhetorician Isocrates. He believed that leaders should be not only great statesmen and philosophers, but also orators. He thought oratorical education essential: it would secure for the city-states of the fourth century BCE "an intelligent and morally enlightened leadership."[21] Another ancient Athenian who wrote extensively about leadership was Xenophon, a general, a historian, and a philosopher. Early in his life he was a disciple of Socrates, which partly explains why later in his life he wrote about how to lead. "A careful reading of Xenophon's works," wrote one expert, points "toward an appreciation of authenticity. . . . Xenophon stressed that acting genuinely and consequentially was essential to outstanding leadership."[22]

Of course, for ancient lessons on how to lead, and for that matter on how to follow, we can also go back to the Old Testament. One student of the Bible goes so far as to maintain that "there is an important leadership lesson in this first tale of human relationships," that "Eve's temptation thwarts God's threat because inspiring, visionary leadership trumps opaque, controlling, and dictatorial management."[23] Another scholar references the New Testament, suggesting that the apostle Paul was an exemplary leader-teacher, a role model. Far from trying to achieve personal or financial gain from, for instance, the Thessalonians, "He became one of them and lavished affectionate care on them. In choosing to lead this way, Paul was following Jesus' command that his followers were not to use a position to lord their authority over others, but rather to serve as he himself came to do."[24] The beatitudes themselves—the blessings put forth by Jesus in the Sermon on the Mount—have been described as "leadership virtues."[25]

Obviously, each of these master leadership teachers was different from the others. Machiavelli promulgated the functionality of duplicity, while Xenophon extolled the virtues of authenticity. Still, as I earlier made clear, they had key characteristics in common. These included *a deep seriousness of pedagogical purpose and the conviction that leadership can be learned, though only after an extended period of education, training, and development.* They also shared the belief that exceptional men mattered most; that the human condition was intermittently if not fundamentally bleak; and that leaders were indivisible from, and dependent on, those they led.

Notwithstanding their understanding that people without power, authority, or influence mattered, it would have been inconceivable to most ancient leadership teachers—men of faith were occasional exceptions—that any but a select few would or could lead. It would have been inconceivable to most that the great unwashed—women and slaves as well as ordinary men—could possibly have a legitimate claim to being agents of change. For it was not until the Enlightenment that fundamental assumptions about leadership and followership were overturned. It was not until the Enlightenment that fundamental assumptions about teaching leading were radically reconceived.

The Recent Past: Government

Beginning in the eighteenth century, leadership pedagogies from the distant past were supplemented or even supplanted by leadership pedagogies from the more recent past. The first major shift was in the public sector—leadership and followership in the body politic. The second major shift was in the private sector—in what by the late nineteenth century was the entirely new and different challenge of leading a large business located in a large organization. In other words, making meaning of leadership education, training, and development changed.

Essentially the old order was one in which a single individual or institution was vested with all the available power and all the available authority. In the West, this individual was likely to be a king or another member of the monarchy; or a pope or another member of the ecclesiastical hierarchy. The institution was likely to be the Crown or, before the Reformation (itself a revolution), the Church. In the distant past, learning to lead meant learning to rule or to govern a collective of some sort, which later typically was a nation state. While there were some exceptions to the general rule, by and large such instruction was, again, only for a select few: for a small or even a very small cadre of men, usually members of an elite, sometimes but by no means always hereditary, who were designated fit for leadership roles. The target audience was so small it sometimes consisted of no more than a single individual—a sage, say, or a philosopher-king, or a prince.

More recently, though, beginning with the Enlightenment, this fundamental assumption was turned on its head. It is not too much to say that if the distant past was the heyday of teaching leadership to the few, the more recent past was the heyday of teaching leadership to the many. One could even argue that it was the heyday of teaching not leadership, but followership. For since the eighteenth century most of the great leadership literature was not about getting leaders, people with power and authority, to create change, but followers, people without power and authority. The idea was, the intention was, to get ordinary people to overturn the existing order, sometimes by any means necessary. Ordinary people were in any case to transition from being passive to being active, to take for themselves what rightfully was theirs—be it liberty or equity, power or property. To reiterate, I am pointing to an entirely new order, one different altogether from the old order. The new order was one in which those who were being ruled, governed, or in any other way led had rights, especially but not exclusively political rights. The new order, moreover, was not fixed. Should leaders in some important ways fail, the led had the right to displace and replace them.

The interesting question is how such a radical change in collective consciousness comes about. What does it take to create a change in which the expectation shifts from power held by the few to power held by, shared by, the many? One explanation is the so-called great-man theory, which refers to someone such as Martin Luther, who in the early sixteenth century dared to challenge the authority of the late medieval Catholic Church. Or someone such as Napoleon, whose Napoleonic Code broke with the past by forbidding privilege based on birth. Another explanation points to a pivotal moment, for example, the signing of the Magna Carta in the thirteenth century, or the American and French Revolutions. And still other explanations claim transformation in consequence of science and industry—the discovery, for example, by Copernicus, that the sun, not the earth, was the center of the solar system; and the invention, for example, by Gutenberg of the printing press. But when I am asked to explain the transition from a world in which leaders had absolute power and authority to one in which they were obliged to share what they had, including power and authority, I point to the life of the mind, to the world of ideas. I argue that the real change agents were philosophers—particularly the great Enlightenment philosophers—who changed forever our conceptions of how leadership and followership should be exercised. Who changed forever our conceptions of power and authority. Who changed forever our conceptions of who had the right to tell whom to do what—to lead.

Of course, even the greatest and most original thinkers—John Locke and Montesquieu, for instance—were situated in a certain context. They worked during a time, they wrote during a time, that was conducive to changing the way people viewed the world in which they lived. In England, constitutional monarchy and parliamentary democracy were in their infancy. And in France, the long-reigning Louis XIV was succeeded to the throne (in 1715) by his five-year-old great-grandson, Louis XV. Not long after was the Industrial Revolution, which, by changing how so many people lived, changed how so many people thought about life. As Adam Smith's classic *Wealth of Nations*, published the year the Declaration of Independence was signed, testified, then as now there was a link between economics and politics, in which the first inevitably impacted the second and vice versa.

So it came to pass that some of the best and brightest who came after Machiavelli, ditched Machiavelli. They transitioned from the idea of a leader as someone who has absolute power and authority to the idea of a leader as someone who does *not* have absolute power and authority. And who, moreover, is morally and legally, even constitutionally, obligated to share power and authority with the led. In other words, the great political philosophers of the Enlightenment transitioned from thinking big thoughts only about leaders to thinking big thoughts, additionally, about followers.

Others have similarly concluded that ideas are, or they can be, all-important, that ideas are the most powerful agents of change. In her remarkable trilogy, the last volume of which is aptly titled *Bourgeois Equality: How Ideas, Not Capital or Institutions, Enriched the World*, economist Deirdre McClosky similarly explains economic enrichment. She writes, "The original and sustaining causes of the modern world . . . were ethical, not material. They were the widening adoption of two mere ideas, the new and liberal economic idea of liberty for ordinary people and the new and democratic social idea of dignity for them. . . . The double ideas of liberty and dignity . . . mattered as causes of the Great Enrichment more than any fresh material incentives, real or fancied."[26]

McClosky's observation—that we in the West came to be persuaded that ordinary people (followers) ought to have, were entitled to have, liberty and dignity—returns us to leadership education, training, and development. I earlier observed that the word "leadership" has been beset by, beleaguered by, many, many different definitions.[27] The disadvantage of this mayhem is confusion. The advantage of this mayhem is autonomy. Every student of leadership and, for that matter, everyone else is free to define "leadership" as he or she sees fit. So, while before the Enlightenment being a leader was virtually always associated with being in a position of authority, after the Enlightenment things changed. After the Enlightenment leadership was divorced, not always but sometimes, from position, from status. After the Enlightenment, it was possible to be an agent of change absent position, absent status, absent any of the resources that even now we tend to associate with being a leader.

Being a leadership teacher in the recent past did not, therefore, necessarily imply what it did in the distant past, that is, teaching leadership only to a precious few. To the contrary. After the Enlightenment teaching leading sometimes implied, often implied, teaching leading to the many, to "ordinary people," McClosky calls them, so that they too could become, would become agents of change. Of course, one could claim that this was not teaching leadership at all, it was teaching followership. Suffice to say here, without getting terminologically and terminally entangled, that during and after the Enlightenment, ideas about who should be taught to exercise power and influence changed radically. Never again was it assumed that creating change was the sole purview and privilege of the high and mighty.

Consider these three master leadership teachers—each associated with the Enlightenment. First, John Locke. Locke shaped the thinking of the American revolutionists, notably of the Founders, as much as any other single individual. How did he, an Englishman who lived and wrote largely in the late seventeenth century, have such a significant impact on men of the late eighteenth century, on the men of the American rebellion? How did he teach how to create change? He did so as did several of the other greatest leadership teachers ever: by putting pen to paper, by penning a classic of the leadership literature, *Second Treatise of Government*. Locke provided the ideological and intellectual foundation for founding a democracy in which, for example, property could be privately held not just by a privileged few but by the ordinary many. ("The labour of his body, and the work of his hands, we may say, are properly his.") At least as importantly, he along with Montesquieu broke with the idea that state power, government power, should be centralized in an executive, in a single leader. Instead they maintained that power should be distributed. Locke held not only that ultimate power resided in the legislature (as opposed to the executive), a legislature that represented ordinary people, but further that it served at the will of, the pleasure of, the "community."

> There can be but one supreme power, which is the legislative, to which all the rest are and must be subordinate, yet . . . there remains still in the people a supreme power to remove or alter the legislative, when they find the legislative act contrary to the trust reposed in them. . . .Thus the community perpetually retains a supreme power of saving themselves from the attempts and designs of any body, even of their legislators. . . . Thus the community may be said in this respect to be always the supreme power.[28]

Think of Locke as opposed to Machiavelli. The latter taught that the leader (the prince) should do whatever was necessary to preserve his power. The former taught that the community, the people, should do whatever they must to assert their rights. Locke wrote that absolute, arbitrary power is one that "neither nature gives, for it has made no such distinction between one man and another." With a single stroke of his pen, then, Locke distinguished himself, divorced himself, from great his predecessor Machiavelli. Locke asserted that absolute power is, or should be, a fiction, that no single man, no matter his station, is superior to any other, and that no legislation can undo nature's intention.

Our second master teacher on leadership was Mary Wollstonecraft. Wollstonecraft was a teacher of a different sort, because her students were of a different sort. They were women. Again, Wollstonecraft was not a leadership teacher as we now conceive of the term. But if you assume, as I do, certainly for the purposes of this discussion, that being a leader and being an agent of change are one and the same, then she did indeed teach how to lead. She taught those without power, authority, or, usually, even influence, women, to think differently, to think of themselves as independent agents who had the capacity to disrupt. Is this teaching how to lead? Or is it teaching how to follow? No matter, for the point I am making is that teaching how to think differently is teaching how to do differently.

Wollstonecraft did what two centuries later, in the 1970s, was called "consciousness raising." She, like Locke, used her pen to send a message, in this case to women "whose minds [were] not in a healthy state." And she, like Locke, was a product of her time, now the height of the Enlightenment, when power was starting in obvious ways to devolve from those at the top toward those in the middle and even at the bottom. Not by chance was her *A Vindication of the Rights of Woman* published in 1792—the year during which the French National Convention abolished the monarchy, Thomas Paine wrote *The Rights of Man*, and there was a vigorous campaign for the abolition of slavery, at least in Britain.

To appreciate the degree of her daring, we must go back to when and where Wollstonecraft was born, in mid-eighteenth-century England. It was a world in which, if you happened to be a woman who was married, your property and your children belonged rightfully, legally, to your husband. Divorce was impossible and marital rape was legal.[29] Wollstonecraft, then, used *A Vindication of the Rights of Woman* to agitate and educate, to exhort women especially, in language as sardonic as sympathetic, to become change agents by changing themselves.

> My own sex, I hope will excuse me, if I treat them like rational creatures, instead of flattering their fascinating graces, and viewing them as if they were in a state of perpetual childhood, unable to stand alone. I earnestly wish to point out in what true dignity and human happiness consists—I wish to persuade women to endeavor to acquire strength, both of mind and body.[30]

If Wollstonecraft was an educator, then her contemporary, Thomas Paine, was an agitator. Paine is the third of the three leading lights of the Enlightenment on which I draw to make my point. Locke taught how to think and do differently regarding power and authority generally. Wollstonecraft taught how to think and do differently regarding power and authority if you were a woman or were considering women's rights. And Paine taught how to think and do differently regarding power and authority if revolution against the existing order was in order. In his fabled pamphlet *Common Sense* (1776), considered by many experts to be the match that lit the American Revolution, Paine's intention was to inflame, to rouse his readers to rage so they would act in their own interest, fight to secure for themselves freedom from tyranny—freedom from England.

Again, the question is whether Paine was a leadership teacher. Did he teach how to lead, or how to follow? The answer depends, again, on definitions, on how "leader" is defined and on how "follower." As I use the word "follower," it does not, at least not necessarily, connote passivity or submissiveness. On the contrary, followers can be active; they can be the ones to decide on and then determine a given outcome. What we can say in any case is this: after the Enlightenment, the line between the two, between being a leader and being a follower, became fungible. Paine incited people without power and authority, colonists who by then were anyway primed, to further indignation. And by inciting further indignation, by whipping up the passions of the people, he incited action. He incited ordinary Americans to shift from rebellion to revolution—to flat out revolt against the king of Great Britain, George III. One might reasonably say, then, that Paine taught how to lead by teaching those without power that, under certain circumstances, they could take power and hold power. They could become agents of change.

Paine made it difficult for anyone even somewhat disposed to refute or resist his argument. He used *Common Sense* to depict the mother country not as a mother, but as a "monster." He used his pen to turn previously passive subjects into revolutionists—men and women hell bent on tearing down the old and building something new.

> But Britain is the parent country, say some. Then the more shame on her conduct. Even brutes do not devour their young, nor savages make war upon their families. . . . Hither have they fled, not from the tender embraces of the mother, but from the cruelty of the monster; and it is so far true of England, that the same tyranny which drove the first emigrants from home, pursues their descendants still.[31]

America's revolutionary genesis had an impact that was pervasive and permanent. Not only did it shape American attitudes toward leadership and followership, but, in time, attitudes toward leadership and followership in the rest of the world.[32] Once democratic theory became entrenched and even enshrined in some semblance of democratic practice, conceptions of who was a leader and who was a follower changed forever—which explains why our ideas on what it means to teach to lead changed over time as well.

Think of the shift from autocracy to democracy as a shift to a measure of equity—between leaders on the one hand and followers on the other. This is not to say that no longer was there inequity—hardly. Nor is it to say that no longer were there any obvious leaders or any obvious followers. Rather it is to indicate that in democratic theory, at least, leaders and followers came to have something resembling moral equivalence. Of course, democratic theory has never been never fully realized in democratic practice. Nevertheless, since the Enlightenment, it has had an impact not only on what we think but on how we democrats behave.

Political scientist Samuel Huntington coined the term "American creed," by which he meant that since the beginning of the Republic Americans have always held views that are antipower, antiauthority, and antigovernment.[33] In time, such "anti" attitudes came to be characteristic not only of American political thought, but, during the nineteenth and twentieth centuries, of Western political thought more generally. The establishment was ultimately upended across Europe, as it had been earlier in the United States and France. Specifically, the fortunes of those previously without even a smidgeon of power, authority, or influence began slowly but certainly to improve. Slavery and serfdom were abolished everywhere in Europe and America; women came gradually to gain some rights; and while the workers of the world never did do what Karl Marx and Friedrich Engels had urged them to do, to unite, they did in time find their collective voice and they did in time flex their collective muscle. In the twentieth century, the trend toward equity continued and it spread, notably to Asia and Africa, where colonialism eventually was out and independence eventually was in.

Which again raises the question: how did such radical change come about? To this question there is, as we have seen, more than one answer. Here I will single out two. First and foremost, again, were changes in how people thought—especially the shift from autocratic theory (Machiavelli) to democratic theory (Locke). Second were changes in communications. In the distant past, ideas that were new and different could be transmitted only by a select few to a select few. But in the more recent past literacy became more widespread and, after the invention of the printing press and, later, the telegraph and telephone, ideas that were new and different could be communicated *by* the relatively many *to* the relatively many. In other words, by the time Western political thought was tantamount to democratic thought, the dream of democracy and everything that it implied, including liberty and equality, was a dream that large numbers of people could come gradually to share.

What I argue, then, is that the greatest leadership teachers of the nineteenth and twentieth centuries taught not *leaders* as conventionally defined, but *followers* as conventionally defined. They were hell-bent on teaching people without status, or station, or sources of power to seize power by taking matters into their own hands. In other words, teaching leading changed. It went from being one thing to being another. It went from being a pedagogy primarily for the few with power and authority, to being a pedagogy primarily for the many without.

If the seeds were planted by the likes of Locke, Wollstonecraft, and Paine, the rows were hoed by the likes of Elizabeth Cady Stanton, Mahatma Gandhi, Betty Friedan, Martin Luther King Jr., and Nelson Mandela. For example, men such as Mahatma Gandhi, Martin Luther King Jr., and Nelson Mandela were great leaders. But they were also great leadership *teachers* who taught by their deeds as well as by their words. They preached to the literally and figuratively disenfranchised to motivate them, provoke them, and incite them to liberate themselves.

Gandhi's mission in life was to liberate India from Britain's colonial rule. Having concluded that to achieve Indian independence he would have to mobilize the powerless many against the powerful few, he developed a system of principles and practices known as *satyagraha*. Satyagraha was, is, primarily a political strategy available to anyone anywhere, with power or without. It was conceived to ameliorate conflict through conciliation—conciliation brought about by nonviolent resistance exercised by the many without power and privilege against the few with. Satyagraha is, in other words, a strategy devised for followers to employ against leaders. Force in a conventional sense is eschewed—instead large numbers of people engage in nonviolent resistance or civil disobedience. "*Satyagraha*," Gandhi wrote, "is not a physical force. A *satyagrahi* does not inflict pain on the adversary; he does not seek his destruction. . . . In the use of *satyagraha*, there is no ill-will whatsoever. *Satyagraha* is pure soul-force."[34]

The Reverend Martin Luther King Jr. was inspired by the Bible: his vision of racial justice was grounded in his Judeo-Christian heritage, and his notion of "creative suffering" was inspired by the suffering of Jesus. But he was also moved, deeply moved, by Gandhi. Like Gandhi, King came to advocate nonviolent resistance or civil disobedience to provide his followers—primarily but not exclusively African Americans—with a strategy for creating change without doing themselves in. During the heyday of the civil rights movement, King was known, therefore, not as a radical but as a moderate. Nevertheless, his words—his writing and his rhetoric—reveal a proclivity to straddle the line between reason and rage. In "Letter from Birmingham Jail" (1963), for instance, he wrote on the one hand that "the dark clouds of racial prejudice will soon pass away and the deep fog of misunderstanding will be lifted from our fear-drenched communities." But he wrote on the other hand that "we know through painful experience that freedom is never voluntarily given by the oppressor; it must be demanded by the oppressed." King was in any case like his hero, Gandhi, in that he was, above all, a leadership teacher, a leadership preacher-teacher of a certain kind, an instructor on the creation of change. King instructed on leadership theory by arguing that the time to demand change was now, not later. And he instructed on leadership practice by arguing for a strategy more constructive than destructive, civil disobedience.

Mandela is a somewhat similar case in point, though at a critical juncture he ditched the nonviolent theory and practice of his young adulthood and replaced it with the violent theory and practice of his middle adulthood. Only toward the end of his life, after his release from prison, where he had served out a sentence of more than twenty-seven years, did he revert again to teaching, preaching, conciliation. Like Gandhi and King, Mandela had a mission, a passion for teaching how to lead, that is, for teaching how to create change. He, like they, taught the powerless how to empower themselves, first by thinking differently, then by acting differently. And he, like they, taught the apparently weak majority to take on the apparently strong minority by taking matters into their own hands. Before he was sent away to jail in 1964, Mandela was given a chance to speak to a South African court, which he did at length. He chose the occasion to teach what was arguably his most important leadership lesson: that sometimes, to bring about change, blood had to be shed. "We felt that without violence there would be no way open to the African people to succeed in their struggle against the principle of white supremacy. All lawful modes of expressing opposition to this principle had been closed by legislation and we were placed in a position in which we had either to accept a permanent state of inferiority, or to defy the Government. We chose to defy the law."[35]

The Recent Past: Business

The American rights revolutions of the late 1960s and early 1970s were the twentieth-century capstone of the changes to which I just alluded—changes in the relationship between leaders and led in the public sector. Of course, this relationship continues to evolve even now. Changing cultures and technologies perpetuate the historical trajectory, in which power devolves from the top down. But it is also true that the events of the 1960s and 1970s, including three tragic assassinations and several failed presidencies, affected our conception of good governance, first in the United States and then elsewhere in the world as well. Individuals and groups heretofore at the margins, heretofore without power, authority, or even influence, experienced, as I previously wrote, "a new sense of entitlement from which nearly no one was exempt: not women or African Americas, or the sick or mentally or physically impaired, not gays or lesbians or, later, transgendered, not the young or the old, not even animals."[36]

But as times changed, our ideas about teaching leading changed in more ways than one. In fact, to understand the explosive growth of the leadership industry specifically, beginning in the 1980s, it is essential to understand the explosive growth of industry generally, beginning in the 1880s. As small and medium-sized businesses grew into larger and then still larger organizations, new and different questions were being raised about how to lead in this new and different context—about how to lead in business, especially big business. Slowly but certainly America's burgeoning business elite came to conclude that new skills were called for, skills that would equip a select group of men to exercise leadership in corporate America. Hence was born the idea of management as a profession. (The word "leader" came into fashion only later. For most of the twentieth century the words "manager" and "executive" were used.)

Harvard Business School professor Rakesh Khurana wrote a very good book that chronicles how American business schools were established precisely for the purposes of professionalizing management.[37] The idea was that managers could and should be taught to become professionals, just as doctors and lawyers were taught to become professionals. Of course, unlike medicine and law, the idea of management was new, as was the idea that it could become a profession, as was the idea that it, management, could be taught in a school of business. Khurana writes that in the early twentieth century managers "faced certain challenges pertaining to the nascent state of their occupation," such as the difficulty of explaining to the public what exactly it was that they did, and the uncertain market for their services.[38] Precisely because of problems like these, those with an interest in establishing management first as an occupation, and then as a profession, sought legitimacy in the university.

In 1881, with a gift from industrialist Joseph Wharton, the University of Pennsylvania established the first "university-based school of business in America." Not long after, in 1900, the Tuck School of Administration and Finance was founded at Dartmouth College, and not long after that, in 1908, Harvard launched its business school. All three institutions shared a single purpose: to foster and facilitate a shift from teaching management by apprenticeship to teaching management in an academic environment "more amenable to the modern age." Their goal was to develop in "young men the specialized knowledge, intellectual breadth, and solid personal character that modern enterprise required of its leaders."[39]

This mission—to educate "young men" to be leaders (or managers)—was based obviously on the assumption that such an education was possible. In fact, once the university became the repository for business education, there was the presumption not only that business could legitimately be taught, but that management and, later, leadership could legitimately be taught as well. It was the university that provided the foundation for what a century later became the leadership industry. In fact, all along it has been higher education that has bestowed on management and leadership something approximating legitimacy, something that comes close to a seal of approval. Leadership teaching that is university based, as well as leadership research and scholarship, have been since the beginning essential to the enterprise, essential to what by the end of the twentieth century had become what I call the leadership industry.[40] The importance of this point cannot be exaggerated, as education is critical to any presumption that professionalization is possible.

While the question of how to teach how to manage clearly was crucial, it was never fully or satisfactorily resolved. Nor has it been to this day. Originally, managers were expected to have a broad liberal arts education, an expectation that informed the curricula of pioneering schools such as Wharton, Tuck, and Harvard. However, the focus on breadth, in combination with only a vague idea of what a business school curriculum should consist of, "left many programs lacking in coherence or underlying logic."[41] Thus the attempt to make management a profession finally failed. Khurana: "The professionalization project that had motivated and guided, however fitfully and unevenly, the first sixty years of American business education would be not only abandoned once and for all but nearly completely forgotten. . . . The era of aspiring professionalism in business would die quietly."[42]

This history of management education is important because it explains why we are now where we are now—why the intention to make management a profession was never realized. Of course, this did not preclude some twentieth-century minds from making some major contributions to the study of management and leadership. I am thinking, for example, of German sociologist Max Weber, who developed a typology of authority: traditional, rational-legal, and charismatic. I am thinking as well of Mary Parker Follett, a pioneer in the study of leadership and management in corporate America, who died in 1933. While in the decades subsequent she was widely ignored, now she is widely respected for her prescient perceptions on flatter hierarchies, participatory decision-making, and employee empowerment. In fact, Follett was so farsighted she focused some of her attention on followers—not just on employers, but on employees. The latter, she argued, were as every bit as important to the enterprise as the former.

- The leader makes the team. This is pre-eminently the leadership quality. . . . Men with this ability create a group power rather than express a personal power.

- A leader is not one who wishes to do people's thinking for them, but one who trains them to think for themselves. Indeed the best leaders try to train their followers themselves to become leaders.[43]

Another pioneer in management thinking was a man who spent the better part of his working life as an executive at AT&T, Chester Barnard. In his pathbreaking book on leadership and management in corporate America, *The Functions of the Executive*, originally published in 1938, Barnard counseled leaders to create a space in which employees at different levels could connect and collaborate. Because these connections and collaborations were intended to be voluntary, not mandatory, the leader was supposed to provide appropriate incentives. Put another way, while as with Follett the spotlight shone most brightly on leaders, it also illuminated followers, specifically on how employers (superiors) could and should get employees (subordinates) to go along because they wanted to— rather than in consequence of being coerced.

> Thus the endurance of organization depends upon the quality of leadership. . . . Leadership . . . is the indispensable social essence that gives common meaning to common purpose . . . that inspires the personal conviction that produces the vital cohesiveness without which cooperation is impossible.[44]

Finally, mention must be made of Peter Drucker, sometimes described as "the founder of modern management." To wit: the Drucker School of Management (at Claremont University), and the Drucker Institute, and the Drucker Forum, and the various Drucker Societies in Europe and the United States. Drucker was born in Vienna and lived in London before immigrating to the United States, where he wrote widely about organizations and about those he called "executives." Drucker bridged the gap between a past (early to mid-twentieth century) during which management had foundered as a subject of study, and a present (late twentieth century) during which it was revived. He recalled that when he first tilled this soil, in the 1940s, there were "pitifully few books and articles . . . on what we now call 'management.'" So far, in fact, was management from being a profession that, according to Drucker, "most mangers did not realize that they were practicing management."[45]

In a series of articles that appeared in the *Harvard Business Review*, Drucker provided executives with no-nonsense, hard-nosed, common-sense advice. He was not a touchy-feely sort of guy, so there is not much here about followers or common purpose. Rather these leadership lessons are purely pragmatic, occasionally dogmatic, with no purpose other than the obvious one of getting the job done as effectively and efficiently as possible.

- Effective executives do not make a great many decisions. They concentrate on what is important. . . . 1) Classifying the problem . . . 2) Defining the problem . . . 3) Specifying the answer to the problem . . . 4) Deciding what is "right," rather than what is acceptable . . . 5) Building into the decision the action to carry it out.[46]
- Executives make poor promotion and staffing decisions. . . . [But] there are only a few important steps to follow. . . . Look at a number of potentially qualified people. . . . Think hard about how to look at these candidates. . . . Discuss each of the candidates. . . . Make sure the appointee understands the job.[47]
- The fundamental task of management remains the same. . . . But the . . . meaning of this task has changed . . . because the . . . work force [was] converted from one composed largely of unskilled laborers to one of highly educated knowledge workers.[48]

Notwithstanding the small number of seminal leadership thinkers and teachers whose work was targeted primarily (though not exclusively) at executives in the private sector, Khurana ultimately concluded that during the last seventy-five years there has been no progress toward the professionalization of management. None was made in schools of business and none was made anywhere else. To the contrary: the "concept of professionalism that had provided the original rationale for university-based business education had been stripped of much of its original content."[49]

Ironically, it was precisely the failure to legitimize management that spawned the leadership industry. Management's failure to become a profession, as, for example, medicine and law had become professions, gave rise to pedagogical practices that bear little or no resemblance to those in the distant past, or even to those in the more recent past. Leadership education, training, and development as we understand them now are, in any case, light years lesser than when Plato penned *The Republic*.

Present

In the 1970s the leadership industry was still incipient. But by the 1980s it had entered a period of rapid growth that until now has not slowed. In fact, it continues to accelerate beyond anyone's early imaginings.

Background

It's tempting to trace the inception of the industry solely to the corporate sector. It's tempting because in the early twentieth century it was business schools that built up the business of management, and, even now, that's where the money is. But the leadership industry has grown so far so fast not just because of what happened in the private sector, but also because of what happened in the public sector. Yes, big business has had a so-far-insatiable appetite for leadership education, training, and development. But learning to lead became an obsession, especially though not exclusively an American obsession, not only because of what happened in business, but also because of what happened in politics.

During the 1960s were three catastrophic assassinations—John F. Kennedy, Martin Luther King Jr., and Robert F. Kennedy—and by the 1970s there was social and political unrest. The various upheavals included but were not limited to the antiwar movement, the civil rights movement, and the women's rights movement, all of which were simultaneous to several successive presidencies that in important ways failed. Because of his extremely costly and contentious escalation of the war in Vietnam—"Hey, Hey, LBJ, how many kids did you kill today?"—Lyndon Johnson felt compelled to withdraw from contention in the 1968 presidential election. Richard Nixon was obliged to resign from the presidency because of the Watergate scandal. His successor, Gerald Ford, was unable to get elected president in his own right. And his successor, Jimmy Carter, could not secure for himself a second term in the White House. Seminal leadership scholar James MacGregor Burns's major tome, *Leadership*, published in 1978, was in part a response to what he perceived as a crisis in American political leadership to which the nation had yet effectively to respond.[1]

Around this same time was a perceptible downturn in the nation's economy. During the postwar years, from the late 1940s through the late 1960s, the United States of America rode high, an economic power that seemed impregnable. But by the early 1970s the postwar industrial system in which the United States was the behemoth began slowly but certainly to unravel. Globalization, including competition from abroad, was making inroads. A series of external economic shocks was compounded by a decline in productivity. And the economy gradually underwent a major shift, from manufacturing to services. These further fueled the perception that America was in decline.[2] In fact, in the late 1960s began a diminishment in trust in government specifically, and in American institutions more generally, that has not since been reversed.

Given the magnitude of the political, economic, and social changes, small surprise that this was precisely the period during which "the professionalization project in American business education finally came to be abandoned."[3] In his previously mentioned book on the history of American business schools, Rakesh Khurana wrote that in the late 1970s "the notion of the CEO as enlightened corporate statesman [became] one of the major casualties in yet another of the periodic contests for control of the American corporation."[4] In other words, while the attempt to professionalize management had slowed by the middle of the twentieth century, by the end of the century the last nail had been hammered in the coffin. Ironically, during the time the attempt to professionalize management was being abandoned, the leadership industry was gaining steam. The idea of educating, training, and developing leaders replaced the idea of educating, training, and developing managers.

But between them was a big difference. Integral to the twentieth-century movement to professionalize management was, necessarily, the belief that professionalizing management was possible. Though this belief waxed and waned over a seventy-five-year period, it was never entirely abandoned. In contrast, those pedaling leadership over the last four decades have not in any serious or sustained way even aspired to professionalism. To be sure, there have been occasional exceptions to this general rule, notably the American military. Nevertheless, since the inception of the leadership industry there has been no serious suggestion that the overwhelming majority of those who are aspiring to be leaders are aspiring to be professionals. I would go so far as to say that being a leader and being a professional have been, with the exception again of the military, mutually exclusive.

Never have leadership experts and educators attempted as a collective to build a broad body of knowledge on a carefully considered theoretical foundation. Never have leadership experts and educators attempted as a collective to develop a set of standards by which leaders should be judged. Never have leadership experts and educators attempted as a collective to require the sort of certification that in other professions, even in vocations, is everywhere in evidence. And never have leadership experts and educators attempted as a collective to develop leadership as a calling, with professional norms that convey certain ethics as well as a sense of service.

As we have seen, "leadership" is defined in many different ways. The same holds for "management." There are many different definitions, and there are many disagreements over the different definitions. While the semantic intricacies do not concern us here, what does, or should, concern us are the implications of these disagreements. During the first half of the twentieth century this was not much of an issue. Scholars as well as practitioners tended to use the word "manager" or even "executive"—not "leader." Moreover, later, after the word "leader" began to appear in the management lexicon, it and "manager" were used interchangeably. For years, no distinction was made between leadership and management, because none was thought necessary. "They were one phenomenon," wrote leadership scholar Joseph Rost. "Leadership was management and management was leadership." The words were used synonymously in books, chapters, and articles, which is why, until the 1980s, only a handful of experts differentiated the one from the other. "Despite all the different... definitions of leadership... there was [near] unanimity among all these scholars about one fact: Leadership is management."[5]

But by the 1970s this began to change. As the intention to make management a profession waned, the impetus to distinguish management from leadership waxed. Moreover, gradually, perhaps inevitably, was a tendency to think one more important and the other less: leadership was favored over management, and leaders over managers. These were the new norms: management was inferior to, lesser than, leadership; and having a good manager was less important than having a good leader. Not only was this sort of thinking prevalent during the early years of the leadership industry, to this day many industry experts shy from "manager" and cozy up to "leader."

Though Rost insisted that any "concept of leadership that dignifies leadership at the expense of management" had to be "defective," by the 1980s this was a train that had left the station. And, by the 1990s, "management" was discredited to the point where business schools faced a "full-blown crisis of identity and purpose." They could no longer claim that their mission was to educate managers, for, as Khurana pointed out, "Traditional managers had been successfully portrayed...as incompetent at best, and venal and untrustworthy at worst. Moreover, increasing numbers of students at the most prestigious schools now shunned traditional management careers altogether."[6] Small wonder that in the early 1990s the Harvard Business School ditched its long-standing focus on managers and management. Instead, it developed a new mission statement that declared a new purpose: to "educate leaders who make a difference in the world."[7]

It was a turning point. Corporate uncertainty led business schools to turn to leadership as a way of redefining their identity and mission.[8] Political uncertainty led professional schools such as schools of government and public administration to introduce leadership into the curriculum. Professional uncertainty led institutions (including professional schools) and individuals to turn to leadership as a way of giving students, clients, customers, and consumers a leg up. And personal uncertainty led schools at every level—including high schools, colleges, and graduate schools—to turn to leadership as a way of developing traits and skills ranging from self-confidence to self-awareness, from negotiating to communicating, from mobilizing to decision-making.

So where are we now? What's happening in the leadership industry? How is leading being conceived, perceived, studied, and systematized? How is leading being taught? Who is learning how to lead and who is teaching how to lead? This chapter and the one subsequent will provide some answers to these questions. But first a few overarching observations.

- Since the early days of the leadership industry, it has been a disappointment. In 1988, a Harvard Business School study found that most executives believed there was a "significant lack of leadership skills in their firms."[9] More than a quarter century later appeared an article in the *Harvard Business Review* titled "Why Leadership Development Isn't Developing Leaders."[10]
- Though the level of satisfaction with leadership programs remains low—one expert writes that "the mismatch between leadership development as it exists and what leaders actually need is enormous and widening"—the investment in leadership learning remains high.[11] The numbers vary, but the authors of an article also in the *Harvard Business Review* estimated that in 2015 the amount spent globally on "employee training and education" was "close to $356 billion."[12] While as mentioned we cannot tell exactly how much of this total was specifically spent on learning to lead, the number is in any case impressive.
- Leadership learning is heavily focused on learning *how* to lead. Scant resources have been or are being invested either in teaching *about* leadership or in building a body of knowledge to buttress the still nascent field of leadership studies. In short, leadership studies as an area of intellectual inquiry has made little headway since the inception of the leadership industry. For all our obsession with leadership, and for all our fixation on individual leaders, leadership scholarship continues to get short shrift.
- Though followers, ordinary people, have gained power and influence, especially in Western democracies, they remain effectively extraneous to the leadership industry. Nearly every nickel is invested in "leaders" and in learning

how to lead. Scarcely a nickel is invested in followers—that is, in everyone else—and in learning how to follow, in learning how to support leaders who are good and how to challenge leaders who are bad.

• Bad leadership, however defined, is ubiquitous. Yet nearly no one in the leadership industry or even in leadership studies invests significant time or energy in carefully considering how to stop it or, at least, slow it. We are almost as ignorant about bad leadership now as we were at the inception of the leadership industry.

• It is widely agreed that the contexts within which leaders and followers operate has changed dramatically, even in recent years. As one research report put it, "We live in a 'VUCA' world—one characterized by volatility, uncertainty, complexity and ambiguity—and it's making leadership harder than ever."[13] Still, contexts get short shrift. The idea that the contexts (plural) should command our close attention remains alien.

• There is no more agreement on leadership pedagogy now than there was four decades ago. By and large, different individuals and institutions pursue their own pedagogical paths. To be sure, there are some exceptions to this general rule. For example, the Inter-Association Leadership Education Collaborative, which consists of eight national/international organizations—including among others ACPA (College Student Educators International), AAUW (American Association of University Women), ILA (International Leadership Association), and NASPA (Student Affairs Administrators in Higher Education)—has worked to foster some connections and collaborations among leadership educators.[14] Still, the lack of greater cooperation in this general regard, notably among the thousands of different leadership pedagogues, is striking.

• Leadership is as far from being a profession now as it ever was. So far as the leadership industry is concerned, being a leader and being a professional remain mutually exclusive.

The leadership industry consists largely—not entirely, but largely, very largely—of countless different programs in countless different configurations in countless different contexts, all claiming to teach how to lead. The rest of this chapter provides some idea of what's out there. These thumbnail descriptions are reflective and indicative. They are not, of course, all-inclusive. But they do give some idea of the many thousands of initiatives that claim to educate leaders, train leaders, and develop leaders.[15]

Learning to Lead in College

"Much of the research on college student leadership fails to provide any definitional parameters or theoretical grounding to frame what is meant by the term. . . .

The lack of a definition is . . . a clear limitation."[16] I'll say! I'll say the lack of "definitional parameters" and "theoretical grounding" is a limitation! There are, as mentioned, some exceptions to the general rule—some efforts to lend cohesion and rigor to the countless leadership programs at the undergraduate level, most of which are targeted at students who want "to make a difference."[17] But, notwithstanding the exceptions and notwithstanding the understanding that many if not most leadership educators at the undergraduate level share a few conventional wisdoms (such as the benefits of community service), the overriding impression is of independent institutions making independent decisions about what their particular attempts to teach how to lead can and should consist of. Again, there is no widely accepted norm to frame what should be done and how. There is no independent body to render objective assessments about what undergraduate leadership programs can and do accomplish. Curiously, given the academic context, there is no clear consensus on anything resembling a cognitive component. (In fact, many if not most undergraduate leadership programs are situated in student services, which means they are separate and distinct from academic affairs.) And there is no rigorous challenge to untested assumptions such as "Leadership can be learned" or "All students can develop leadership."[18] (Of course, these claims depend, among other things, on how "leadership" is defined.)

Withal, while there are countless colleges and universities with no undergraduate leadership content at all, there are countless others in which learning how to lead or, occasionally, learning about leadership constitutes a considerable component of the curriculum. This means that there are countless students for whom learning leading is a significant part of their undergraduate experience and that there are countless faculty and administrators for whom teaching leading is a significant part of their workload. In fact, the evidence suggests that those "tasked with developing leadership in others become socialized to thinking of themselves as leadership educators."[19]

Two schools that have what could be called standard or typical leadership programs are Ithaca College and the University of Texas at Austin. Ithaca believes that "leadership development is integral to a student's college experience and overall educational process." Therefore, the Office of Student Engagement and Multicultural Affairs "offers a wide variety of leadership development opportunities designed to help students identify their leadership paths." There is a Student Leadership Institute featuring a series of interactive workshops. There is an opportunity to earn a leadership certificate. There is a conference intended for students interested in applying their leadership skills in professional settings. And there are other activities such as, in 2016, a "Women in Leadership Experience."[20]

The University of Texas at Austin has a Leadership and Ethics Institute located in the Office of the Dean of Students. It runs ProjectLEAD, "an empowerment program" for undergraduates interested in continuing their "leadership curriculum path." Students must apply for the program and, if they are accepted, spend eight hours a week "engaged in instructive workshops, community presentations and group project management in both the fall and spring semesters." Additionally, once a month they are expected to attend interactive workshops for their personal and professional development. The benefits of participating in ProjectLEAD are said to include the acquisition of certain skills, a heightened awareness of leadership styles and strengths, and field experiences in the city of Austin.[21]

Leadership learning at Williams College is something altogether different. Williams is one of the few undergraduate institutions that provides students with the opportunity to do rigorous *academic* work in leadership studies—as opposed to focusing on their own leadership development. A legacy of James MacGregor Burns, who was a professor at Williams for most of his long professorial life, leadership studies at Williams "focuses on the universal phenomenon of leadership in groups." The program explores leadership in different contexts, and the dynamics between leaders and followers. To meet the requirements of the concentration, students at Williams choose either a track in Leadership Studies or in American Foreign Policy Studies. Either way, they have a relatively wide range of leadership courses from which to choose, many of them signaling even by their titles that leadership is a serious subject worthy of serious study.[22]

One model of learning to lead—the social change model of leadership development (SCM)—claims to be the most widely used such template on American campuses, as well as in Canada, Japan, and Turkey, among other countries.[23] SCM approaches leadership as a "purposeful, collaborative, values-based process that results in positive social change." Created specifically for college students aged, typically, eighteen to twenty-two, who tend to be attracted to the idea that leadership can be exercised in a socially responsible way, SCM is based on a core set of values.[24] It defines leadership not as a position or as a quality of a single individual, but as an activity rooted in a commitment to, among other values, self-knowledge, service, citizenship, and collaboration.[25]

Pomona College is an example of a school that uses the social change model. The program at Pomona takes several years to complete, during which students earn three certificates: one in individual leadership, another in group leadership, and a third in values-based leadership.[26] Reed College has also adopted SCM: it asks students to examine leadership development on three levels, each of which is roughly analogous to Pomona's three certificates: (1) the individual level—what personal qualities are we attempting to foster? (2) the group level—how can we collaborate to effect positive social change? and (3) the community level—toward which social ends is leadership being directed?[27] Another example is the intensive, ambitious four-year scholarship program, the President's Leadership Fellows (PLF), at the University of Tampa. It too is based on the social change model. But Tampa's program, which each year selects thirty freshmen as participants, is more rigidly defined and carefully structured. For example, for fellows to receive their $1,000 annual scholarship, they are required to adhere to an "honorable code of conduct." And they are asked, literally, to sign and return a contract in which they commit to, among other things, integrity and service. The PLF "Program Handbook" is fully twenty-two pages long.[28]

Learning to Lead in Graduate and Professional Schools

If leadership programs at the undergraduate level are what might be called a mixed bag, leadership programs at the graduate and professional levels might be called the same. The focus is nearly entirely on learning leadership practice, not on learning leadership theory, on learning *how* to lead, not on learning *about* leadership. Though some graduate and professional programs make something of an effort to teach *about* leadership, mostly such efforts are minor and meager. Most of these programs are designed to offer a practical, professional master's degree of some sort, say in education or in business, not an academic one. And most are designed to teach how to lead as an adjunct to teaching how to do something else.

To this general rule there are some exceptions. The University of San Diego (USD), for example, offers a master of arts in leadership studies. The program is in the Department of Leadership Studies, which is affiliated with Education Sciences. While the program's purpose is clearly practical ("The program prepares students for leadership positions in a wide variety of organizations, including but not limited to education, mentoring and consulting"), and while students are described as "practitioner-scholars," not scholar-practitioners, USD's courses are somewhat more academic than most.[29] Another exception is Harvard University's Graduate School of Education (HGSE). HGSE offers a doctoral degree in leadership or, more precisely, a doctor of education leadership, which is a full-time, three-year multidisciplinary program intended to prepare graduates for "system-level leadership positions" in school systems, departments of education and other nonprofits, as well as "mission-driven for-profits."[30]

The leadership program in the College of Education at the University of Washington is more typical. In keeping with a modest tradition that connects leadership to education, the school offers a master of education in instructional leadership intended for "passionate" teachers who feel "called to lead." The program differs from its competitors by targeting students who do *not* "currently aspire to become principals or administrators," but who are instead intent on improving student outcomes. To this end, the curriculum "blends teacher leadership coursework, content-specific coursework, and inquiry-focused leadership practice."[31] The Rossier School of Education at the University of Southern California similarly connects leadership to education. It offers an EdD program called global executive doctor of education. Described as a "first-of-its-kind program designed to meet the needs of senior leaders in education by providing them with the skills and knowledge necessary to succeed in the 21st century," Rossier's executive program is designed for "full-time working leaders" who already have a master's degree as well as "significant leadership experience."[32]

Westminster College in Salt Lake City has a different orientation. It offers an MA degree in community leadership that prepares graduates "for leadership positions in a variety of community organizations that work to strengthen communities and democratic processes." To receive a certificate in community leadership, students are required to complete approximately twenty hours of core courses, including Public Policy and Advocacy, Social Change and Community Organizing, and Executive Development. To receive the master's degree, students must complete a minimum of thirty-five credit hours in courses oriented toward the development of leadership and management skills such as speaking, writing, and budgeting.[33] Somewhat similarly, though it is larger and more ambitious, the mission of the Hubert H. Humphrey School at the University of Minnesota is to "inspire, educate, and support innovative leaders to advance the common good in a diverse world." Leadership and management are the central focus of the Humphrey School, which presumes that such work will enable nonprofit organizations, philanthropic efforts, and the public sector "to solve problems, serve the public interest and advance the common good."[34] The school offers an array of related degree programs and centers, such as the Public and Nonprofit Leadership Center, the Center for Integrative Leadership, and the Minnesota Senior Leadership Institute. The school also bestows the Hubert H. Humphrey Public Leadership Award, which "honors individuals who have contributed to the common good through leadership and service."

Finally, there are professional schools—such as medical and law schools—that integrate learning to lead into their curriculums. At Omaha-based Creighton University, for example, the School of Medicine has a Program for Leadership Development that supports faculty, residents, and students in the "development of their leadership potential within the health care environment." Harvard has something similar. Its T. H. Chan School of Public Health offers several leadership programs, including the Ministerial Leadership in Health Program, which works with ministers from Africa, Asia, and Latin America to "achieve enduring health sector strengthening and improved national well-being," and the National Preparedness Leadership Initiative, which "encourages a new connectivity to manage emergency situations whether on a local, national or global scale."[35]

Creighton is unusual, however, in that its Program for Leadership Development is completely integral to its medical school curriculum. By offering courses in, for example, team building, situational leadership, and mentoring, Creighton, a Jesuit institution, seeks to address "the need for compelling and compassionate leadership" in healthcare.[36]

Nor are law schools immune to the trend. For example, Stanford Law School offers a course titled Law, Leadership, and Social Change, which examines "the responsibilities and challenges for those who occupy leadership roles and those seeking to use law as a vehicle for social change."[37] Similarly, Columbia Law School has a course titled Leadership for Lawyers. Harvard Law School has an executive program it calls Leadership in Law Firms. And the Law School at the University of Chicago has an optional Professionalism and Leadership Program that provides its students with "additional opportunities to gain professional, strategic, interpersonal, practical, and leadership skills that are critical and necessary for career success."[38]

Learning to Lead in Business Schools

Change is afoot. Traditional master of business administration (MBA) programs are getting fresh, stiff competition from master in management (MiM) programs. Though the word "management" is, as we have seen, less fashionable than it used to be, at least in comparison with "leadership," it continues to send a persuasive message: that to learn to manage is to learn to be competent in ways that relate to running a business, or for that matter running anything else.

The *Financial Times* describes the MiM degree as "the star of 21st century business education."[39] Unlike traditional MBA programs, MiM programs demand little or no previous work experience, which means among other things that they attract younger students eager to get well-paid jobs shortly after their formal education is complete. Moreover, MiM programs take only one or one and one-half years to complete, as opposed to two, which further means that they cost much less. And they are especially attractive to women, who make up nearly half of all MiM students, in contrast to only a third of MBA students.

To be clear, most MiM programs do not emphasize learning to lead over learning anything else. But some master's programs do, for example, at Switzerland's University of St. Gallen, which, I might add, has topped the *Financial Times* ranking of the best MiM programs worldwide for the last six years.[40] In addition to a master's in management, the University of St. Gallen offers a master's in management, organization studies, and cultural theory that promises to provide students with "new perspectives on demanding leadership tasks, for instance as an entrepreneur, change manager or organization developer."[41]

Because of the competition from sleeker and cheaper master's programs, traditional two-year MBA programs are being obliged to reassess both their curricula and their methods of delivery. As Columbia Business School dean Glenn Hubbard pointed out, for most students the cost of attending a lower-tier, two-year MBA program is prohibitive. He went on to add that even for top-tier schools "the opportunity cost of getting a two-year MBA is going to get achingly high."[42] (The Harvard Business School's class of 2019 has an annual tuition fee— that is, fee for tuition only—of $72,000.) In addition to the question of cost is the question of whether spending two years earning an MBA degree is necessary or even desirable. (Again, women particularly "balk at the opportunity cost of MBA study.")[43] In 2016 the school that ranked highest among all full-time MBA programs was INSEAD. Located just outside Paris, INSEAD distinguishes itself from the competition in various ways, not least by having an MBA program that takes not two years to complete but just one—ten months to be precise.

INSEAD claims that it "develops successful, thoughtful leaders and entrepreneurs who create value for their organizations and their communities."[44] However, a closer look at its courses reveals a somewhat more modest ambition, at least as it pertains to leadership. INSEAD'S MBA program is divided into five periods, each of which lasts eight weeks. But the fourteen core courses are not about learning to "lead." Instead they are about gaining a "solid understanding of the key management disciplines," such as financial accounting, marketing management, and operations management. Moreover, most of the seventy-five electives are similarly oriented—toward management skills, that is, not toward leadership skills. I should note that this is in stark contrast to INSEAD'S executive education programs, which do focus, laser like, on *leadership*, not on management. They focus on courses and curricula that promise to transform "effective managers" into "strong leaders."[45]

I return to INSEAD'S executive programs below, but first some examples of leadership learning in traditional two-year MBA programs. The four semesters at Tulane University's Freeman School of Business concentrate on classes that "teach business fundamentals including leadership, management, operations, accounting, statistics, and analytics." As usual in such programs, the distinctions between courses in "leadership" and "management" are almost impossible to discern. They do not, in any case, despite the program "overview," get equal time. At least twice as many MBA courses at Tulane have the word "management" in their titles as "leadership."[46]

At the University of Chicago's Booth School of Business students have a choice of four MBA programs, including one offered in the evening. Its curriculum is flexible; the only requirement is a single course, LEAD. In other words, the program considers learning how to lead to be "so critical that it's the only required component." LEAD stands for Leadership Exploration and Development: it "enhances students' self-awareness and interpersonal effectiveness" by having them work on "key management skills such as interpersonal communication, relationship building, and conflict resolution." (Again, amazingly, the words "leadership" and "management" are used virtually interchangeably.) Part of the program is designed to have students "learn more about themselves as experienced by others through a feedback process." Additionally, students are asked to complete a leadership development plan that will require them to take leadership courses and attend leadership development workshops, all offered by Booth's Leadership Development Office.[47]

The two-year MBA program at Arizona University's W.P. Carey School of Business is also strong on learning to lead. Students engage in self-assessment and team-building exercises even before the start of classes. Once school begins, they take Future Focus MBA, a component of which is Future Focus Leadership. Its purpose is to prepare students to deal with "ambiguous situations by building skills in design thinking, improvisation, and super-flexibility." Though the "future focus" is on "leadership," the present focus is, again, on management. In the first year of the program particularly, the words "manage," "manager," and "management" appear far more frequently in the various course titles than the words "lead," "leader," and "leadership."

It will be obvious by now that most full-time, two-year MBA degree programs have courses and, or, other sorts of curricular or cocurricular activities dedicated to the idea that many, if not most or even all, of their students should learn how to lead. Emory University's Goizueta Business School has a Leadership Coaching Fellows Program and an Advanced Leadership Academy. The academy takes "leadership to a higher level" by providing leader learning experiences including a Capstone Challenge. (In 2013 the challenge consisted of a five-day sailing adventure.)[48] Somewhat similarly, Carnegie-Mellon's Tepper School of Business offers its full-time MBA students the opportunity to affiliate with the Accelerate Leadership Center. The center's programs include the Accelerate Leadership Program, one-to-one leadership coaching, one-to-one communication coaching, and customized workshop and trainings.

But Stanford University's Graduate School of Business (GSB) seems to take learning how to lead to a whole other level. The GSB asserts flat out that the "traditional leadership" curriculum—in other words, the leadership curriculum of its competitors—"often fails to challenge students," which presumably justifies Stanford's notably more assertive approach. For example, GSB requires all first-year students to take a course titled Leadership Labs, in which they "practice core leadership skills in a team setting." As well, the school provides the Executive Challenge, an annual exercise in which some 500 students and some 250 alumni and faculty get together to test students' strategies and leadership skills. Stanford also has a leadership fellows program, in which second-year

MBA students selected through a "highly competitive process" coach and mentor first-year MBA students.[49] Stanford's Graduate School of Business is, in short, trying to distinguish itself by having a *leadership* (not management) curriculum that is considerably more focused, rigorous, and, arguably, creative than most of its competition.

More generally, in 2016 Stanford launched its Knight-Hennessy Scholars Program, which is open to all graduate students, including but not limited to those at the GSB. Its purpose is "to prepare a new generation of global leaders with the skills to address the increasingly complex challenges facing the world." The program has a $750 million endowment, which makes it the "largest fully endowed scholarship program in the world." Not incidentally, under its rubric is the King Global Leadership Program, which has "a distinctive [leadership] training and development curriculum in which all Knight-Hennessy Scholars will participate to complement their core degree studies."[50]

Of course, if you really want to learn how to lead in business school, perhaps best to do so through a program in executive education. It might cost you—or your organization—an arm and a leg. But it will allow you to focus full time, full tilt, on leadership. Let's be clear: executive education (Ex Ed) leadership programs, especially in business schools, especially in schools that are top tier, are enormous profit centers. In 2017, a three-week course in Executive Leadership Development at Stanford's Graduate School of Business cost $34,000. (This included private accommodation, all meals, course materials, and three one-on-one coaching sessions. Additional leadership coaching cost $3,000.) Similarly, a three-day executive education program in Leading Organizational Change, offered in 2017 at the University of Pennsylvania's Wharton School of Business, set someone (or, more likely, some organization) back $8,600. No wonder Ex Ed programs, courses, workshops, whatever, in learning to lead are ubiquitous!

Though executive education programs designed to teach people how to lead are located mostly in schools of business, they are by no means located only in schools of business. My own institution, the Harvard Kennedy School, is a school of government that has a good number of leadership programs on its Ex Ed roster. For instance, in 2018, its program called Women and Power: Leadership in a New World will run for five days at a cost of $8,500. While this is still a hefty fee, it is notably lower than at an equivalent business school. Still, it is in business schools that executive education as an engine of leadership education (or training) most prominently resides. Three examples.

First, INSEAD. As earlier indicated, while its MBA program does not focus on "leaders," its executive education programs do, in a big way. INSEAD states that "to influence and inspire those around them," managers "have to learn new skills and gain new self-awareness." As well, they must learn "to *lead* [italics mine] across cultures and borders." Thus, the school offers thirteen different leadership executive education programs, including The Challenge of Leadership, The Leadership Transition, Leading Successful Change, High Impact Leadership Program, and Learning to Lead. What becomes apparent, then, is that while INSEAD does not really expect its relatively young MBA students to become leaders in a ten-month time frame, it does send to more seasoned managers a different message. They can, INSEAD in effect claims, transition from being merely effective (managers) to being strong (leaders), notwithstanding the short time frame.[51] (Most such INSEAD programs are five days long, though some run up to twenty.)

Second, the University of Pennsylvania's Wharton School of Business. The most striking thing about Wharton's executive education program is the sheer number of its leadership offerings. They include but are by no means limited to Boards That Lead, CEO Academy, Executive Development Program, Global CEO Program, Global Resilient Leadership, Global Strategic Leadership, The CFO: Becoming a Strategic Partner, Creating and Leading High-Performing Teams, High-Potential Leaders: Accelerating Your Impact, Leading and Managing People, Leading Organizational Change, The Leadership Edge: Strategies for the New Leader, and The Leadership Journey: Reimagine Your Leadership. In 2017 most of these programs were four days in length, though not all. For example, the Advanced Management Program ran for one month.[52]

Third, the Harvard Business School (HBS). HBS has among its many different Ex Ed programs one especially ambitious leadership initiative—the Program for Leadership Development (PLD). The PLD is billed as an alternative to the executive MBA: an "accelerated learning experience," an "ongoing transformational experience" designed to put "up-and-coming mangers" on the "fast track to leadership." (Note that like INSEAD, HBS implies that managers can, and ideally should, develop into leaders.) The program consists of four modules and an optional fifth. Module 1 has tutorials and a "leadership learning path assessment." Module 2 provides a "cross-functional business approach." Module 3 is on strategy. Module 4 centers on "Leading Change." And module 5, titled "Personal Leadership," promises a "new perspective" on leadership challenges and "new insights" into participants' "leadership development path."[53] In 2017 the cost of the Program for Leadership Development was $48,000.

Learning to Lead in Large Corporations

In recent years learning to lead in business schools has been aggressively rivaled by learning to lead in-house, particularly in large corporations. Rather than spending big bucks to outsource leadership education, training, and development, countless companies now provide what is, in effect, their own customized leadership programs. A pioneer was General Electric's legendary CEO Jack Welch. His significant investment in GE's large leadership development campus in Crotonville, New York, provided a model, while he personally paved the way for other CEOs who came similarly to believe that they too should support in-house leadership learning. Henry Paulson, Goldman Sachs's CEO from 1998 to 2006, is an example of someone who, in this regard at least, followed where Welch led. In a 1999 letter to shareholders Paulson made clear that Goldman should and would devote "more time and attention to the formal training and development of leaders, particularly senior leaders."[54]

Of course, leadership programs like those at Goldman Sachs are not even vaguely reminiscent of the social change model of leadership development. Nor are they intended to be. Goldman's primary interest is not in service, citizenship, or leadership for the common good. Rather, Goldman's leadership programs are like other corporate leadership programs: they are largely if not entirely self-serving. Goldman's leadership training is for the purposes of training Goldman's leaders to lead in Goldman's best interest. In fact, after Paulson's letter, Goldman went on to develop a series of leadership initiatives, of which Pine Street is the best known. Pine Street is targeted at senior managers worldwide. It provides executive coaching, leadership acceleration initiatives, and master classes, and it has, for various reasons, been frequently described and carefully studied. For example, in 2006, the Harvard Business School published a case study titled "The Pine Street Initiative at Goldman Sachs."[55]

Other examples of learning to lead in large corporations include IBM's General Management Leadership Development Program (GM LDP). GM LDP is an ambitious three-year initiative in which participants rotate though assignments "designed to accelerate advancement to key leadership positions around the globe."[56] IBM also has other "innovative leadership programs," such as the Joint Leadership Development Program, a two-year initiative that enables "select senior leaders to enhance their leadership capabilities."[57] Boeing, in turn, rather like GE, has its own Leadership Center, located just north of St. Louis. It's a 285-acre campus where "current and future leaders" can "immerse themselves in the company's leadership education programs." The campus's large size is said to be "symbolic" of the "huge investment that [Boeing] has made in leadership." Each year thousands of Boeing's "current and future leaders" travel to the Leadership Center, where Boeing's senior leaders do most of the teaching and coaching. At Boeing, it is said, "Leaders [teach] leaders."[58]

Ford also has several leadership programs, including (1) the Global Leadership Summit, aimed at executives and general managers; (2) the Global Executive Leadership Program, geared toward directors and senior managers; and (3) the Experienced Leadership Program, for middle managers. Ford's leadership programs focus on self-awareness, developing others, team effectiveness, building relationships, operating in a global environment, and creating a leader-ship environment.[59] Pearson, in turn, which self-describes as "the world's leading learning company," has the Pearson Leadership Development Program (PLDP). PLDP is a full-time, salaried, twenty-four-month rotational program that "com-bines on-the-job experience with leadership workshops, rigorous training, sen-ior leader mentorship and support from all areas within Pearson." The program is selective: it seeks candidates with proven leadership skills, a passion for mak-ing a difference, perseverance, grit, and the capacity to adapt to change.[60]

Two final corporate cases: Whirlpool and Bank of America. Whirlpool has a Global Leader Program that emphasizes cross-functional and cross-regional experiences "complemented by mentoring, coaching, and a comprehensive learning and development framework." It is not, the company claims, a "one-size-fits-all leadership development program." Rather, the senior leaders who serve as guides are there to ensure that participants embark on their own "unique career path." The program is presented as an outstanding opportunity, but only for some—it is targeted at "driven" individuals "looking to build [a] career in a challenging, innovative and growing customer-focused environment."[61] Finally, there is Bank of America, which features a yearlong Accelerated Development Program that selects eighty to one hundred "high-potential leaders" (from a pool of five thousand nominees), who are considered the bank's next generation of senior leaders. The curriculum is a "blend of self-paced, Web-enabled con-tent, instructor-led classroom learning, assessment, coaching and ongoing, vir-tual instructor-led learning." The program is not, however, for the faint-hearted. Those who enroll are required to "submit to a multifaceted assessment regimen with a combination of online simulation, individual instruments, 360-degree feedback and structured career history interviews."[62]

Learning to Lead in the Federal Government

Opportunities for leadership education, training, and development in govern-ment are, of course, notably less extensive, expensive, and elaborate than those in business. The leadership industry is, after all, like every other industry: as much about money as it is about anything else. But, limitations notwithstand-ing, the US government does offer leadership programs that provide people in government with opportunities for learning to lead.

For instance, the Center for Leadership Development (CLD), located in the US Office of Personnel Management, is described as the "leading provider of leadership development solutions for the public sector." CLD's website puts it this way: "As the government designated provider of agency, interagency and tri-sector leadership development, we offer government-to-government

educational courses, certificate programs, tailored solutions and technology systems . . . to respond to your immediate challenges and emerging needs."[63] CLD
provides a range of different programs to a range of different constituencies,
from "seasoned" executives to fledgling recruits at the "pre-supervisory level." It
provides "training" in both management and leadership. It enables networking
at "all leadership levels." And it offers a Leadership Education and Development
(LEAD) Certificate. How is all this supposed to be accomplished? Above all,
quickly. That is, through a range of programs and courses that typically last from
three to ten days. For example, in 2016, a four-day course titled Extraordinary
Leadership; a three-day course titled, Coaching and Mentoring for Excellence;
and a ten-day course titled Collaborative Leadership" were offered.

There are exceptions to this general rule. A few leadership programs run
longer and are, therefore, more rigorous, such as Leadership for a Democratic
Society, which takes nearly a month to complete, and (in 2016) cost $19,875.
Another even more extensive and expansive program is the Senior Executive
Service Candidate Development Program (SESCDP), described as a "management tool" for agencies "to identify and prepare aspiring senior executive
leaders." SESCDP lasts at least twelve months; and it requires an individual
development plan, a minimum of eighty hours of formal training, four months
of "developmental assignments outside the candidate's position of record," and a
Senior Executive Service mentor.[64]

The National Institute of Health (NIH), an agency of the US Department of
Health and Human Services, has its own small, select leadership program. The
NIH Executive Leadership Program (ExLP) is primarily targeted at the small
number of NIH officials most likely to become senior leaders in the next five
years. The six-month program partners with the Brookings Institution, a prominent Washington think tank, which is charged with conveying an "understanding of executive attributes and the unique role of the executive leader." ExLP also
collaborates with Washington University of St. Louis, which has a highly ranked
school of medicine, to "successfully prepare leaders for executive ranks of leadership at the NIH."[65]

Of course, the federal government has leadership programs in addition to
these. For example, the Department of Defense has an Executive Leadership
Development Program. NASA has a sixteen-month Training and Leadership
Development Program. The Department of Commerce has an Executive
Leadership Development Program that "provides leadership development
opportunities and addresses key competencies." And the Department of the
Interior has leadership development programs that "provide a planned, systemic, competency-based approach to developing future leaders, at all levels"—from "emerging leaders" to "executive-level training." However, the
public and nonprofit sectors do not and cannot compare with the private

sector, where the investment in leadership education, training, and development is singularly large.

Learning to Lead Elsewhere

Though the sample in this chapter is, compared to what's out there, small, it will be evident by now that programs providing lessons in how to lead are everywhere in evidence. They are widely available, though mostly only at a steep price and mostly only to a select few. But . . . not always at a steep price and not always to a select few.

For instance, Kentuckians for the Commonwealth (KFTC) is a grassroots organization that aims to teach new power (ordinary people) how to challenge old power (the establishment, the leadership class). While KFTC is exceedingly democratic in its ideology, it is also exceedingly practical in its methodology. It has a New Power Leader program specifically intended to "deepen the impact of grassroots organizing." New Power Leaders typically organize people in groups of five, and then engage them at least four times a year. KFTC claims to represent "ordinary people instead of powerful interests," which is precisely why its New Power Leader initiative is low key rather than high maintenance—or high cost.

The J. W. Fanning Institute for Leadership Development at the University of Georgia is another example of a program intended for those who cannot shell out big bucks. Its Community Leadership Program is a "basic leadership skill development program for emerging leaders in communities throughout the state," while its Nonprofit Leadership Program "helps strengthen nonprofit organizational leadership."[66] Similarly, the Kansas Leadership Center (KLC) was established in 2007 to "equip people with skills to make positive change for the common good." KLC believes that "leadership is an activity, not a particular role or position." And it conceives of the civic arena as a collective: a "means of sharing responsibility for acting together in pursuit of the common good."[67] There is also the New Leadership Academy (NLA) at the University of Michigan, sponsored in part by the American Association for Hispanics in Higher Education. Its mission is to foster diversity by empowering "individuals with the knowledge, tools, and courage needed to lead effectively on their campuses and across the system of higher education." Finally, PICO (originally the Pacific Institute for Community Organization), a national network of faith-based community organizations, is dedicated to solving community problems. PICO is, if you will, antileadership in that it is antistatus, antiposition, and antiauthority. It deliberately employs a community-organizing model to bring people together to enable equal relationships. But PICO is by no means averse to the word "leadership." In fact, it engages in "intensive leadership training," which is, however, training of a different sort. PICO aims to get people to use the tools of democracy, which is why its groups "are led by ordinary people," and which is why it tasks leaders with "listening to the concerns and ideas of their neighbors."[68]

It's no surprise that "learning to lead in other places" is not only about learning to lead in the nonprofit sector. The Marshall Goldsmith Group is an example of a freestanding enterprise, in this case based on the work of one man, Marshall Goldsmith. Goldsmith is a well-known executive coach who has parlayed his individual success into an institutional one. He and his colleagues develop leaders who want to "earn the trust and respect of followers." They work with teams that want to "succeed in today's complex organizations." And they provide support to enable "large systems to change and adapt to their complex environments."[69] The Center for Creative Leadership (CCL) is another freestanding enterprise that is all about teaching how to lead. Headquartered in Greensboro, North Carolina, CCL is a durable operation dedicated entirely to leadership education, training, and development. CCL provides customized services—based in part on its own leadership research—that enable organizations to develop their "leadership competencies," to address their leadership "challenges," and to face their leadership "realities." It offers some leadership programs that build the "most critical skills for success at each leader-level." It offers other leadership programs that provide "immersion into specific leadership topics." And it offers still other leadership programs tailored for specific groups.[70] CCL does not, of course, come cheap. In 2017 a three-day program called Maximizing Your Leadership Potential would have set some individual or institution back $4,400.

Finally, McKinsey, the management consulting firm of worldwide repute, provides its clients with choices among several leadership programs.[71] The Bower Forum, for example, is a "platform for CEOs to counsel with and learn from fellow chief executives."[72] McKinsey also features a Centered Leadership Program that helps organizations "to accelerate their transformations and achieve greater impact by building inspiring role models at the top."[73] And there is Leadership Accelerator, in which participants "embark on a 9-month development experience that lets them realize their full potential as the next generation of leaders."[74] Leadership Accelerator includes among its learning goals deepening self-awareness, mastering challenging conversations, leading and motivating teams, influencing and inspiring others, and managing change.

Learning to Lead in the US Military

Let me state this as plainly as I can: *Learning to lead in the American military is unlike learning to lead anywhere else in America. Learning to lead in the American military is better. Learning to lead in the American military is harder, broader, deeper, and richer. And it is longer. In the American military learning to lead lasts a lifetime.*

How did this happen? First, the US military is the only American institution that invested significant resources in learning how to lead long before, over a century before, such an investment became fashionable, that is, before the inception of the leadership industry.

Second, this tradition, this legacy if you will, especially but by no means exclusively oriented toward officers, continues. In the twenty-first century, learning how to lead, even learning *about* leadership, remains central to any educational endeavor associated with the American military.

Third, leadership education, training, and development begin early in the American military. For example, the various military academies, which enroll students beginning at around age eighteen, all put leadership front and center. Case in point: The United States Air Force Academy (USAFA). Its mission is "to educate, train, and inspire men and women to become officers of character motivated to lead the United States Air Force in service to our nation."[75]

Fourth, leadership education, training, and development in the military are full throttle, and they take place in tandem. Air force cadets, for example, don't just get trained, as if for a vocation of some sort. They also get educated, as if for a profession of some sort. In fact, they get the kind of liberal arts education that used to be the hallmark of any educated adult—and that, in the old days, used to be the hallmark of a management education. "A comprehensive liberal education has been the cornerstone of the USAFA's curriculum from its inception." Notice that a liberal arts education is not considered *a* cornerstone. It is considered *the* cornerstone.

Finally, learning to lead in the American military is a process, a developmental process far more extensive, complex, richly textured, and multifaceted than anywhere else in America. All other leadership-learning efforts pale in comparison. This process is not, I should note, leader-centric. The American military is impressively aware that leadership development depends not only on what lies within, but on what lies without, that is, on others, on followers, and on the contexts within which leaders and followers are located.

I will have more to say about leadership learning in the American military later. For now, just a few quick takes on leadership education, training, and development in the army, navy, marine corps, and air force.

For a select few, learning to lead in the army begins at the undergraduate level, at the US Military Academy at West Point. West Point has a Department of Behavioral Science and Leadership in which students can major in management. But the Academy's "primary vehicle for influencing leadership development both on and off post" is the West Point Leadership Center. The Center is "an academic agency responsible for leadership development, practice, and research," and an "essential component of the Academy's ability to continually refine its Cadet Leader Development System in order to successfully meet the leadership challenges of the 21st century and beyond."[76] The Center has several different programs intended to "transform cadets into leaders," such as an annual Cadet Leadership conference and a World Leadership Conference. Additionally, West Point has a leader development "system"—the Cadet Leader Development System (CLDS)—which provides the framework for "transformational" change. "Philosophically, CLDS is influenced by the strategic environment into which our graduates are launched, the social environment from which our students are drawn, and higher educational accreditation standards and practices."[77]

Learning to lead in the US Army occurs not only at West Point, but in the army more generally. A 2012 Department of the Army publication titled *Army Leadership* has a foreword by (four star) General Raymond Odierno, who at the time was army chief of staff. He writes, "Leadership is paramount to our profession. It is integral to our institutional success today and tomorrow."[78] Odierno made his expectations clear—for example, a leader should have a vision, a leader should have a moral compass, a leader should build high-performing teams, and a leader should empower subordinates. How are such high expectations to be met? The concluding section of *Army Leadership*, titled "How Leaders Develop," is a solid summary of what it takes to learn how to lead. On the one hand is the importance of individual dedication and perseverance, and on the other is the importance of the institutional context within which leadership programs take place. "Leadership develops when the individual desires to improve and invests effort . . . and when the organizational climate values learning."

Like West Point, the US Naval Academy at Annapolis also invests heavily in learning to lead. It has a Division of Leadership Education and Development (LEAD), whose primary mission is the preparation of junior officers for "combat and operational leader roles through a four-year immersion program of leadership and ethics education and training, as well as leader development experiences and opportunities."[79] LEAD also has under its rubric a Department of Leader Development and Research; a Department of Leadership, Ethics, and Law; and the LEAD Company Officer Master's Program, which is offered in conjunction with George Washington University. The US Navy also operates the Naval Postgraduate School, which grants master's degrees, engineer's degrees, and doctoral degrees, and which has an Executive Leaders Program. And it has in its bailiwick the Naval War College, which awards students in some of its programs a master's degree, and which is dedicated first and foremost to "developing strategic and operational leaders."[80]

The marines focus laser-like on leadership as well. Eleven principles form the "foundation of leadership in the Marine Corps," principles that are supposed to guide marine corps officers in everything they do. Together, says one marine manual, these principles constitute the traits and values that define "character as a leader."[81] The principles are:

1. Be technically and tactically proficient.
2. Know yourself and seek self-improvement.
3. Know your Marines and look out for their welfare.
4. Keep your Marines informed.
5. Set the example.
6. Ensure the task is understood, supervised, and accomplished.
7. Train your Marines as a team.
8. Make sound and timely decisions.
9. Develop a sense of responsibility in your subordinates.
10. Employ your unit in accordance with its capabilities.
11. Seek responsibility and take responsibility for your actions.

The US Air Force Academy has a Center for Character and Leadership Development, which serves as the "integrating focal point" of the Academy's "commitment to developing leaders of character." Developing leaders of character depends on a four-year "Leadership Growth Model" (LGM) which unfolds in four stages: expectation, instruction, feedback, and reflection. Notably, the air force thinks in terms of what I call the "leadership system."[82] The LGM describes "key relationships" among leaders, followers, and contexts. In fact, the air force pays special attention to the importance of followers and followership, quoting approvingly from the late leadership expert Warren Bennis: "In many ways great followership is harder than great leadership. It has more dangers and fewer rewards, and it must routinely be exercised with much more subtlety."[83]

So what, in conclusion, does this look at the leadership landscape tell us? Some facts to extract:

- Programs that teach how to lead (or profess to) are ubiquitous, available at every level, in every sector, for every type of customer, client, and consumer, including students from, at least, college through graduate and professional school.
- Programs that teach how to lead (or profess to) do not, generally, make much if any distinction between teaching leadership and teaching management.
- Programs that teach how to lead (or profess to) define "leadership" in different ways.
- Programs that teach how to lead (or profess to) have very different purposes and very different pedagogies.

- Programs that teach how to lead (or profess to) attract various individuals and groups who want to learn how to lead for various personal, professional, and, sometimes, political reasons.
- Programs that teach how to lead (or profess to) tend to shortchange or even ignore leadership education and development, and to focus instead on leadership training. The military is the exception to this general rule.
- Programs that teach how to lead (or profess to) are usually of short duration. Again, the military is the exception to this general rule.
- Programs that teach how to lead (or profess to) are generally expensive. They are generally expensive to provide and to attend. Usually, some individual or institution is obliged to cough up big bucks for the privilege.
- Programs that teach how to lead (or profess to) are presumed important not only professionally, but personally.

Suffice to say that anyone with any interest in professionalizing leadership—or even in making leadership learning more serious and rigorous—would conclude that where we are now is disheartening. Moreover, so long as leadership experts and educators remain content to provide leadership pedagogies that are hasty and superficial, that are minor and meager, so long will leadership stay stuck. Leadership will be an occupation—not a profession. No wonder we incline to devalue and disparage our leaders. Many, if not most, are ill-prepared to take on the task. Similarly, no wonder the military is much the most highly esteemed of all American institutions.[84] Its leaders are well prepared, singularly well prepared, to do what they are expected to do, to lead.

3

Future

Chapter 1 was about teaching how lead in the past. Chapter 2 was about teaching how to lead in the present. This chapter turns to the future. It's the first in a series about teaching how to lead in the future. Here I will explore three different domains to which close attention must be paid. The first is meaning-making—specifically the meaning we make of becoming a leader. The second is developing—specifically changing and growing during adulthood. The third is learning—specifically learning how to lead lifelong.

Meaning-Making

Up to now I have written about leadership (1) education, (2) training, and (3) development, as does everyone else who takes up the subject: as if, for all intents and purposes, they were one and the same, synonymous, with no real reason to distinguish the one from the other.

Some leadership programs profess to *educate* leaders. Others aim to *train* leaders. And still others claim to *develop* leaders. Rarely are these verbs defined; rarely are these verbs operationalized; and rarely is it made clear why one of these three words was chosen over the other two. What does it mean to *educate* a leader? To *train* a leader? To *develop* a leader? What meaning are we making of each of these words? What is the message that each of them sends? And, if learning to lead is the common thread, what are the differences, if any, in the messages that we receive?

A small number of leadership experts have distinguished among leadership education, training, and development, though none of these distinctions have stuck. A few decades ago Dennis Roberts differentiated leadership education from leadership training, and both from leadership development, arguing that leadership education should focus on the most important concepts, and leadership training on the most important skills. Together, he presumed, they would contribute to leadership development.[1] Somewhat similarly, one of the pioneers of the leadership industry, John Gardner, wrote that leading wisely and well required cognition before action. "The first step is understanding," he wrote. "The first question is how to think about leadership."[2]

But, as we saw in the preceding chapter, the distinctions among leadership education, training, and development are now blurred or simply absent. Among other reasons, learning *about* leadership (education) tends to be disconnected from learning *how* to lead (training). Gardner's caution notwithstanding, seldom is "understanding" the first step—seldom is leadership education required before leadership training. In fact, adult learners overwhelmingly want to learn leadership not because they want to learn *about* leadership, but because they want to learn *how* to lead. They have no obvious intellectual interest in or curiosity about leadership; rather they see the practice of leadership as the means to an end. The nature of this end varies, of course, depending on the individual. For one it might be professional success, for another political action. The point in any case is that most people participate in most leadership programs not to satisfy any cognitive craving, but because they hope to become leaders, or they hope to become better leaders than they already are. Leadership education and, in turn, leadership scholarship—that is, leadership as an area of intellectual inquiry—is something of a stepchild, something to be tolerated but primarily for the purposes of achieving more proficient leadership practice.

"Understanding," therefore, is being shortchanged. Or, more precisely, the quest for understanding is confined. It is confined nearly entirely to understanding the self. (The American military is, again, an exception to this general rule.) Leader learners are taught about authenticity and self-awareness; they are taught to reflect about their own leadership experiences and trajectories, and they are taught to develop their own special skill set. But they are not typically taught about whoever is the other, or about the context(s) within which the self and the other necessarily are embedded. Nor is there much if any learning in the broader, deeper, richer sense of this word—as in learning how the liberal arts pertain to leadership. As in learning the history of leadership. As in learning the great leadership literature. As in learning how country and culture impact on leadership. As in learning how the hard sciences pertain to, for example, gender and leadership. There are, of course, several reasons for this lack of learning, this lack of "understanding." Foremost among them is, arguably, time—the lack of it. *I cannot emphasize enough that limiting leadership learning to a limited period limits leadership learning—period.*

If leadership education in any meaningful sense of this term is given short shrift, this leaves us with leadership training and development. The mission of my own institution, the Harvard Kennedy School (HKS), is first and apparently foremost (it is the first part of a two-part mission statement) "to train enlightened public leaders." What exactly this means is not, however, immediately obvious. The "public" part is clear enough. Presumably it is to distinguish leadership learning at the Harvard Kennedy School from, for example, leadership learning at the Harvard Business School (HBS). The Kennedy School is primarily (though not exclusively) dedicated to training leaders in the public and nonprofit sectors; the Business School is primarily (though not exclusively) dedicated to educating leaders in the private sector.

But if we remove the word "public" from the phrase "to train enlightened public leaders," the waters get murky. Does "to train enlightened leaders" mean to train leaders who already are enlightened? Or does it mean to train leaders to become enlightened? Or does it mean to train Harvard Kennedy School students to become leaders who are enlightened? And what is meant by the word "train"? Why does this mission statement use the verb "train"—as opposed to "educate" or "develop"?

The mission statement of the Harvard Business School provides an interesting contrast. HBS states that its mission is to "educate leaders who make a difference in the world." Why the Kennedy School chooses to say that its mission is to "train" leaders, while the Business School chooses to say that its mission is to "educate" leaders, is not immediately apparent. What is immediately apparent is that while HKS is silent on the question of what exactly its mission statement means—it seems to presume it is self- evident—HBS goes to some lengths to expand and expound on the message it sends. With one telling exception, nearly every word in the Harvard Business School's mission statement is elaborated on, explained. A "leader" is defined by HBS as someone who embodies "a certain type of competence and character," someone who has "earned the trust of others." To "make a difference" is defined by HBS as "creating real value for society." Leaders must create value "before claiming value." Moreover, HBS makes plain that it seeks to create "value" not only in one area—in business—but in many areas. There are "many ways of making a positive difference." HBS even expands on the phrase "in the world." It reflects the school's focus on the "rapidly changing, dynamic environment," and its awareness of the "fact that many of the world's most challenging issues will require a global perspective."[3]

There is, however, one word, one key word, in the HBS mission statement that the school fails to elaborate on. Why the exception? It was either an oversight or a decision not to expand on the word "educate" because elaboration was unnecessary. What we might surmise, in any case, is this. First, that HBS thought long and hard before choosing the verb "educate" over the verbs "train" and "develop." And second, that HBS ultimately concluded that the message it intended to send was better encapsulated in "educate" than in either of the two obvious alternatives. Of course, I am only surmising. It's possible obviously that the all-important verb "to educate" was chosen without much deliberation.

Stanford's Graduate School of Business (GSB) is a similar top-tier institution that, however, made a different choice. Unlike the Harvard Kennedy School, which aims to "train" leaders, and unlike the Harvard Business School, which aims to "educate" leaders, Stanford's Graduate School of Business aims to "develop" leaders. Its mission statement declares GSB seeks to "develop innovative, principled, and insightful leaders who change the world." Moreover, this sentence is succeeded by this one: "We seek to attract faculty and students with high leadership potential."[4] Again, I can only imagine the thinking that went into the choice of language, but logic suggests this sequence: GSB will admit primarily if not exclusively students who have already demonstrated "high leadership potential." The word "potential" suggests that these students are not yet leaders who are "innovative," "principled," and "insightful." Rather they are to *become* such leaders—*develop* into such leaders. Hence the word "develop" in GSB's mission statement—as opposed to "educate" or "train."

Though in the past the distinctions among leadership education, training, and development have been few and far between, I argue that it's past time for this to change. The leadership industry has matured to the point where such distinctions can and should routinely be made. I, for example, maintain that most leadership programs do not provide leadership *education* in any meaningful sense either of "to educate" or "to be educated." The teaching we typically provide is too hasty and superficial, the learning too meager and shallow to justify the verb "educate." This does not mean that there is no leadership education at all. Rather it means that the instruction that takes place is nearly always inadequate to the task of providing a first-rate or even a good enough educational experience—an education befitting a professional leader.

The term "leadership training" can be confusing, but it is, arguably, more forthright and straightforward. It is confusing because, among other reasons, we do not explain what we mean when we say we "train," and because we do not distinguish between training people to become leaders and training people who already are leaders to become better leaders. There is, presumably, a difference that should, presumably, affect pedagogy. But for the word "train," this much can be said: it does not suggest, not to speak of promise, more than it can reasonably deliver. "To train" and "to be trained" ordinarily imply the introduction or improvement of certain skills. The verb "train" does not imply, as does the verb "educate," a more ambitious agenda, as in providing learners, here leadership learners, with new information, fresh ideas, and original insights.

The word "development"—as in "leadership development"—suggests something different yet again. First, unlike leadership education and training, which almost always indicate outside intervention of some sort, by, say, a teacher, or a trainer, or a coach, leadership development implies work that is largely or even entirely done on our own. Others can somehow support us, encourage or nudge us to develop, and contexts can also be more, or less, conducive to development, to movement from one stage, level, order, or plateau to the next. But in the end leadership development is like adult development: the journey is ours to undertake because development work is internal, not external. I can readily demonstrate to you, maybe even prove to you, that I have mastered a body of knowledge. I can readily demonstrate to you, maybe even prove to you, that I have mastered a certain skill. But usually it is difficult if not impossible for me easily to demonstrate to you, to prove to you, that I have developed, transitioned from one way of thinking and being to another.

Second, as Roberts suggested, leadership education and training can be subsumed under leadership development. They can even be considered necessary precursors or, at least, integral to the developmental task. But it is not at all clear that leadership development can be subsumed under either leadership education or leadership training. I am as ardent a believer in leadership education as any other leadership teacher. I am firmly in the camp of those who think it critical that there be a cognitive component to leadership learning. However, I would never suggest that cognition, that knowing, is all, that to know *about* leadership is to know *how* to lead. Similarly, it seems that honing certain skills, say communicating and negotiating, can be extremely useful to anyone who is learning how to lead. But I would never equate skill improvement with leadership development. I would never suggest that "to train" people—to teach them a certain skill or to modify a certain behavior—is to develop them, to fundamentally change them. Leadership development, on the other hand, suggests just such a change, a fundamental change in who the individual is, in how the individual thinks, and in what the individual has the proclivity and capacity to do. Precisely because leadership development connotes a change more profound than either leadership education or leadership training, it should, ideally, be undertaken more sparingly.

Words matter. It matters, or it should, whether we are talking about educating leaders, training leaders, or developing leaders. To be sure, each implies a process of some kind, so that someone who is successfully educated or trained presumably is different at the end of the process than at the beginning—somehow better equipped to lead. But the process of development usually is conceived of as more profound. It implies a significant transition or even transformation of some sort, one that takes time, a long time. The terms "adolescent development" and "adult development" are indicative. They suggest change over a span of years, not months or weeks, not to speak of days.

The term "leadership development" is, then, more encompassing than "leadership education" or "leadership training"—or, at least, it should be. Not only are our conceptions of education and training more limited, but our conception of development is more expansive, extended, and inclusive. Leadership development implies not only the acquisition of a body of knowledge or of a special skill but "a qualitatively different state of being."[5] A transition from being one thing to being another—from having "high leadership potential" to being a leader. From being a leader to being a better leader.

Developing

This book is a discourse on professionalizing leadership, professionalizing the process of producing a leader. It is, then, presumably not adequate only to educate or only to train. But since *developing* a leader cannot, by definition, be accomplished in a short time, it must be presumed, as the ancients presumed, that it takes years to learn how to lead or, at least, to learn how to lead wisely and well. It takes, among other things, education and training, practice and experience, reflection and maturation. It takes external work and internal work, all of which can be accomplished only in due course, not during a single week of executive education, or during a single term of a leadership course, or even during a year or two of a degree program.

Of course, by choosing to settle on the word "develop" I do not mean to suggest that the Graduate School of Business at Stanford is superior to the Business School at Harvard, just because the former uses the word "develop" in its mission statement while the latter uses the word "educate." What I do mean to suggest is that if we reflect on the meanings of these words—on the differences in what they imply and on what, in turn, these differences imply for professionalizing leadership—then the leadership industry should be dedicated to leadership *development*. This is precisely why, when we speak of leadership education, training, and development, we owe it to our clients, customers, consumers, and students to clarify just what we mean.

It used to be that psychologists thought child and adolescent development important—but not adult development. However, forty years or so ago this began to change. In what might not be an accident of timing, interest in leadership development began to grow just when interest in adult development began to grow. One of the early pioneers in human development was Jean Piaget, a twentieth-century Swiss psychologist who found that cognitive growth was accomplished in stages, developmental stages, in which children made the transition from one level to the next once they had reached a certain level of cognition. This finding, it turned out, had implications for change not only during childhood but during adolescence and adulthood as well.

In time, other researchers built on Piaget to pursue work that was in some ways similar and in others different, among them Lawrence Kohlberg. Kohlberg's research on the development of moral reasoning has been described by biologist Robert Sapolsky as "monumental," as "canonical."[6] Kohlberg built on Piaget: he extended the notion of development from adolescence into adulthood to postulate six stages of moral development. In the first, we obey rules set by others only to avoid being punished. But by the time we reach stages five and six, which Kohlberg's disciples claim most of us never consistently do, the content of our moral reasoning is completely different. By then we have our own code of ethics, our own ideas about what is right and good and true. By then we act in accordance not with what others expect or even dictate, but with our own consciences, no matter the consequences.[7] Developmental psychologist Robert Kegan named this sort of work constructive-developmental theory. The theory is "constructive" in that it focuses on how people construct, or interpret, their experience. It is "developmental" in that it explores how these constructions, or interpretations, grow more complex over time. "Constructive-developmental theory thus takes as its subject the growth and elaboration of a person's ways of understanding the self and the world. It assumes an ongoing process of development in which qualitatively different meaning systems evolve over time."[8]

As Kohlberg built on Piaget, so Kegan built on, among others, Kohlberg. In one of his early books Kegan suggested that we can progress through five stages in adulthood, each of which represents not just change but growth.[9] Each of these five stages constitutes a different "order of consciousness"—a different way of making sense of the world.[10] While Kegan's original, five-stage model has since been modified, his overarching point has remained the same: that all of us can develop in adulthood, can elevate or increase the level of our mental complexity. In a recent book, *An Everyone Culture,* Kegan and his co-author, Lisa Lahey, write: "Looking at a population as a whole, mental complexity tends to increase with age, throughout adulthood, at least until old age."[11]

Management professor William Torbert found a correlation between the level of a leader's development and the level of a leader's performance: the higher the leader's stage of development the more effective he or she was likely to be "at leading transformational change."[12] Not surprisingly, Kegan and Lahey argue similarly. In *An Everyone Culture* they maintain that the highest of the three (down from five) "adult plateaus" is the "self-transforming mind." The self-transforming mind enables leaders to think in complex ways, so that they can, if necessary, not simply run organizations but reconstitute them. Incidentally, Kegan and Lahey themselves have changed. By now they acknowledge that what we need are not only more highly developed leaders, but more highly developed *followers.* Whereas in the past, they argue, it generally sufficed to have workers with "socialized minds," that is, workers at the lowest or first plateau, what we need now, in the twenty-first century, are workers with "self-authorizing minds," workers at the second plateau.[13]

The details of constructive-developmental theory need not concern us here. What should concern us are several underlying principles: first, that adults (like children and adolescents) can and often do change in ways that can be of consequence to the exercise of leadership. Second, that adults can and often do *develop*, or grow. Third, that adults have a greater tendency to develop, to grow, when they are in situations or contexts that challenge and support them. Fourth, that no single theory of adult development supersedes all the others. And fifth, again, that development does not mean merely adding something, such as more facts and figures, or additional skills, but implies instead an evolution toward greater moral and cognitive complexity.[14]

Other theories of adult development relate to leadership development as well, for example, those that are age related. Erik Erikson, a German born psychologist and psychoanalyst, was a pioneer in adult development theory whose work led him to conclude that over the course of our lifetimes we go through various stages, each of which is characterized by conflicts between competing forces. For example, he claimed that middle adulthood is characterized by the tension between self-absorption and stagnation on the one hand, and generosity and generativity on the other. While Erikson's work is now out of fashion—in the 1970s he was something of an intellectual hero—his theory of adult development generally led to work on leadership development specifically, some of which remains important. I am thinking particularly of his two groundbreaking biographies—also called psychobiographies, or psychohistories—one of Martin Luther and the other of Mahatma Gandhi, in which he applied his ideas to the lives and times of legendary leaders.[15]

Another pathbreaking book about age-related adult development, this one by psychologist Daniel Levinson, was titled *The Seasons of a Man's Life*. Levinson posed this question: "Is there an underlying order in the progression of lives over the adult years, as there is in childhood and adolescence?"[16] As the title of his book suggests, Levinson found there was just such a progression, just such a sequence if you will, from adolescence into adulthood, right through old age. "I am *not* talking about stages in ego development or occupational development or development in any single aspect of living," he wrote, taking pains to distinguish his work from work that preceded it. "I am talking about *periods in the evolution of the individual life structure*. The periods, and the eras of which they are a part, constitute a basic source of order in the life cycle. The order exists at an underlying level."[17]

While Levinson postulated several developmental periods in early and middle adulthood, and one in late adulthood, all of which may be said to pertain to leaders and, for that matter, to followers, for our purposes again, the devil is not in the details. Rather it is in the underlying finding, which other researchers, such as psychiatrist George Vaillant, who studied some eight hundred people, mostly men, over a span of fifty years, have uncovered as well. This finding is that to progress successfully, healthily, through adulthood is to resolve certain conflicts, including residual ones from early in our lives, and to complete certain tasks, all in some sort of natural sequence. And it is that to be an adult is inevitably, necessarily, to change. Sometimes it is to change in major ways; sometimes in minor ways. It is not, in the event, to remain the same.[18]

A constructive-developmental theory of adult development is obviously different from an age-related theory of adult development. For example, the first refers to change that is positive or even optimal, while the second does not, or, better, in the second change is not necessarily positive. Just as clearly, these theories have in common two key components: *both posit changes during adulthood that can be and often are enduring; and both posit, certainly implicitly, that learning to lead involves learning lifelong.*

How precisely adult development relates to leadership development remains unclear because different experts and educators define development differently, because different experts and educators define leadership differently, and because some theories of adult development are based on populations that might not be relevant to leadership development. Here is another example of how language—in this case the word "development"—can maximize rather than minimize the confusions. The term "identity-based leader development" does not refer either to developmental stage or to age. It refers instead to the extent of leadership experience. The theory of identity-based leader development is based on the common-sense finding that the more leadership experience we have, the more likely we are to identify ourselves as leaders. In other words, experience, specifically leadership experience, is "inextricably integrated with the development of the persons' self-concept as a leader."[19] Conflating (1) leadership, (2) development, and (3) identity led to the construction of the leadership identity development model (LID), which consists of six stages "that describe the increasingly complex ways in which individuals [in this case college students] define leadership and identify themselves as leaders."[20] So, for example, when these individuals are at stage 3, they view leaders as people in positions of authority. But by the time they reach stage 4, they have changed, they have developed. They now see leaders as those who contribute the most to the group. Those who reach stages 5 and 6 have continued to evolve, in large part in consequence of their own leadership experience. Now they internalize being a leader—now being a leader is part of who they are.

My point is not that the work on adult development (in this case early adult development) is infallible, or that it is so clear and consistent that it can be taken, so to speak, to the bank. It does not, in fact, consist of theories so repeatedly and rigorously tested that we should think of them as being gospel. Rather it is that conceptions of adult development, findings relating to adult development, have major implications for leadership development. They all imply changes that take place over extended periods of time. They all imply changes that are meaningful as opposed to superficial. They all imply changes that are permanent as opposed to transitory. And some have the additional virtue of implying changes with benefits. These changes represent improvement, betterment, growth, not only early in life, but later in life as well. It's why leadership development generally should subsume leadership education and training. It's why leadership education, training, and development should not be confused or conflated.

I earlier suggested that leadership learning in the military is singular in several ways. Among them is the emphasis on development, as opposed to only education or training. For example, learning to lead at West Point—where students are mostly between the ages of eighteen and twenty-two and in residence for four years—centers on the word "development." This suggests, correctly, that at West Point leadership development and adult development are entwined. Consider these lines, from a West Point publication titled *Building Capacity to Lead*. Development, it says, "occurs in stages." Developing college-aged students "involves many of the same processes as those employed to develop more experienced adults, albeit at potentially different stages of development where values, experiences, and even roles are viewed differently."[21]

My point is that leadership teaching that purports to be serious must be serial. My point is that leadership teaching that purports to be serious cannot be brief, confined to a brief burst over a brief time. My point is that leadership teaching that purports to be serious cannot be limited to education, or to training, or even to education and training. My point is that to professionalize leadership, learning to lead must come to include development, which necessitates, among other things, prolonging the process.

Learning

We do not normally educate and train children, or even adolescents, to become professionals. We do, however, educate and train some adults some of the time to become professionals, to become doctors and lawyers, for example. That is why when we think about professionalizing leadership, we must think about how adults learn.

The term "adult learning" suggests just what it is intended to suggest: that adults learn differently from children and adolescents, that how a fifty-year-old best learns is not necessarily the same as how a fifteen-year-old best learns, not to speak of a five-year-old. This returns us to the subject of adult development, for the connection between how adults develop and how they learn is direct. As one group of authors put it, referencing Piaget as pioneer, his understanding of how individuals interact with their environments "clearly had a major impact on our understanding of cognitive development."[22]

The connection between development and learning exists because experience, the stuff of it, the stuff of life, is instructive. Experience also accumulates. I have more of it, experience, at fifty than I did at fifteen, and more of it at fifteen than I did at five. "Adult intellectual and cognitive growth centers on the accumulation of experience in dealing with the concrete problems adults encounter. For this reason, the particular content of a problem and the context within which it is set become increasingly important with age."[23] In other words, because of the additive effects of experience, as we age we gravitate toward learning that is specific as opposed to general. Thus, the particularities of a problem, and the particularities of the context within which the problem is located, are presumed more important to learning in early adulthood than to learning in adolescence, and to learning in middle and late adulthood than to learning in early adulthood.

The idea that context is of special importance to adult learners is of special interest to me. For as I will later elaborate, I myself have learned in adulthood, learned over time, so that the way in which I think about leadership in the present is different from the way in which I thought about leadership in the past. I think of leadership now as being less narrowly focused (on individual leaders) and more broadly expansive. I think of leadership now as a *system*—the "leadership system," I call it—with three parts: leaders, followers, and contexts. On the one hand the system is simple—it has only three parts. But on the other hand, the system is complex. It is complex in that each of the three parts is of *equal* importance—which, in turn, has implications both for teaching how to lead and for learning how to lead. To see leadership as a system in which leaders are of no greater importance than followers (others), and in which leaders and followers are of no greater importance than the contexts within which they are situated, inevitably affects the pedagogical process. To be sure, this process includes learning about the leader, which, in most leadership programs, is tantamount to learning about the self. But I have found that it equally includes learning about everyone else—and learning about the contexts within which leaders and followers relate.

Piaget's work explains why the ways in which we make meaning depend on our experience.[24] Any change in this experience, from one that is primarily or even exclusively narrow to one that is more expansive and inclusive, is what development is about. Well-known studies conducted by Harvard educational psychologist William Perry in the 1950s and 1960s chronicled precisely this process, the cumulation of experience, in young adults. When Perry interviewed a group of Harvard undergraduates (then all male) about their educational and personal histories, he found that freshmen approached life simplistically. That is, to most freshman it seemed that on most issues there was only a single valid opinion, theirs, and that to most problems there was only a single good solution, theirs. Over time, though, during their sophomore and junior years, these same students supplanted this narrow approach with one that was broader and more complex. In other words, as they grew older, as they lived longer, had more experiences and exposures and accrued more information and ideas, Harvard students changed. They developed. They developed a more nuanced, more complex way of seeing the world. By the time Perry's subjects had their undergraduate degrees in hand, typically at age twenty-two, for reasons both internal (they were older and more experienced) and external (they had spent four years in the culture and context that constituted Harvard), they had changed yet again. By then they had reached a different developmental level, one that enabled them to complete the transition from having only one perspective, their own, to having several perspectives in addition to theirs.

It is difficult if not impossible to extract from Perry's studies whether the students he followed changed, developed, largely because by the end of the study they were four years older, or largely because they had spent four years learning and living at one of the world's leading undergraduate institutions, or largely because of a reason other than these, or largely because of an amalgam of all of the above. In any case, one of the implications of Perry's studies and of others like it is that how adults best learn and develop is different from how children best learn and to develop. Hence different pedagogies for different populations—which is why more pedagogies are being, and should be, particularized.[25] Certain populations are presumed optimally taught in certain ways—which raises the question of why most of us in the leadership industry teach how to lead to large numbers of people not only simultaneously, but similarly.

For the purposes of this discussion I further focus on three themes particularly pertaining to adult learning: *expertise, experience,* and *embeddedness.* First, *expertise.* In chapter 1, I described Plato's conception of the ideal state, one in which kings are philosophers and philosophers are kings. Precisely because he imagined rulers as philosophers, as wise men of great learning, Plato prioritized the pursuit of knowledge. This pursuit was to be tireless, relentless, and lifelong. "Plato's ideal republic was a place where individuals who displayed emerging expertise were supported and encouraged to assume their place of honor and to hone their particular talents through the continued pursuit of knowledge."[26] How does Plato's ideal apply to learning to lead in the twenty-first century? What does Plato's ancient emphasis on the pursuit of knowledge suggest for here and now?

It turns out that Plato's prescription is by no means dated. It still pertains. The development of what we now call multiple intelligences, and the acquisition of different sorts of expertise, are still considered essential to learning in adulthood, to learning lifelong. Which raises these questions: What are the kinds of intelligences and sorts of expertise that particularly apply to learning to lead? And what are the kinds of intelligences and sorts of expertise that can reasonably be taught to leadership learners? The answer to both these questions is . . . it depends. It depends on the nature of the leader, and of the followers, and of the situation. There simply is no single answer to questions as complex as these. Additionally, the meanings, even the definitions, of words such as "intelligence" and "expertise" have changed. It no longer suffices to conceive of intelligence simply as "computational power." We now think in terms of several intelligences, of practical, applicable, multiple intelligences in addition to those that are more traditional.[27] Moreover, whereas in the past an expert was someone whose primary qualification was the ability to solve a problem, now the bar is higher. Now we presume that an expert already possesses a considerable body of relevant knowledge, a body of knowledge already well organized; and has extensive prior experience that will enable problem-solving that is current as well as efficient.

Additionally, we now associate the process of acquiring expertise with the process of gaining experience. In keeping with our current conceptions of adult development, we assume that becoming more expert in adulthood usually takes place over time. We are not, simply, either a novice or an expert. More likely we are somewhere in between—and we can move over time from one end of the spectrum, from being a novice, toward the other, to being an expert. What this suggests, again, is the importance of age and of experience, in addition to traits such as ambition, curiosity, diligence, and persistence.[28] This also suggests that those interested in leadership development would do well to borrow from what we know about adult development, and that those interested in leadership learning would do well to borrow from what we know about adult learning.

The second theme is *experience*. If expertise is still acquired partly in the classroom, experience is acquired largely and sometimes entirely outside the classroom. In recent years, experience as pedagogy has moved to center stage. It has come to be considered critical to adult learning and development—and to leadership learning and development. Experiential learning is thought part of adult learning, period; leadership learning without experiential learning is considered leadership learning that is lacking. In fact, one of the main reasons that leadership development programs are said often to fail is that often they are divorced from the world of work. The problem? "Adults typically retain just 10 percent of what they hear in classroom lectures, versus nearly two-thirds when they learn by doing."[29]

No wonder the emphasis in recent years has been on "action learning," on learning not just outside the classroom but on the job. Jay Conger and Beth Benjamin described action learning as a process by which "managers learn . . . from their own companies."[30] Action learning is learning by doing: it typically addresses workplace issues, involves work conducted in teams, and places participants in problem-solving roles. Conger and Benjamin argued that when they are done right, action learning programs are among the few "training designs" that translate principles of adult learning into leadership learning. This is their way of saying that most trainings leave a lot to be desired. A decade ago they wrote, "Leadership programs of the future will have to do a better job of leveraging adult learning principles if they hope to accelerate and enhance ... critical and complex [leadership] capabilities."[31]

Several articles in a May 2017 issue of the *Financial Times* confirm that action learning, whether within the workplace or without, is where the action is. This pertains especially to executive education, which, by definition, is delivered in brief bursts and is targeted at adults who remain on the job. Not only are companies less interested than they once were in paying for executives to "sit passively in classrooms listening to experts," they are similarly disinclined to foot the bill for people "to take online courses made up of video lectures." The future of executive education, then, of education aimed at mature leaders and managers, lies in less talk and in more action, in pedagogies that "force executives to rely on their wits" by obliging them to "think creatively about how to stand out."[32] While some innovations in instruction are taking place in traditional schools, such as in France's Grenoble School of Management, which has an entire laboratory dedicated to executive role-play, others are in start-ups, which use new technologies to shake up old pedagogies.[33]

As if to drive home the point, in 2016 the Association to Advance Collegiate Schools of Business (AACSB) came out with new guidelines that urged all MBA programs to get practical, to provide their students with "real world" experiences and exposures, nearly all of which were to take place outside the conventional classroom. While traditional academics worry that changes like these will sideline their expertise and intellectual rigor, ineluctably they are being pushed and prodded by practitioners, especially former executives valued for their skills and contacts, who hold increasing sway.[34] Tellingly, before issuing the new guidelines, the AACSB welcomed input not only from professors at schools of business, but from executives with long years of practical experience, for example, from Michael Arena, chief talent and development officer at General Motors.[35]

Of course, the benefits of experience are by no means presumed confined only to those in the private sector. They are regularly touted for those in the public and nonprofit sectors as well. To be clear, though, most of the newer pedagogies are no more foolproof than the older ones. Most research findings on adult learning, as on adult development, have not been rigorously tested and confirmed. As one observer put it, "The question of whether or not service-learning and civic participation is an influence on adult development and if so, which developmental outcomes are most likely promoted is an important one for which there is little empirical evidence. The relationship is . . . speculated and presumed, but not well researched and understood."[36] Still, notwithstanding cautionary notes such as this one, there is by now the widespread presumption that experience, especially experience involving others, contributes not only to development in adulthood, but to learning in adulthood. Further, there is the related assumption that experiencing leading is essential to learning leading.

While what exactly it is about experience that encourages development (adult development, leadership development) remains unclear, the following three statements are considered by some to be gospel: (1) placing individuals in contexts that introduce dissonance and disequilibrium prompts them to adopt increasingly complex views of themselves and their environments; (2) encouraging individuals to engage with the outside world, especially in civic contexts, encourages an ethic of empathy; and (3) engaging individuals in the world of others facilitates the acquisition of certain skills, particularly those relating to emotional intelligences such as connecting and communicating.

The third theme of learning in adulthood is *embeddedness*. It focuses on the importance of embedding leadership learners in larger social contexts. The importance of other people to adult development, and to leadership development, is repeatedly emphasized. This is not to imply that time spent in solitude is devoid of benefits. In fact, leaders are repeatedly encouraged to carve out quiet time, time for reflection and self-reflection, time spent alone, not in the company of others. Moreover, certain ideas and information are more quickly and easily acquired alone than in groups. But by and large adult learners are strongly encouraged to immerse themselves in the world of other people. In fact, if we disaggregate even the small number of studies on development that I reference in this chapter, we can see that development—again, both adult development and leadership development—is thought dependent on engagement, engagement with others and, yes, also with the circumstances shared with others. As West Point's manual *Building Capacity to Lead* puts it, "Leadership development increases one's capacity to understand the world, especially other human beings in social situations." Leadership development, it continues, "requires meaningful interaction."[37]

It is not unusual, in fact, for leadership programs to presume that being embedded is itself being socialized to lead. City Year, for instance, is a national service organization that engages young adults in a year of full-time citizen service. To a striking degree, City Year's theory of leadership development is grounded in the idea that being a member of a group or organization itself provides "a wide variety of seemingly disparate leadership development tools, concepts, processes and practices." As Max Klau, director of leadership development at City Year, described the theory that underpins its practice, "By intentionally creating an organizational culture that allowed corps members to quickly embrace a shared identity as idealists, City Year sought to rapidly transform a diverse group of strangers into a cohesive, effective, and inspiring service corps [and] into a generation of civic leaders."[38]

Being embedded is presumed of both theoretical importance and practical consequence. As I have mentioned, I never talk or write any more about "leadership," but only about the leadership *system*, including followers and contexts. Similarly, others have pointed out that leadership is, necessarily, both social and situational. Rob Goffee and Gareth Jones, professors at the London Business School, write first that leadership is relational. "You cannot be a leader without followers." They write second that leadership is situational. "The ability to observe and comprehend existing situations, *situation sensing*, is vital to leadership. . . . Effective leaders . . . tune into the organizational frequency and penetrate beneath the surface."[39]

The best way to think about the themes of expertise, experience, and embeddedness is in tandem. Each is central to learning in adulthood. Each is central to learning to lead. Each is different from the other, but relevant to the other, even dependent on the other. It is difficult if not impossible to acquire expertise without experience, and it is difficult if not impossible to acquire experience without being engaged in the world of other people.

Meaning, Developing, Learning

I began this chapter by exploring the meaning we make of three words invoked virtually interchangeably in relation to learning to lead: education, training, and development. I then suggested that we stop using the words synonymously, and that we consider subsuming "education" and "training" under "development." The assumption I make is that "education" and "training" are necessary prerequisites to "developing," part and parcel of the developmental process, whereas the reverse is not true. It is possible to be educated but not trained. It is possible to be trained but not educated. It is also possible to be educated and trained but not in any meaningful way to be developed (except insofar as development is age related). Further, I presume that it is possible to develop without being formally educated or trained. Withal, given the nature of leadership, and given the requisites of leading wisely and well, the term "leadership development" seems more promising and encompassing than either of the two typical alternatives. Moreover, since this chapter is about the future of leadership, and since this book is about *professionalizing* leadership, the idea of focusing on development, as opposed to education or training alone or even in tandem, is compelling.

Again, the word "development," as in, for example, leadership development, necessarily implies both the process of change and the passage of time. It suggests that what we are in, say, middle adulthood is qualitatively different from what we were in early adulthood. We are not merely more educated and more trained. We are, instead, something quite different, not only older but wiser. We are wiser and better leaders at fifty-five than at thirty-five. A doctor can be wiser and better at fifty-five than at thirty-five not merely because he or she knows more or has become more skilled. In addition, he or she has in some ineffable way and for various reasons changed, matured, developed from being one sort of person to being another sort of person. The precise nature of what constitutes leadership development is not important here. What is important is that the difference to which I allude is qualitative in addition to being quantitative.

This is why the word development—adult development, leadership development—necessarily implies the passage of time. As the members of the American military seem to grasp, it takes years to develop a leader, to professionalize a leader, many years. It takes much, much longer to *develop* a leader— to *professionalize* a leader—than it does to educate a leader or to train a leader. There is no way in hell that anyone can teach how to lead, or learn how to lead, in a month or even a year. Therefore, institutions and organizations (other than the military) that declare their mission is to "educate" or, especially, to "train" leaders are more precise in their intention than those who declare their mission is to "develop" leaders. For the work that can reasonably be accomplished in, for instance, a one or two-year master's program, not to speak of a five-day executive education program, can never be said to "develop" a leader, though it might, arguably, be said, at least in a modest way, to educate a leader or to train one. Here is General Fred Franks, former commanding general of the army's Training and Doctrine Command on just this subject: "The longest developmental process we have in the United States Army is development of a commander. It takes less time to develop a tank—less time to develop an Apache helicopter—than it does to develop a commander. It takes anywhere from twenty-two to twenty-five years before we entrust a division of soldiers to a commander. . . . [Leaders] must continue to grow and to learn and to study [their] profession, to learn by [their] own experience. To learn by study, school, reading and . . . from others. . . . It [requires] total professional involvement."[40]

It is impossible to make the point more persuasively than did General Franks. Impossible to argue more convincingly than did he that learning to lead takes decades, years and years of involvement and investment by leadership teachers and leadership learners. Impossible to express more exactly than did he the idea that learning to lead takes expertise, experience, and embeddedness. Impossible to say more succinctly than did he that when the goal is "development"—as in the "development of a commander," or the development of any other leader— what is required is "total *professional* involvement."

A few closing points, some that bear reiterating, on developing in adulthood, on learning in adulthood, on developing in adulthood into a leader, on learning to lead in adulthood. For those with a personal as well as professional stake in leadership development, I should note that some of the relevant methodologies and pedagogies can and should be implemented in small groups, or one on one, or even alone. However, there are others that imply an investment of institutional resources, an institutional (or group or organizational) commitment to changing the culture and sometimes the structure to foster individual development at every level.[41] While development is not something that can be done "to" someone, creating a context and a culture that support growth and change sometimes is consequential.[42]

- Intelligence and expertise are as important to leadership as they ever were. However, the way we think of them in the present is different from the way we thought of them in the past. We conceive of them now as being more complex, more multifaceted—as in, for example, multiple intelligences.
- Adults learn best when what they learn seems to them to be "grippingly relevant."[43] Leadership development programs should be rich in relevance and experience, especially if relevance and experience are defined broadly. History, for instance, can and should taught so that it obviously is "relevant." In short, pedagogies matter, for learners in adulthood as for those in childhood and adolescence. Withal, instruction that is innovative is not, by definition, superior to instruction that is traditional.
- Experience does not imply experience only on the job—experience that obviously is task related. To the contrary: for all the interest in action learning on the job, the evidence suggests that our conception of experience should be inclusive and cumulative. People with "high leadership potential" should, therefore, be evaluated not only in terms of performances that are task-related, but also on the bases of the lives they lived.
- Contexts matter. They matter at every point in the life cycle. We are the products of the relationship between who we are as individuals, and the circumstances within which we were and are situated. Contexts matter especially to those learning to lead. Too few institutions understand what West Point does—that learning to lead without learning the various "environments" (strategic, social) within which we are located is like trying to learn to swim without getting wet.
- People matter. Context is not an empty construct. It's a construct that, literally, contains other people. Moreover, while there are exceptions to the general rule, the general rule is that because power and authority have declined in the twenty-first century, both in liberal democracies and in many, if not most, large organizations, influence is more important than it used to be. That is

precisely why more than before leadership skills imply people skills: the ability to persuade people voluntarily to follow your lead.

- Leadership development and adult development are entwined. It is wrong-headed to think about the first without thinking about the second.
- Finally, there is this. Leadership is, as we have seen, defined in scores of different ways. My own definition is simple and value free: a leader is an agent of change, for good (a good leader) or ill (a bad leader). However, without exception, leadership programs define leadership differently. Without exception, they claim, if only by implication, to educate, train, or develop people to be *good* leaders—good as in, simultaneously, *effective* and *ethical*. It's one of the reasons why leadership programs and management programs should not be confused or conflated.

On this last point, this last note. Adulthood has come to be viewed not as a period of stasis and stability, but as a period of change and growth. Ideally, at least, change and growth take place on every level—intellectual, social, psychological, professional, emotional. Moreover, ideally, this growth takes place lifelong. It should not come to a grinding halt in early or middle adulthood. Ideally, it should continue into later adulthood. This more than anything else is why learning to lead needs to be reconceived. This more than anything else is why learning to lead needs to be reconceived as learning lifelong.

One way to think about all this is to consider the difference between becoming a competent amateur and developing into a skilled professional. It takes not much talent and not much time to become, say, an amateur cook or even an amateur pianist. I'm thinking here of cooking and piano playing as occupations—not as vocations and certainly not as professions. However, it takes considerable talent and time to develop into a professional cook or a professional pianist, a cook or a pianist who is so good—who so clearly has achieved professional status—that people are prepared to pay for their services. Moreover, the small number of cooks and pianists at the pinnacle of their professions are, typically, fiercely determined to stay there, fiercely determined to get better and better, to become more brilliantly accomplished than they already are. This means that they must keep at it—must continue to work exceedingly hard to learn, to remain creative, to concentrate deeply, to expand their repertoires, and to stay focused lifelong until they decide to surrender their professional status.

The analogy is, of course, imperfect. Becoming a cook or a pianist and becoming a leader are not one and the same. There are, though, some similarities that those of us with an interest in leadership development would do well to bear in mind. As well, there is one striking dissimilarity. We assume that only a relatively few have the innate talent and extreme ambition to learn how to cook wonderfully well or to learn how to play the piano wonderfully well. However, for some curious reason, we make a different assumption when it comes to learning how to lead. When it comes to learning how to lead the mantra everywhere in evidence is not only that everyone *can* lead wonderfully well, but that everyone *should* lead wonderfully well.[44] Why the difference? Because in leadership there is no clear distinction between leading like an amateur (leading as an occupation), and leading like a professional (leading as profession). The line between them is so indistinct as to be nearly nonexistent.

We can agree that it usually takes years or even decades to develop a first-rate professional cook. We can agree that usually it takes years or even decades to develop a first-rate professional pianist. We cannot and do not, however, agree that it usually takes years or even decades to develop a first-rate leader. For some reason, to leadership we apply a different standard. We have a different sense of what is required for excellence to emerge. That is precisely the problem—our refusal to recognize any sort of parallel. We continue to be deeply dissatisfied with and disappointed in leaders, and in leadership programs, because we insist on teaching in short bursts that which requires learning lifelong.

If the future of leadership, the future of learning how to lead, is to be better than the past, this more than anything else must change. There is no shortcut to becoming a professional leader—any more than there is to becoming a professional cook or pianist or a professional anything else. How would you like your head sawed open by a brainy brain surgeon who, however brilliant, had no continuing education or training in thirty years? Who in thirty years had not in any meaningful way developed? If leadership education, training, and development are to be better in the future than in the past, our abbreviated, aborted sense of what it takes to learn to lead must change.

PART II

BEING A LEADER

4

Occupation

Earlier I distinguished among an occupation, a vocation, and a profession. Given that these distinctions are critical to this discussion, and that the point of this discussion is to galvanize a transition from leadership as an occupation to leadership as a profession, in both this chapter and the next I further explore the differences among them.[1]

Practice

The lines of demarcation among occupations, vocations, and professions are thin. However, in general, an occupation—an activity in which a person engages sometimes but not always for the purposes of making money—does not require extensive training or specialized schooling. A vocation, in contrast, or a trade, is an activity in which a person usually engages for the primary purpose of making money. Vocations require those who enter them to have some training, schooling, and, typically, some experience as well. A profession is also an activity in which a person usually engages for the primary purpose of making money—though some professions are also thought of as having a higher calling. In contrast to vocations, in any case, professions nearly always require extensive education and experience and, sometimes, in addition, a period of specialized training. Medical residencies are an example: they involve extended experience that generally consists of training in a specialty or subspecialty. Many professions and some vocations are, moreover, overseen by various governing and licensing bodies. These bodies monitor and regulate. They also set clear standards, and, sometimes, they develop a similarly clear code of conduct.

Society generally accords higher status and greater rewards to those who practice professions than to those who practice occupations, or even vocations. As one expert on professions put it, "Professions are somewhat exclusive groups of individuals applying somewhat abstract knowledge to particular cases"—emphasis on "exclusive."[2] Doctors and lawyers typically rank higher on the various pecking orders than do hairdressers and truck drivers—not to speak of grape pickers and street-sweepers—and the former are better compensated. Still, people in vocations are usually required to take tests that resemble those for people in professions. For example, the state of Connecticut, in which I live, strictly regulates hairdressing and truck driving.

To work in Connecticut as a hairdresser, that is, legally to earn money as a hairdresser, a person must acquire a Connecticut hairdresser licensure. To acquire a Connecticut hairdresser licensure, a person must clear, among other bureaucratic hurdles, the following: (1) successful completion of the ninth grade or its equivalent; (2) successful completion of a course entailing no fewer than fifteen hundred hours of study in a school approved by the Connecticut State Board for Barbers and Hairdressers (or its equivalent); and (3) successful completion of the Prometric Licensing Examination (it pertains to insurance). Should someone somewhere in the state want to open a new barber or hairdresser school, he or she will be required to secure from both the Office of Higher Education and Connecticut's Board of Examiners for Hairdressers, Barbers and Cosmeticians a certificate of authorization. This certificate can be obtained only after completing several tasks, including submitting for state approval the school's curriculum and the list of instructors.

Should you be interested in working not as a hairdresser but as a truck driver, the demands on you will be fewer. Nevertheless, you too will be required to meet certain criteria and adhere to certain standards. First, in accordance with federal rules and regulations you must secure a commercial driver's license (CDL). To secure a CDL, you must pass a written exam. Once you have passed said exam, you will be eligible for a CDL learner's permit. To progress from having a learner's permit to having a regular CDL, you will need to pass a skills test, including a road test. After you pass the requisite tests, you will be issued a full, formal CDL. However, should you wish to drive a specialized vehicle, such as, for instance, a school bus or a hazmat truck, you will be required to clear additional hurdles. In any case, in all cases, before you obtain a CDL, you must have a physical exam. And, in any case, in all cases, after four years you must renew your CDL, which will require an updated background check and another physical examination, including one that tests your vision.

The point here is not to draw parallels between vocations and professions. As I will make clear in the next chapter, the demands on those in most professions are far more stringent than on those in most vocations. Rather it is to point out that many if not most vocations are in some ways regulated and governed by certain standards, even if these are no more than minimum standards of performance. This is in sharp contrast to leadership, which is not only not akin to a profession, it is not even akin to a vocation. Connecticut does not require its leaders to be in any way regulated. And it does not require its leaders to prove to the state that they are in any way qualified. Leadership is, in short, not a profession nor even a vocation. It is an occupation.

This raises the question of why. What is it about the exercise of leadership that makes us think that it can be learned so quickly and easily and taught so superficially and haphazardly to so many different people in so many different situations? Additionally, what is it about the practice of leadership that allows it to be so vague and unregulated, so free of the standards and practices that we generally apply to vocations and professions? Is it that this thing, leadership, is a breed apart, something that can grow on its own and then thrive on its own without any support? Without any control?

It was not, as we have seen, always so. It was not, as we have seen, always anticipated that leadership could be so easily mastered. To the contrary, in the distant past it was assumed by some of history's greatest intellects—Confucius and Plato are examples—that learning to lead was learning deeply, richly, and extensively, lifelong. Plato's leadership learners, a small, elite cadre of the best and brightest, were, after all, some fifty years old before they were deemed ready to rule. So how did we get from there to here?

Some of the reasons are grounded in theory. Some of the reasons are grounded in practice. Purely on a practical level, any leadership development program that even vaguely resembles the one envisioned by, for example, Plato, would require now, as it did then, an enormous investment of resources, financial, intellectual, pedagogical, professional, personal, and temporal. As I suggested, in our own time and place the only institution that approximates making an investment of this size and scope is the military. Only the American military can fairly be said to put, so to speak, its money where its mouth is. It recognizes and responds to the idea that leaders cannot possibly be developed on the cheap or on the fly.[3]

Put differently, to invest extensively in leadership education, training, and development implicitly involves a two-step process: first, the recognition that learning to lead requires a considerable investment over a considerable time; second, the willingness and readiness to make such an investment. Rarely are these steps taken. Rarely does it occur to members of the leadership industry—whether pedagogues or practitioners—that leadership development of the first rank, which subsumes education and training, requires a significant investment over a considerable time. And rarely is there an individual or institution that is willing and able to make such an investment—again, other than the military. We think, or we pretend to think, that minimal leadership education and training will suffice—as opposed to maximal leadership development. And we think, or we pretend to think, that because leadership education and training can be accomplished quickly and easily, doing so is as politically, pedagogically, and fiscally viable as justifiable.

Think of it this way. Think of leadership experts and educators as both specialists and realists. They, we, specialize in teaching how to lead in a certain way, and they, we, have a vested interest in continuing to do so. Moreover, they, we, recognize that the chances of substantially changing the system, either within the academy or without, are slim. The academy, higher education particularly, has been demonstrably resistant to the idea that leadership curricula should in any fundamental or significant way be reconsidered and reconceived. Of course, outside the academy it is efficiency that rules: the desire to have leadership learning that is extremely efficient trumps the desire to have leadership learning that is extremely effective.

Additionally, we—we putative leadership experts and educators—know which side our bread is buttered on. We who teach how to lead, sometimes for large sums of money, we card-carrying members of the leadership industry, recognize that the power structure is allergic to the idea that leadership education, training, and development are consuming and complicated. Furthermore, we recognize that it is not in our interest to challenge the industry norm, which is why, generally, we do not.

I want to be clear here: I recognize and have testified to the fact that numberless institutions and organizations are committed to the idea of leadership development, and that to this end they invest resources, sometimes even considerable resources. Corporate America, for example, continues to pour large sums of money into one or another kind of leadership learning experience. And so, for that matter, do other institutions, including institutions of higher education, which, as we have seen, are stuffed with leadership programs at the undergraduate and graduate levels, and in professional schools as well. Still, again excepting the military, the expectation is always the same: that learning to lead can be accomplished reasonably cheaply and easily and within a reasonably short, or even a very short time. That is the irony, the vicious cycle if you will: the inability to recognize, to acknowledge, that leadership development requires significant investment over an extensive period by everyone concerned, not least leadership learners, explains the disappointment in leadership development. As long as the leadership industry promulgates the fantasy that leadership learning can be, simultaneously, wonderfully efficient and marvelously effective, so long will leaders retain their dubious, their unprofessional, status.

I cannot emphasize this point enough. There is a correlation between these refrains: first, that in the first quarter of the twenty-first century leaders in America are, by and large, perceived as inadequate to the task at hand; second, that in the first quarter of the twenty-first century leadership programs are, by and large, inadequate to the task at hand. Whatever the protestations to the contrary, most extant programs in leadership training, education, and development are just not good enough. They bear no resemblance whatsoever to what they would look like if leadership was perceived as a profession—as opposed to an occupation.

Theory

Part of the problem is leadership theory. Think leadership theory supports leadership practice? Think again. Leadership theory is inconsistent to the point of being incoherent. More precisely, it *is* coherent if it is confined either to a single leadership theorist or to a group of leadership theorists who happen to share a similar perspective. But it is *not* coherent or comprehensible if you have the temerity to go beyond, to explore different leadership theories put forth by different theorists with different areas of expertise, or with different disciplinary lenses, or with different research interests, or with different points of view—those who seem to have little or even nothing in common with their intellectual, academic, or pedagogical peers.

Think of it this way. If you are learning to become a physician, or an attorney, you have a single, reasonably coherent body of knowledge that you are expected to master. A core curriculum in other words, in, say, medicine, in which case anatomy would be a required course. If, in contrast, you are learning to become a leader, not only is there no coherent body of knowledge that you are expected to master, there is no coherent body of knowledge period. Or, at least, there is no coherent body of knowledge that most leadership teachers would agree ought to be taught to most leadership learners.

As I write I have before me a well-respected volume titled *Handbook of Leadership Theory and Practice.* The editors are Nitin Nohria and the previously mentioned Rakesh Khurana, both of whom have, among their other credentials, faculty status at the Harvard Business School.[4] (Nohria is also the current dean of the Harvard Business School; Khurana is also the current dean of Harvard College.) They began the book with an introductory chapter in which they declared, no holds barred, that "the current state of scholarly research on leadership" is weak. The existing research does not, they pointed out, provide an answer to this basic question: are our institutions "developing leaders who have the competence and character necessary to lead" in the twenty-first century? In other words, Nohria and Khurana began their own edited volume on leadership theory and practice by asserting flat out that there is no "vision or model of leadership" that allows us to "develop better leaders who can serve society,"[5] or that allows us "confidently" to teach how to lead.

Given their high standing as academics and administrators, Nohria and Khurana were being refreshingly, even remarkably, candid. (Of course, it was precisely *because* of their standing that they could afford to be so straightforward.)

One could go so far as to say that they were undercutting their own institution, the Harvard Business School, by admitting to the gap between what even a business school of the first rank claimed to do and what it did. They admitted to the gap between "purpose and practice," and then went on to speculate about why: maybe because leadership is an elusive concept; maybe because the academy does not reward leadership scholarship; maybe because if you have never led, leadership is hard to grasp, to teach. Or maybe, I would add, the gap is because leadership scholarship requires inquiry into more than one discipline; or because leadership is as much art as science; or, conversely, because in the twenty-first-century inquiry into leadership mandates inquiry not only into the social sciences but into the hard sciences; or because leadership is still so constricted a conception—limited largely to a single-minded focus on single individuals.

I could go on. The bottom line is that leadership theory is as Nohria and Khurana describe it: a "vast and sprawling field with no clear contours or boundaries, which has been pursued in fits and starts across different disciplines and intellectual traditions."[6] This sorry state and statement is hardly a heartening introduction to a handbook of leadership theory. Nor is it a heartening assessment for someone like me, looking to nudge leadership from uncertain occupation to confident profession. The problem is not, however, confined to the various confusions, or to the "vastness" of the field, or even to the fact that the field is "sprawling." The problem goes deeper, to two questions so fundamental that they throw into question the field itself. First, what is this thing called leadership? Second, does leadership even matter?

"What Is This Thing Called Leadership?" happens to be the title of a chapter written by the late psychologist Richard Hackman for the above-mentioned *Handbook*. After suggesting that leadership seems sometimes "little more than a semantic inkblot, an ambiguous word onto which people project their personal fantasies, hopes, and anxieties about what it takes to make a difference," Hackman asserted, albeit with more hesitation than conviction, that there "*is* something there." He did not, however, contradict the bleak assessment offered by Nohria and Khurana. In fact, Hackman concluded his chapter by predicting that leadership as a field of intellectual inquiry would continue to face an uphill climb. It remained, he wrote, for us to identify leadership, "to tame it, and set it off on a course that generates knowledge . . . that is more robust, cumulative, and useful than what we have collectively produced so far."[7]

Hackman was not above irony. He was not above pointing out an unusual specimen: the "master leader." A master leader is a great leader—a leader who seems to know just what to do and how to do it. Odd thing is, though, that most master leaders never participate in a leadership program. Master leaders, Hackman could not help but remark, "seem able to do the right thing at the right time without having any formal training at all."[8] Put differently, unlike a master doctor or a master lawyer or most other master professionals, it appears that leaders can, if only rather rarely, become masters of their craft without any instruction or intervention whatsoever. Hackman did not, I think, intend to suggest that there is nothing about leadership that can be learned. What he did, however, intend to suggest was that there was something about leadership that remained ineffable, elusive, singularly resistant to learning in any conventional sense. At the close of Hackman's chapter, the question he raised—"What is this thing called leadership?"—remained unanswered. Leadership, he concluded, is "a mystery."

To the second fundamental question—does leadership, do leaders, matter?—the answer remains similarly inconclusive. Even when there is a leader who stands out, who transcends the norm, it is difficult to prove that this single individual could account for what happened in any given group or organization. Human agency is just one of many variables that pertain, that determine what happens, that are responsible for complex outcomes. Which raises this question. Do we turn to human agency, to leaders as explicators, because they really do have a major impact most of the time? Or do we turn to leaders as explicators because they help us to make sense of a world that would otherwise be experienced as overwhelmingly, exhaustingly chaotic?[9]

This question has been so vexing for so many years that it has come to be known as the "hero-in-history debate." Historically, famously, on the one side has been Thomas Carlyle, who in his nineteenth-century essay titled "On Heroes, Hero-Worship, and the Heroic in History," wrote, "Universal History, the history of what man has accomplished in this world, is at bottom the History of the Great Men who have worked here." And on the other side have been those such as the nineteenth-century English philosopher and sociologist Herbert Spencer, who took issue with Carlyle. Spencer argued that in the event we were "dissatisfied with vagueness," we should look more closely, and that if we did, we would discover that the hypothesis of the great man was "utterly incoherent." We would discover that the great-man theory "breaks down completely."[10]

The hero-in-history debate remains, of course, unresolved. It remains unresolved because it addresses a question impossibly complex and because the answer varies, depending on the circumstance. Leaders do make a difference, but, arguably, they make a major difference only in certain circumscribed circumstances. Nevertheless, notwithstanding a common-sense middle ground, the hero-in-history debate is framed by the extremes. On the one hand are those who dominate the leadership industry, which itself is predicated on the presumption that leaders matter, matter a great deal nearly all the time. On the other hand are the minority, those who remain skeptical that leaders make much of a difference. Leadership, they argue, is "principally mythological." Events are driven not by individual actors "but are derived from and perhaps even deter-mined by the organization's environment."[11]

It is, in any case, impossible to exaggerate leadership's hold on our collective consciousness. The idea that leaders are important, even all-important, domi-nates the leadership industry, which is undergirded by two deep-seated beliefs. The first is that programs in leadership education, training, and development will, of their own, produce good leaders—leaders who are both effective and ethical. The second is that good leaders result in good outcomes. That all it takes for good things to happen is a good leader.

Incidentally, American culture more generally is similarly besotted: it pre-sumes, without sufficient evidence, that leadership is all, that leaders are all. To take just one obvious example, any American not living in a cave during the numbingly long 2016 presidential campaign—with its relentless fixation on Hillary Clinton and Donald Trump—will have ended being indoctrinated with the idea that the nation's destiny would be determined largely if not entirely by who is elected president of the United States. The full-throated personalization of American politics, relentlessly and endlessly amplified by the American media, is the best evidence we have of the general assumption to which I allude: that leaders are the drivers, the rest be damned. I would argue, in fact, that the main reason the outcome of the 2016 presidential election was such a surprise, such a shock even, is because nearly everyone, including the media, was so fixated on the key players, Clinton and Trump, that the secondary ones, American voters, were ignored. Also ignored was the context within which American leaders and American followers were necessarily together tethered. Still, to reiterate, among a vocal if small minority of contemporary leadership experts the conviction that leadership is "mythological" remains strong. I hasten to add that this is not some random conception loosely promulgated. Rather it is a research finding grounded in relevant studies, one of which, a study of organizational behavior, concludes that "most organizational action can be understood not as an exercise of individual agency but as an organizational response to the demands of exter-nal actors."[12] Here is another disciplinary perspective, more generally sociolog-ical than specifically organizational, that comes to the same conclusion: "The creation of 'leaders' arises out of the need for meaning and the tendency to make inferences within the confines of the prevailing explanatory systems. . . . It may be that with the increasing routinization and disenchantment of the modern world, the need to believe in heroes and great figures becomes greater as the probability of their appearance becomes less likely."[13]

Notwithstanding the doubts, disclaimers, and disagreements, Nohria and Khurana's *Handbook* tries to tame the beast. It contains twenty-six different chapters by more than twenty-six different authors, all of whom bring their own professional perspectives to leadership theory and practice. To be sure, the editors attempt to group the different perspectives in accordance with some logic: the twenty-six chapters are divided into different sections, for example, "The Impact of Leadership," "The Theory of Leadership," and "The Variability of Leadership." Still, the book mirrors the field. It is full of different explorations and explanations, for example, one chapter on psychological perspectives on leadership, one on organizational perspectives, one on sociological perspectives, one on economic perspectives, one on historical perspectives, one on political perspectives, one on cultural perspectives, and one on gender perspectives. Additionally, the section "The Development of Leaders" has several different chapters set on several different theoretical foundations, such as, for example, the link between leadership and identity, the link between leadership and experience, and the link between leadership and (adult) development.

In the end, precisely because the book reflects the field, we are left with a hodgepodge. Instead of a reasonably cogent and coherent narrative, we are left with random chapters that do not form a cogent and coherent whole. We are left instead with contributions to the conversation that remain disconnected, the one from the other. We are left instead with lots of leadership theories, but no single leadership theory, and no strong sense of how the various theories might connect to each other, might complement or even conflict with each other. In sum, we are left with the sensation, the suspicion, that we had when we started: that, as the editors themselves acknowledged, leadership as a field of intellectual inquiry is weak. It lacks a firm foundation based on theory. It lacks the impact of cumulative empirical evidence. It lacks now, as it has for the duration of the forty-year history of the leadership industry, a cadre of intellectual leaders. And it lacks a cadre of widely recognized and properly acknowledged cutting-edge leadership scholars who are also collaborative. With few and only occasional exceptions, leadership experts and educators continue to do their own thing, which explains why leadership remains a field in which, while one hundred flowers bloom, the crop, the yield, whatever the proper agricultural analogy, is poor.

As I look around me, at the shelves in the room in which I write, the impression remains the same. The leadership books that line my shelves are not only more different than they are similar, they are, by and large, independent of each other. People who write about leadership tend not to borrow from each other— more significantly, they tend not to build on each other. Contrast this with other professions in which the knowledge base is cumulative, and in which researchers from one generation tend to stand proudly on the shoulders of researchers from previous generations. Gene theory has progressed by leaps and bounds from when Gregor Mendel founded (in the nineteenth century) the modern science of genetics. But the appreciation of Mendel, the reverence for his work, only grows over the years. Conversely, who can say that Plutarch's great work on leadership, *Lives*, from which there is so much to be learned, has had any discernable impact on twenty-first-century leadership scholarship? Ironically, Plutarch's progeny, biographies of leaders, abound. But not only do contemporary leadership teachers and researchers tend to ignore Plutarch's *Lives*, they, we, tend to ignore its contemporaneous incarnations. In other words, biography is at the margin of leadership theory and practice—not at the center.

Of course, to the general rule—that leadership experts and educators tend to neglect rather than incorporate the work of their predecessors—there are, as is usual in these matters, some exceptions. For example, the distinction drawn by James MacGregor Burns, between transactional and transformational leadership, has had a significant impact on leadership scholars.[14] And Joseph Nye's distinction between soft power and hard power has been so influential as to become part of our leadership lexicon.[15] But even Burns's impact seems to have diminished somewhat in recent years. And for all of Nye's considerable contribution to the language of leadership, his work remains outside the leadership field rather than integral to it. His distinguished career is perceived to be in the fields of international relations and foreign policy—not so much in leadership. That, of course, is one of the problems. Leadership as a field of intellectual inquiry has failed by and large to integrate relevant work from other, notably more mainstream, disciplines. In the event, Burns and Nye are the exceptions. They do not change the fact that in leadership theory, the wheel is regularly reinvented.

Most of the late twentieth- and early twenty-first-century leadership literature does, however, have one thing in common. There is a single premise, a theoretical premise, if you will, that most authors of most books about leadership share: it is that leadership can be taught and that leadership can be learned. The unspoken assumption, of course, is that their own books about leadership will be especially instructive. Some small number of these books intend to instruct on theory—instruction as intellectual exercise. The great majority, though, intend to instruct on practice—instruction as manual, a manual on how to lead based, in many cases, on findings that grew out of the authors' own earlier work or on ideas that grew out of their earlier experience.

Warren Bennis was an example. He was a scholar with experience as a leader, who became later in his life a prolific writer of books and articles about leadership. Each had a different angle, though each was based on the same two fundamental assumptions: that leaders are of major importance and that how to lead can be taught. Other leadership experts have been similarly astute at bringing their own personal and professional perspectives to the study of leadership. An example is social psychologist Edwin Hollander, whose early studies of small-group psychology informed his work lifelong not only on leadership, but on followership. And there is Archie Brown, along with Burns and Nye an esteemed political scientist, who came over the course of his career to focus on leadership, a focus shaped both by his conceptions of political theory and by his observations of political practice. Still other experts developed a model of leadership that remained throughout their professional lives the center of their attention, such as, for example, psychiatrist Ronald Heifetz, whose work on adaptive leadership has continued for more than four decades to inform his teaching and scholarship.

Other books on my shelves look at leadership through a narrower lens, for instance, on women and leadership. In *Through the Labyrinth: The Truth about How Women Become Leaders*, Alice Eagly and Linda Carli made no claim to explore leadership broadly. Instead their focus was limited, informed by the inordinately important finding that women have leadership issues that are in addition to those of men. As Eagly and Carli described it, they were motivated by the fact that many more men than women were in "positions of power and authority" and that, of itself, this "demanded an explanation."[16] Other leadership books with a narrower focus are those on ethical or moral leadership. Despite the lack of rigorous research in this area, or maybe because of it, these books ask fundamental questions, such as these by Deborah Rhode, in her edited volume *Moral Leadership*: "How do leaders form, sustain, and transmit moral commitments? Under what conditions are these processes most effective? How do norms and practices vary across context and culture?"[17]

Yet another example is books by leadership experts who are not by any stretch leadership scholars, not to speak of theoreticians, but who are, or, more typically, were, leadership practitioners. Mostly they are men who held what Eagly and Carli call high "positions of power and authority." Though they do not generally so state, there is in fact a theory or at least a theoretical assumption, that underlies their work as well: it is that (their) exceptional leadership experience generates (their) exceptional leadership expertise. Countless books fall into this category, by, among others, entrepreneurs and elected officials, military officers, chief executive officers, and prominent coaches. Examples are by Lee Iacocca, Pat Riley, Andy Grove, Rudolph Giuliani, Colin Powell, General Stanley McChrystal, and, most impressively, former secretary of defense Robert Gates.[18] (Gates's book is titled *A Passion for Leadership*. It is, atypically, first rate.)

Finally, I include in this section books by leadership theorists who instruct on leadership practice—and whose instruction is based on their empirical research. In this group, I put a book such as Herminia Ibarra's *Act Like a Leader, Think Like a Leader*. Ibarra wrote that during her career she had been a researcher, author, and educator, experiences that enabled her to examine "how people navigate important transitions."[19] This led her, in turn, to develop what she called "the outsight principle," a theory that proposes "the only way to think like a leader is . . . to experiment with unfamiliar ways of getting things done."[20] In this group I also put Sydney Finkelstein's *Superbosses: How Exceptional Leaders Master the Flow of Talent*. Finkelstein "spent ten years conducting more than

two hundred interviews; sifting through thousands of articles, books, mono-
graphs, and oral histories; and writing three dozen case studies in the most
extensive and rigorous research project of its kind." This led him to develop
a theory about "superbosses," a theory that, when extended and extrapolated,
was supposed to instruct those with "with no special training in management"
to nurture "precisely the kind of curious, energetic, open-minded people companies need."[21] Of course books such as these are based on the familiar assumption that leadership can be taught and that it can be learned by reading a book
such as the one now in hand.

Obviously, there are many ways of organizing the many thousands of books
and articles about leadership. My intention here is simply to indicate that these
works do not in any obvious way congeal or coalesce. They do not provide a
theory or body of knowledge widely considered seminal. They do not comprise
information and ideas widely considered foundational. They do not constitute
a core curriculum widely considered essential. Clearly the problem is not lack
of leadership theory. There is leadership theory aplenty. The problem is that it
is strewn. Not only has no single individual done the requisite integrative work,
no group has joined together over an extended time to do this work in tandem.
Or, more precisely, no individual or group has done this work in a way that the
rest of us are ready and willing to buy into, to adopt, to acknowledge as being
so rigorous and persuasive that we are willing to support it, to use it to expand
and enrich the leadership field. Instead, again, we have preferred over the forty-
year history of the leadership industry to till our own soil, to cultivate our own
garden.

To this state of affairs there is no professional or even occupational analogue.
In hairdressing and truck driving are suppositions, or principles, or systems—
theories, premises, facts and figures, information and ideas on which the pedagogies and practices of hairdressing and truck driving are based. That is why there
is wide agreement on what a hairdresser must learn to get a license. And that is
why there is wide agreement on what a truck driver must learn to get a license.
Similarly, more impressively, since we are focused here primarily on professions,
it is important to point out that medical theory and practice and legal theory and
practice are sufficiently robust to allow for considerable consensus on what a
doctor absolutely must learn, and on what a lawyer absolutely must learn. This is
not to say that the curricula of all medical schools or all law schools are the same.
Rather it is to say that in medical and law schools, certain fundamental theories constitute organizing principles; certain fundamental facts are uncontested;
certain fundamental bodies of knowledge are required to be acquired; certain
fundamental practices are part of the process; and certain criteria must be met.
Leadership is different. For all of Sidney Finkelstein's prodigious research, it is
unlikely that five years from now *Superbosses* will be considered by leadership

educators or experts to be required reading. This says more about us than it does about him or his book.

Pedagogy

Given the state of leadership theory, it's no surprise that the state of leadership pedagogy is similar. It's all over the place. Some organizations and institutions have given careful thought to how to teach how to lead or, less frequently, how to teach about leadership. I've already pointed to the American military as one such example. Another is the Jepson School of Leadership Studies at the University of Richmond (UR), which falls into the second category. As its name suggests—it is, after all, a school of leadership studies—its primary focus is on leadership as an area of intellectual inquiry.

The Jepson School is in a singularly privileged position. It was established courtesy of business leader Robert Jepson, a 1964 UR graduate, and his wife Alice, who provided the University with an initial $20 million challenge gift to develop a leadership studies program. The School opened in 1992 and graduated its first class in 1994.[22] Since then it has by most measures thrived, in no small part because it has had the resources—human, fiscal, and temporal—to think long and hard about what an undergraduate leadership studies program should look like.

The program is a rarity: an undergraduate program that focuses on leadership through the prisms of the liberal arts and social sciences. The Jepson School does not, directly, purport to teach how to lead.[23] Rather it uses the "academic lenses of anthropology, economics, history, literature, philosophy, politics, psychology, and religion" to focus on leadership. But the school connects theory and practice: one of its premises is that studying leadership prepares students for practicing leadership. Statements such as these—"Jepson students step into organizations and life after college with deeper knowledge about leading change" and "We believe that our students are enriched when they have the knowledge and skills to contribute to organizational, political, and social life"—make clear that while the short-term purpose of Jepson is intellectual inquiry, its long-term ambition is to graduate students who will become in time leaders who are ethical and effective.[24]

UR undergraduates who want to major or minor in leadership studies must work for the privilege. They must apply for admission to the Jepson School during the fall semester of their sophomore year. Then, if they are accepted, they must enter the program through one of two gateway courses: Leadership and the Humanities or Leadership and the Social Sciences. Eventually both courses are required, along with a capstone course and an internship. In the end, to graduate with a major in leadership studies, students must successfully have completed seven core courses and four advanced courses grouped into three areas: ethics, history, and social/organizational.

I provide this information not to suggest that other institutions emulate Jepson's model. As indicated, Jepson has been and still is in a privileged position. Among its other advantages, it has always had faculty dedicated to leadership studies who have had, in turn, decades to hone their leadership curricula. However, there are some propositions that might be borrowed from Jepson, propositions that any group or organization professing to teach how to lead, or to teach about leadership, would do well to bear in mind. First, there is a connection between the study of leadership and the practice of leadership. Second, there is a preferred sequence to learning leadership. Jepson suggests a broad base to begin, grounded in theory, and a defined end, grounded in practice. Third, learning leadership at Jepson connotes an extended commitment both by teachers and by students—again it cannot be accomplished on the fly or on the cheap. Finally, leadership learners should receive from their leadership teachers this simple message: leading is not, simply, an occupation or a vocation. It is a profession.

Of course, the more important question is what the pedagogies in other leadership programs are, those that are less well endowed, less clearly focused, and less strongly committed than a wealthy, dedicated undergraduate institution such as Jepson. Two years after editing their initial handbook on leadership theory and practice, Nohria and Khurana, this time with Scott Snook (also Harvard Business School faculty), sought to answer this question by editing a second handbook, this one titled *The Handbook for Teaching Leadership: Knowing, Doing, and Being.*[25]

The editors began by acknowledging the explosive growth of the leadership industry (my term), noting that their Google search (in 2011–2012) of "leadership books" returned more than 84 million hits. Sad to say that they found not the slightest correlation between quantity and quality. Their overarching assessment of leadership pedagogy was no more heartening than their assessment of leadership theory. As before, the editors made immediately clear that their assessment was bleak. The flaws in leadership education, they wrote in their introductory chapter, are "easy to enumerate." They included course content that rarely conforms to the norms of the scientific method; teachers who employ casual and often self-serving empirical evidence; approaches rarely grounded in well-established theoretical traditions; few credible groups and organizations that are dedicated to developing and sharing best practices; and scant empirical evidence that any of the current pedagogies work. Their conclusion, then, was that the "current state of leadership education lacks the intellectual rigor and institutional structure required to advance the field beyond its present (and precariously) nascent stage."[26] In short, leadership education and training are, to put it politely, problematical.

Despite lambasting the state of leadership education, Nohria Khurana, and Snook, tackled the task at hand—to edit a volume about leadership education. As their subtitle suggests, the chapters written by the various leadership teachers are organized (with one exception) into three different parts: knowing, being, and doing. The assumption, apparently, is that there are certain things that leaders ought to know, certain ways that leaders ought to be, and certain skills or behaviors that leaders ought to acquire or adopt. The last section of the book is based on another assumption entirely: that some leadership learning should be other than leader-centric—it should center on context.

The Handbook for Teaching Leadership has thirty different chapters, which is another way of saying that the book has thirty different pedagogies promulgated by more than thirty different pedagogues (most of them academics)—of whom I, not incidentally, am one. While some of the pedagogies outlined in the book bear some resemblance to some of the others, many do not—such as mine. The course that I describe in the book bears no similarity to any of the other courses described in the book, which in some ways is good and in other ways is not so good.

I wrote in the *Handbook* about a course that I developed at the Harvard Kennedy School (HKS) titled Leadership Literacy"[27] Like most leadership teachers, I had no rigorous, reliable evidence that students who took such a course would be better leaders than those who did not. Moreover, I was aware that Leadership Literacy was an elective, a stand-alone course that was not integrated into the HKS curriculum. By offering a traditional liberal arts course in a professional graduate school, I was also taking a risk—the professional risk that student enrollment would remain rather low. Which it did. Nevertheless, I went ahead and developed an approach to teaching leadership at HKS that was one in which I deeply believed—for I deeply believe that leaders, nascent or otherwise, should be exposed to the liberal arts. It was also as new to HKS as it was different and, counterintuitively, as new and different as it was ancient and conventional. (Course content consisted primarily of readings from the classical leadership literature: Lao-tzu to Lenin, Elizabeth Cady Stanton to Betty Friedan, Rachel Carson to Martin Luther King, Peter Singer to Larry Kramer.) I write about this experience, this course, not to defend its importance, even for students who want to learn something *about* leadership, as opposed to those who want only to learn *how* to lead. Rather it is to point to questions such as those immediately below.

How is leadership education different from leadership training and development? What are the purposes of leadership education, training, and development? What constitutes a good leadership education, or good leadership training? Is there a seminal body of work—a core curriculum—with which every serious student of leadership should be familiar? If yes, what does it consist of? How to compare the benefits of learning, say, the classics of the leadership literature with learning about leadership in large organizations; or with learning about autocratic or entrepreneurial leadership; or with learning about the natural obverse of leadership, followership; or with skill-based trainings; or with the virtues of experience in the field? How, in short, should leadership experts and educators establish and sequence their priorities? How for that matter should leadership students establish and sequence their priorities? Does it depend entirely on who they are and on what they particularly want and need? Or are there fundamentals that all students of leadership should learn, just as there are some fundamentals that all students of medicine and law, and all students of hairdressing and truck driving, should learn? And, finally, what is the connection between questions such as these and transitioning, transforming, leadership from an occupation to a profession?

Back to the *Handbook*'s twenty-nine other pedagogies. Again, they're grouped into four categories. This said, they are also, the grouping notwithstanding, discouragingly disparate. Professor Deborah Ancona writes that faculty at MIT's Sloan School of Management teach four capabilities: sense-making, relating, visioning, and inventing.[28] University of Pennsylvania professor Michael Useem describes his work at the Wharton School to "create and instill a leadership template" that offers a set of "essential principles that are generic enough to apply to many situations yet specific enough to provide tangible guidance for each."[29] In his chapter, City Year's aforementioned Max Klau asserts that the experience of extended national service represents a "uniquely powerful context for developing civic leaders."[30] Louis Csoka, of Apex Performance, explains how his experience training athletes and soldiers led to his teaching "extraordinary" leadership "though mental skills development," skills such as stress management and attention control.[31] And Manfred F. R Kets de Vries (INSEAD and European School of Management and Technology [ESMT]) and Konstantin Korotov (ESMT) describe "transformational programs" based on a "clinical paradigm that underscores the illusion of rationality, the challenge of seeing what's happening beyond the level of consciousness, the impact of the past on current behaviors and thinking, the importance of transference and countertransference, the role of emotions, and the motivational need systems important for human functioning."[32]

Need I say more? Need I go on about how leadership pedagogy, like leadership theory, is strewn—like one hundred flowers—across a field? To be sure, in addition to the military and a few other places such as Jepson, there have been efforts to integrate the whole, to provide a single pedagogy that is internally consistent and reasonably coherent. I am thinking, for example, of a book by Susan Komives and colleagues titled *Exploring Leadership: For College Students Who*

Want to Make a Difference.[33] It targets a very particular audience and aims, given its audience, to be reasonably complete and comprehensive. But how is it related to, for instance, sense-making? Or to transformational leadership programs that explore what's happening "beyond the level of consciousness"? If sense-making and going beyond the level of consciousness are such important parts of leadership pedagogy, why are they not part of undergraduate leadership pedagogy? Is it that sense-making and going beyond the level of consciousness are important for leadership learners who are fifty years old, but not for leadership learners who are twenty years old? If yes, where is this written down, demonstrably proven? Is it that sense-making, to take a single case in point, is perceived as being of extreme importance at the Sloan School, but not elsewhere, not, for instance, in other graduate or professional schools? Is it that only so much can reasonably be learned at the undergraduate level—and sense-making can come later? Is it that the time and space we provide for learning to lead are woefully inadequate to the task, which means that vast amounts of what ought to be taught are left on the cutting room floor? Is it that the critical task of establishing pedagogical priorities has been largely avoided? Or is it some or all of the above?

I defy anyone who picks up the *Handbook for Teaching Leadership* to develop an obvious leadership curriculum based on its thirty different entries. I use the word "obvious" because there are some markers in the *Handbook*, implicit and explicit ideas about what ought to be taught and why. But there are no indicators provided by the editors or by anyone else of what is pedagogically indispensable, or of what the pedagogical priorities should be, or of what the curricular sequencing should be, or of what the curricular requirements should be. In other words, the key questions remain unanswered.

There's another problem: striking gaps in the literature on how to teach how to lead. Two come immediately to mind—followers and failures. If followership is important to leadership, followers to leaders, you would never know it from the literature on teaching leadership, which is relentlessly leader-centric. And if failures are important to leadership—failures that signify bad leadership along with successes that signify good leadership—you would never know it from the literature on teaching leadership, which is almost relentless in its sunniness. The literature on leadership teaching and learning is, in other words, woefully narrow. Followers are largely excluded. And failures, not to speak of disasters, are largely sidelined. Such research as there is on followers and failures—which is, to be sure, scant—is marginalized by the leadership industry, in this case, specifically by those proselytizing pedagogies.

We fail similarly to address the question of whether teaching how to lead in organizations and institutions that are entirely self-interested is, or should be, obviously different from teaching how to lead in organizations and institutions that are not. The first have an interest in teaching people how to lead only insofar

as it accrues to their own benefit. Certainly, most if not all businesses fall into
this category. As we have seen, and as common sense would dictate, companies
such as General Electric, Pierson, and Bank of America do not exactly think
teaching leadership for the common good is their top priority. Their top priority
is teaching leadership for the good of the company: for the profit-making, share
price-climbing purposes of General Electric, Pierson, and Bank of America.[34]
It might make sense though for such sorts of leadership teaching to be distinguished from other sorts of leadership teaching, especially when the motivations underpinning these teachings are radically different. The social change
model of leadership development, which, as mentioned, is used at more colleges
and universities than any other leadership development model, has the benefit
of having a name that distinguishes it from other models of leadership development. Most do not; most leadership programs and their respective pedagogies
remain unnamed. In other words, most leadership programs are simply referred
to in some vague way as "leadership programs," There is no clear indication of,
or obvious justification for, what the leadership program consists of or, more
importantly, what motivates it. Who is supporting it and for what purpose, what
end? Bottom line: we apply the same appellation to leadership education, training, and development programs that are entirely different from one another.

This returns us, not incidentally, to the distinction between leadership and
management. For one could reasonably make the argument that learning to provide direction in the interest of the common good is learning to *lead*. And one
could reasonably make the argument that learning to provide direction in the
(self) interest of a certain group or organization is learning to *manage*.

As we hack our way through the underbrush, it becomes clear that neither
the theories of leadership nor the pedagogies of leadership suggest professional
practice or status. Of itself, this chapter provides eloquent testimony to why
leadership remains an occupation and a sloppy one at that. It lacks the widely
accepted rigors and rules, ideas and information, pedagogies and practices, and
standards and measures that characterize the professions and even various vocations, such as hairdressing, trucking, and plumbing.

If you want to be a licensed plumber in the state of Connecticut you must
first learn how to be plumber; then you must prove that you have learned how
to be a plumber. How to do this? You might begin by signing up for training at
a technical high school or community college. Training in such a setting would
cover the basics, such as water systems, heating systems, air conditioning, valves,
vents, welding and piping. Alternatively, you might try getting into Connecticut's
apprenticeship program, Plumbing Apprenticeships in Connecticut, which is
run by a union, the State of Connecticut Plumbers and Pipefitters Local 777.
In this case, during your five-year apprenticeship, you would earn a living wage,
but the program is demanding. It requires forty hours of work a week and, to

learn the fundamentals of plumbing, six weeks of all-day classes for each of the five years. After your education and training are complete, to work in the state of Connecticut, either as a plumbing contractor or journeyperson plumber, a license is required. One of the requirements for such a license is passing two exams: one in business and law, the other in the techniques and technicalities of plumbing. You have five hours to answer 120 questions.

Easy enough to get my point. It seems more forethought has been given to what it takes to be a reasonably good plumber in the state of Connecticut than what it takes to be a reasonably good leader in the state of Connecticut. (No wonder the state has been grappling for years, so far to no avail, with a deep fiscal crisis!) Among the other virtues of the plumbing apprenticeship program is the sense that the basics are being covered, and that they will have been learned by any plumber in the state of Connecticut who has proven worthy of having a license. Of course, none of this guarantees that when I, a resident of the state, need a first-class plumber I will get a first-class plumber. Nevertheless, it is reassuring to know that if a licensed plumber walks through my door, odds are that he or she will be able to fix what's broke and, one hopes, be reasonably honest in the process. I wish I could say the same for a leader—I wish I could say that Connecticut was putting in place a licensure called Leadership Apprenticeships in Connecticut. Such a program would not make leadership a profession. But it would go some way toward transforming leadership from disrespected occupation to respectable vocation.

What I describe in this chapter is not a mess impossible to address. Not by any means. This is not rocket science. But cleaning it up would require something that's been absent during the forty-year history of the leadership industry. Cleaning it up would require leadership—good leadership and, as importantly, good followership.

5

Profession

Why is leadership an occupation and not a profession? How is a profession different from an occupation? What does a profession look like? How does an area of human endeavor transition, or evolve, from being an occupation (or a vocation) to being a profession? And why does no one even question that medicine is a profession, and that law is a profession, but that leadership and management are not professions? This chapter will answer these questions by exploring, in turn, leadership and management, and medicine and law.

Management

First a few words, again, about a few words: "leadership" and "management." I already discussed the distinctions between them, made by some, though by no means by all, of the experts. In fact, most of the time the lines are blurred— the words are used interchangeably. Finally, I made note of the fact that in the modern literature on leadership and management, the word "management" came first and the word "leadership" second. I noted that our fixation in recent decades on the words "leader" and "leadership" was the unintended outcome of a failure: the failure of American schools of business to make "management" a profession.

The title of this book is *Professionalizing Leadership*. However, in this chapter on the meaning we make of "profession" I will use the words "management" and "manager" more frequently than "leadership" and "leader" because, until the twenty-first century, when the subject of the discussion was professionalization, the former, or "executive," was used, not the latter.

In 1930, prominent author and social critic Abraham Flexner leveled a broadside at management education, warning of its deficiencies. "Modern business," he wrote, "does not satisfy the criteria of a profession: it is shrewd, energetic, and clever, rather than intellectual in its character; it aims . . . at its own advantage, rather than at noble purpose within itself."[1] Flexner's charge was on two counts: business education, management education, had failed to build a solid theoretical or pedagogical base; and business education, management education, had failed to provide a proper moral imperative. At around the same time (in 1927), pioneering management expert Mary Parker Follett published an article that contained the same cautions. Titled "Management as a Profession," Follett reminded her reader that "a profession is said to rest on the basis of a proved body of knowledge, and such knowledge is supposed to be used in the service of others rather than merely for one's own purposes."[2] For both Flexner and Follett, then, the word "profession" connoted two virtues, both of which were essential to professional status: science *and* service. This is precisely why Follett insisted that "men must prepare themselves as seriously for this profession [management] as for any other," even though, as she would have been the first to admit, there was no good evidence as yet of a science of management and no good evidence as yet that management was seen as a service.[3]

Close to a century has passed since Flexner and Follett penned their critiques—to little effect. Which is why I've written the present book. For I, like they, believe in the extravagant importance of professionalizing management—of leadership. I, like they, believe in "preparing" people to be managers, leaders, as thoroughly as for any profession. And I, like they, am frustrated by what has—or, better, has not—happened, especially during the forty-year history of the leadership industry. Of course, others have argued similarly, that management should be professionalized. But though experts and educators in management and leadership have, as Follett pointed out, drawn "a good many conclusions" and though they have "certain principles," to this day they have not taken the next step. They have not taken the "relation between these conclusions or these principles" and transformed them into a pedagogy that is intellectually rich and rigorous, as well as morally powerful and persuasive. They have not, in other words, developed the widely accepted core curriculum or the widely accepted code of ethics that are essential to educating, training, and developing professionals.

In recent years, two prominent academics and administrators revived the argument that management should evolve from an occupation to a profession. To be sure, it's not immediately apparent to whom they were preaching their gospel. Among other reasons, they themselves are in positions of considerable authority, positions that presumably would enable them to create meaningful change—which raises the question of why they have not. Why haven't they themselves done more to move toward the goal to which they aspire—to professionalize management? I refer to the previously mentioned Nitin Nohria and Rakesh Khurana. In fact, based not only on the articles to which I refer immediately below, but also on their *Handbooks*, and on Khurana's history of American business schools of business (all also previously mentioned), it's fair to say that no two of my contemporaries have given more thought to the sorts of questions that I raise in this book than they.

The first of the two articles, published in 2004, is titled "Management as a Profession." It was motivated mainly by shocking then recent revelations of corporate wrongdoing—of which Enron was the most famous/infamous example—and by polls indicating that the American people's trust in business leaders was starting to mimic their trust in political leaders. That is, it was in steep decline. "Executives, as a class," the authors wrote, were increasingly perceived as "greedy and dishonest."[4] So the questions they sought to address were, first, why was this happening? And second, what could be done to stem the tide? To the first question the answers were obvious—and not so obvious. It was obvious that corporate malfeasance was the result in good part of simple human greed, humans by nature being capable of inordinate self-interest. It was less obvious, or it had been, that such rules and regulations as were in place were inadequate to the task of holding extreme self-interest in check. Though this conclusion pertained to whole classes of careerists, including accountants, bankers, and stock market analysts, Khurana, Nohria, and coauthor Daniel Penrice, were concerned not with them, but with those at the top, with those who ultimately were responsible for the wrongdoing. Their interest was in "CEOs and other senior executives" who had failed to uphold "their professional obligations."

"Yet to speak of the 'professional obligations' of individuals such as CEOs and other executives," they wrote, "is to imply that business management itself is a profession. But is it really?" They went on to explore what constitutes a profession, and settled finally on four criteria that were "the essence of professionalism." The result was a comparison between "true" professions, on the one hand, such as medicine and law, and occupations, on the other hand, such as management, which, obviously, was less truly a profession. According to Khurana, Nohria, and Penrice, the criteria for achieving professional status are

- a common body of knowledge resting on a well-developed, widely accepted theoretical base;
- a system for certifying that individuals possess such knowledge before being licensed or otherwise allowed to practice;
- a commitment to use specialized knowledge for the public good. . . ;
- a code of ethics, with provisions for monitoring individual compliance with the code and a system of sanctions for enforcing it.[5]

Most discussions of management and leadership are generic. They apply across the board, to, say, management and leadership in business, in politics, in education, and in the military. Other times, though, discussions of management and leadership are specific—they are set in a certain context. In this instance, in

"Management as a Profession," the discussion focused on management in the private sector, on the professionalization, or the lack thereof, of management in business. Because of the scandals that were plaguing corporate America, Khurana, Nohria, and Penrice used their platform to propose that professionalizing management would provide a "remedy for the crisis of legitimacy now facing American business."[6]

But, contrary to what the authors presumably wanted and intended, each of their four criteria for achieving professional status amounted to a very high hurdle—not least, certification. The practice of medicine requires an MD degree, and of law a JD degree. So, naturally, Khurana, Nohria, and Penrice focused on the rough corporate equivalent, the MBA degree. However, the MBA presents two obvious problems. First, the MBA is not, per se, a degree in management or leadership. Second, it is not mandatory. Unlike MD and JD degrees, which are required before practicing, the MBA degree is by no means a prerequisite for practicing management or leadership—not even in the corporate sector. It might be considered desirable, but it isn't essential.

In keeping with their obvious concern for the future of American business, and with their obvious interest in making management a profession, some four years later Khurana and Nohria published another article, rather like their earlier one, this time in the *Harvard Business Review*. It was titled, more forcefully, "It's Time to Make Management a True Profession."[7] This second article on more or less the same subject making more or less the same point was written primarily for practicing professionals, so their analysis was less sweeping and their focus narrower. Their focus was on just one of their four criteria for a "true" profession—on a code of ethics, or, as they termed it, a "Hippocratic Oath for Managers."

The authors' argument was by now familiar: "In principle, there's no reason why management couldn't strive to become a profession."[8] They explored why management had stayed stuck, and why it had failed to do even that which it relatively easily could: to adopt the stringent knowledge and competency standards required by the true professions. Then they touched, briefly, on the all-important issue of academic politics—specifically disputations among academics. One of the problems, Khurana and Nohria wrote, if not *the* problem, was gaining acceptance, especially by their faculty colleagues, of the idea that setting strict educational standards would improve the practice of management. "Many management scholars and practitioners," Khurana and Nohria pointedly observed, "believe that management is as much art or craft as science, better mastered through experience than through formal education."[9]

Though it's a view with which the authors took issue—they distanced themselves from the position that formal education has no place in management education—they made clear nevertheless that this is the view held not only by many of their faculty colleagues, but also by practitioners, by leaders and managers in the so-called real world. "In the absence of empirical evidence," wrote Khurana and Nohria, "the idea that people can improve the practice of management by mastering some body of knowledge rests on faith. If you believe that the only value in management education is derived from signaling dedication to the field or building networks, it makes no sense to advocate the professionalization of management.... But if you believe, as we do, that the practice of management can benefit from judgment that draws upon a coherent body of formal knowledge, then pushing management in the direction of the true professions makes a lot of sense."[10]

The authors do not, in their article, say what this "coherent body of formal knowledge" should consist of. Instead, they take an easier, less controversial path: they focus on establishing a management code that would "have enormous influence" because such codes "provide guidelines for how an occupant of a role ought to behave."[11] Why is this path easier—a relatively low-hanging fruit? Because it is less politically fraught. It is harder to fight the idea of, and the specifics of, a code of ethics than to fight the idea of, and the specifics of, a core curriculum. In fact, at the Harvard Business School at least, the idea of an "MBA oath" had some traction, though only briefly. For even this well-intentioned effort soon petered out. This does not, however, mean that Khurana and Nohria do not deserve credit for pushing the idea that would-be leaders and managers, in this case MBA graduates, should swear that they will "act with the utmost integrity" and pursue their work "in an ethical manner."[12]

However, while a code of ethics is important, it would be more morally persuasive if it were implemented only *after* some of the other pieces have been put in place. Only *after*, for example, there was a generally agreed-on body of knowledge resting on a well-developed, widely accepted theoretical base. Only *after* there was a system for certifying that individuals possess such knowledge, as well as some relevant skills and experiences. Only *after* said individuals had committed to the idea that some of their knowledge and skills were to be used for the benefit of the common good. And, arguably, only *after* there was an association or some other sort of licensing body that was charged with protecting the profession and providing it with a modicum of cogence and coherence. In other words, building a profession is like building most everything else. It must be done slowly and carefully, and in some sort of sensible sequence. Ideally at least, a code of ethics should be drafted and implemented toward the end of such a process, not before any of the other building blocks have been put into place.

Moreover, such a code must be crafted by experts, not by amateurs, not by students such as those who played a considerable part in spearheading the initiative at Harvard. In short, the effort to transform management from an occupation to a profession must be *led* at every turn by professionals themselves. This is work that cannot be outsourced or democratized. If ever management and leadership are to be transformed from occupation to profession, the process, however gradual, must be led largely by those already in possession of professional credentials. Professionals in management and leadership must take responsibility—just as did doctors for the medical profession and lawyers for the legal profession.

Medicine

The Hippocratic oath is one of the oldest binding documents in history—it dates back two and a half millennia. Its purpose was, is, to get physicians to swear to uphold their professional obligations *before* beginning to practice medicine as professionals. To some the oath seems dated. But to most in the medical profession its core principles, such as treating the sick to the best of one's ability, remain sacred to this day. In fact, the number of medical schools administering some form of the Hippocratic oath to its graduating students has increased in recent decades, not decreased.[13] Put another way, Western medicine has an ancient tradition of invoking professionalism that is venerated to this day.

While the accumulation of more medical theory led gradually led to more proficient medical practice, for hundreds and even thousands of years, progress remained slow. While all along had been some advances in anatomy, physiology, and pharmacology, only in the sixteenth and seventeenth centuries did progress became more exponential and less incremental. By 1700 knowledge of gross anatomy was especially well advanced: valuable work was being done on specific organs, and there were many first-rate anatomical atlases.[14] In fact, anatomy was the first practical medical subject to be brought into the university curriculum. From the time of the Renaissance onward, medical "professors were expected to be experienced in dissection, and all students were required to attend anatomical demonstrations."[15]

But attendance at anatomical demonstrations was increasingly inadequate to the challenge of developing a distinct professional, medical identity. By the end of the seventeenth century, then, several universities had introduced another sort of study to medical education, clinical experience. "The University of Leiden was one of the first medical schools to make use of a local hospital to provide clinical lectures, where actual patients substituted for the case histories presented in lectures."[16] Suffice to say here that during the eighteenth century medical practice and theory were increasingly entwined, so that students of medicine might, for example, serve first as apprentices with local surgeons and then get their degrees at a university.

By the late eighteenth century there were new opportunities for medical education, especially at universities, which offered increasing numbers of courses in what gradually was regarded as medical *science*. Such courses were available not only to university students but also to practitioners who had no ultimate interest in getting a university degree. In time, universities themselves were faced with competition: first, from medical professionals, especially surgeons, who, intent on enhancing their own professional status, began to form exclusive guilds; second, from schools dedicated exclusively to medicine, that is, medical schools; and third, from so-called hospital schools, which, as the name implies, were hospitals that offered students additional clinical experience.

But only at the beginning of the nineteenth century, as the hard sciences took root, did medicine acquire most of the trappings of professions. Above all was a growing body of knowledge that was considered mandatory learning for anyone who wanted to practice. This knowledge base was grounded in reason and science, as opposed to dogmatism and superstition. This is another way of saying that modern, Western medicine was affected by, even shaped by, the Enlightenment, a set of ideas and ideals that valued open and objective inquiry, and by an empiricism freed from the shackles of the blinkered past. Several Enlightenment luminaries were, in fact, physicians themselves, notably John Locke, who was medically trained, and whose body of political thought was, as we have seen, so influential that it provided the ideological underpinnings of the American Revolution. Tellingly, the eminent historian Peter Gay concluded that contemporaneous medical practitioners and Enlightenment thinkers had something of a symbiotic relationship, in which the one fed the other, each contributing to the "recovery of nerve" vital for the "pursuit of modernity."[17]

During the eighteenth century, medicine became increasingly professional. Universities offered more medical courses. Surgeons' guilds extended their authority by offering certificates of competence that required more formal study, including lectures, examinations, and dissection. Clinical experience went from being the exception to becoming the rule. And licenses to practice professionally were beginning to be required, for instance in France, where midwives received permission to practice only after completing a course of study.

By the beginning of the nineteenth century, requirements for the practice of medicine had become notably more rigorous. Lisa Rosner described the process as a "kind of inflation of medical education," the demands on those wanting to practice medicine becoming distinctly more stringent. She wrote that by about 1800 "students who might previously only have served an apprenticeship with a local practitioner now began to take courses at a university, and students who might have taken only one or two classes began to attend many classes, for several years."[18] Universities remained in the game by co-opting some of the competition, by incorporating into their own curricula most components of medical study. Similarly, surgeons' apprentices were expected to attend more university classes, and medical students were expected to become proficient in anatomy and surgery. If apprentices had previously excelled in "skill" and students had previously excelled in "science," the distinction between them began to blur. In time, both groups were expected to be accomplished in both skill and science. In other words, medicine was becoming professionalized.

During the nineteenth century, medicine's transition from occupation to profession was completed. The reasons included the changing nature of medical education, which became in time the most rigorous of any profession. Interestingly, though medical education in the twenty-first century is not exactly what it was in the nineteenth century, it is not very different. A good liberal arts education was assumed even then. There followed at least three years of concentrated medical study. Finally, after graduation from medical school, came a year or more of clinical experience in a hospital, now called internships and residencies. In sum, by the middle of the nineteenth century, it was determined that the best possible medical education and training were a combination of length and depth, of hard study and clinical experience, all of which would necessarily take place over a protracted time, several years or more. The rigorousness of this requirement served several purposes. It admitted to the medical profession only those who were highly motivated and extremely accomplished. It conveyed to this elite cadre of medical professionals a sense of community and camaraderie. And it excluded from the medical profession everyone who did not meet the high standards that by then the profession had set.

These standards were supported by a national professional association, the American Medical Association (AMA), which was established in 1847. Virtually from its inception, the AMA took an active role in defining the qualifications of medical professionals. Moreover, it grew over time to become one of the most powerful professional associations in the world. American physicians have become, in other words, a "classic political interest group" of prominence and power, one that by nearly every measure is successful.[19] As one expert put it, "The nebulous world of proprietary medical schools, patent medicine, and unregulated practice vanished under the clear organization radiating from a powerful, nationally united organization."[20]

The AMA today has one of the largest political lobbying budgets of any organization in the United States. It is deeply, sometimes controversially, involved in public policy issues such as Medicare and the Affordable Care Act. And it publishes the *Journal of the American Medical Association*, which has the largest circulation of any weekly medical journal in the world. Above all, though, the AMA is the ultimate professional organization—the ultimate organization of professionals fiercely determined to protect, as they see fit, their status in every aspect. The AMA's mission statement is grounded in the rhetoric of public service: "to promote the art and science of medicine and the betterment of public health." And, of course, the AMA is committed to guiding principles, such as charting "a successful course for health care delivery that will improve the health of the nation."[21] But, more than anything else, the AMA is committed to its members, to addressing the needs, wants, and wishes of medical professionals who are physicians.

Recently, one of the several journals of the AMA, the *AMA Journal of Ethics*, published an article titled "Professional Socialization in Medicine." It described what about medicine makes it a profession, as distinguished from a vocation or occupation. Moreover, it detailed how the profession of medicine inculcates professional norms. For example, socialization to the profession of medicine begins early on, in medical school, where norms are established that dictate the nature of interactions between superiors and subordinates and between physicians and patients, criteria for evaluation, and ideas and beliefs considered right and good and true, such as, in recent years, the importance to the profession of diversification. (Fifty years ago, physicians were, overwhelmingly, white males. This was the norm, considered not only acceptable but appropriate.)[22] In short, the research on medical socialization is clear. One of the purposes of a medical school is to socialize medical students to the medical profession. Medical school is considered a "rite of passage during which neophytes are structurally separated from their former environments . . . stripped of their former external identities, and finally are collectively incorporated into their new roles."[23]

Sociologists use the term "professional culture" to convey the idea that every profession sends to its members messages intended for them only. These messages are sent through professional structures, such as medical schools. But they are also sent by conveying norms about what is expected of (or considered unbecoming to) medical professionals. Finally, they are sent through habituation, that is, through beliefs and behaviors that are repeatedly reinforced, so that they become in time second nature. Thus are those within the profession separated from, distinguished from, those without. A profession is, then, a kind of club to which membership is gained through various rites of passage. Some of these rites are open and obvious, such as graduating from an accredited medical school. (Accreditation is, not incidentally, another means of gaining and maintaining professional control—which explains why the AMA has long played a large part in the accreditation process.) Others of these rites are less obvious, hidden transcripts of sorts in which norms are conveyed covertly, such as, until relatively recently, the norm that a physician was a man. (Note: the gender gap in medicine persists. While the number of women in medical school is now roughly on a par with men, in 2016 only 21 percent of full professors at American medical schools were women.)[24]

Medical professionals continue to take medical pedagogies especially seriously. More specifically, they take seriously the need to update pedagogies and to reform them. We know that for a variety of personal, professional, and political reasons, pedagogies tend to stay stuck—medical pedagogies among them. This explains why, despite remarkable recent progress in science, technology, and medicine, medical education remains in important ways unchanged. "Compared with the dramatic changes that have occurred in biomedical science and the practice of medicine, the fundamental model of clinical education in American medical schools has changed little since the time of Sir William Osler, a century ago," concluded the authors of a recent article in one of the leading medical journals. "Students are still assigned to specialty-specific teams of interns, residents, and supervising faculty physicians for relatively brief, randomly sequenced rotations. . . . And the core clinical credentialing experience continues to be this same series of rotations, primarily in the third year of the traditional four-year . . . curriculum."[25]

The charge obviously is that while medicine has radically changed, medical education has stayed more or less the same. Among the concerns is that medical educators have failed to incorporate some of the research on learning in adulthood. It's why some have become interested in "progressive professional and personal development," the idea that learning is a process that takes place over time and is intended to support continuing personal as well as professional growth.[26] For example, there is considerable interest now in the concept of "continuity." Continuity in this context implies, among other things, a medical education that is more integrated, enabling students to follow their patients as long as necessary to "observe the course of the illness and the patient's experience of the illness, and . . . the effects of their management decisions."[27] This explains at least in part why one of the reforms most often recommended is the tearing down of walls—such as the wall between medical education and medical training, and the wall between basic science learning and clinical science learning.[28] None of this is easy. Educational reform in medicine is like educational reform everywhere else: it presents "substantial financial, organizational, and cultural difficulties."[29]

A final note. It is impossible to look at the literature on medical education without being struck by the fact that it is no longer the province only of the young. Physicians, it is now believed, must extend their education and training into middle adulthood and, if they are still practicing professionals, into later adulthood as well. As one physician and medical school dean put it, "The centrality of lifelong learning and critical thinking reflects the rapidity with which knowledge in the field of medicine is evolving. It is accepted as a truism that much of what is learned in medical school will be outdated in less than 10 years. Consequently, the majority of learning occurs after a student graduates medical school."[30] In fact, as a result of changes in medicine and in what we expect of medical professionals, certification programs have become staples of the profession. In other words, especially in some specialties, to be certified as a medical professional lifelong you must be recertified as a medical professional lifelong. For example, the Maintenance of Certification Program (MOC) of the American Board of Psychiatry and Neurology (ABPN) states that its mission is to ensure that its diplomates continue to "adhere to the highest standards in medicine and pursue excellence in all areas of care and practice improvement." Those diplomates who were board certified after 1994, but who do not recertify in accordance with ABPN requirements, will lose their board certification.[31]

The process of professionalizing medicine took a long time, as does the professionalization of every occupation, every vocation. It happens in stages and in some sort of reasonably logical sequence. Moreover, it takes a cadre of dedicated and determined individuals, leaders if you will, who are hell-bent on drawing a line between those who are professionals and those who are not. Fifty years from now, even five years from now, the context within which medicine is practiced will inevitably have changed. But the overarching parameters of the medical profession have been long since established. Whatever the challenges to twenty-first century medical professionals, they will not in any major way be diminished. Physicians will maintain and retain their professional status.

Law

To James Brundage, the author of a book titled *The Medieval Origins of the Legal Profession*, the word "professional" meant more than "simply a body of workers who do a particular job on which they depend for support." To him being a professional meant (1) mastery of a substantial body of knowledge; (2) acquisition of this knowledge though a lengthy period of dedicated study; (3) a clear commitment to public service; and (4) a pledge to observe ethical rules more stringent than those applied to the rest of society. Remarkably, by the mid-thirteenth century "Professional lawyers were doing all these things."[32]

In fact, the legal profession goes back even further, to Roman times. Moreover, by the late twelfth and early thirteenth centuries the profession had developed to the point where men were learning the law through the systematic study of legal texts, including readings, lectures, review sessions, and disputations; where their legal studies were taking place in university settings; and where they were taught by faculty who were legal experts. Additionally, some practicing lawyers had law degrees that attested to their superior performance in rigorous examinations and permitted them to serve, in effect, as law professors. Finally, lawyers were professionals in that they had been "formally admitted to practice in one or more courts, and at the time of their admission had pledged themselves to observe the rules of a special body of ethics peculiar to their calling."[33] Because lawyers had demonstrably high levels of accomplishment—this was during a time when most people were still illiterate—it's no surprise that during the thirteenth and fourteen centuries lawyers occupied positions of high status and considerable authority.

The enduring and complete transformation of the law from occupation to profession had its inception in the courts of the medieval church. Canonists were the first to develop a clear legal identity, one that provided a model not only for other lawyers, but for other professionals as well, such as university-trained physicians, who also came gradually to adopt the sorts of trappings that distinguished persons practicing professions from persons practicing occupations or vocations. Tellingly, even in medieval times lawyers insisted on being considered separate and distinct from those around them. They regarded themselves and their professional colleagues with pride, as an intellectual elite that deserved its considerable power, prestige, and privilege precisely "because what they did was difficult, demanding, and vital to the well-being of society."[34] Indeed lawyers considered themselves every bit as important as soldiers—they thought that they, like soldiers, were critical to the general welfare.

During this period, the law was itself transformed. Legal disputations led to the gradual creation of legal doctrine, a body of law that, because it was formally codified, became core to the professional culture. Ideas and ideologies about, for example, representative assemblies and limits on the power of rulers first appeared in university lectures, only later to become central elements in the reshaping of social and political institutions. Brundage wrote that "these doctrines owned their inception to law teachers, while the lawyers whom they taught became instrumental in applying those ideas to practical problems in both church and state."[35]

By the middle of the thirteenth century, then, two components critical to the legal profession, as to any profession, were in place. The first was an elite that was highly educated and supremely well trained and that was considered distinct from, and superior to, almost everyone else. The second was a body of knowledge essential not only to the profession, but to professionals, whose main claim to fame was to have mastered it. In due course was added a third critical component: a code of ethics that legal professionals had to swear to uphold. Judges presiding in church courts began to demand of those who appeared before them that they vow to follow certain rules pertaining to how they conducted themselves vis-à-vis the courts and their clients. So, in addition to physicians, who since ancient Greece had the Hippocratic oath, and to men of the cloth, who had pledged themselves to follow the dictates of the Catholic Church, was now a third group of professionals who swore allegiance to a set of ethical principles as a condition of admission to practice law.[36] The specifics of these principles sound familiar, contemporaneous as opposed to ancient. For instance, every lawyer had to promise that he would perform his duties faithfully; that he would not steal his clients' documents or cause them to be purloined; that he would not put forward perjured testimony or forged documents; and that he would not conceal the truth from the judge. But, of course, that's precisely the point. Professional codes of ethics are supposed to be timeless. Similarly, once a professional, always a professional—unless the code that was sworn to be upheld has been violated.

In America, the legal profession goes back to the days of the colonists. But, given that colonial America was America divided—divided into different colonies, each of which was founded separately and operated independently— questions arise. At which point was there a clear class of professional lawyers? And, since the colonies all had their own governments, their own courts, and their own laws, what was it about their legal systems, if anything, that they had in common?

The variations among them were clear. Some colonies sought to ban lawyers altogether. Others were more dependent on English common law and less on Scripture. And still others were the converse, less dependent on English common law and more on Scripture. But, by and large, legal doctrine in early New England was reminiscent of what it had been in Great Britain: both were based on the Bible and on English law. Similarly, lawyers in Puritan New England did not greatly deviate from lawyers in medieval Europe: Puritan magistrates, along with Puritan clergy, were in control of community affairs. In other words, in early America as in Europe magistrates held sway along with clergy. In fact, both magistrates and clergy thought of themselves as professionals, as members of a group or a class that was separate and distinct from, and arguably superior to, other members of their community. However, as the colonies matured and the zeal for independence from Britain grew, so did the movement to separate American law from English law. Because of this growing defiance, because American society was a pioneer society, and because in early America there were only a few trained lawyers, "Each colony gradually developed a sort of common law of its own which often differed greatly from that of England as well as from that of any other colony."[37] In other words, in the waning days of colonial America, justice was as dispersed as dispensed, between the Crown and the clergy, and among the various cities and boroughs, each of which had its own courts of justice.[38]

Withal, on the eve of the American Revolution, lawyers were viewed as being at the apex of the colonial gentry. After a century or more of some disarray, lawyers had by then, by and large, achieved economic success, social standing, and professional prestige, which enabled them in turn to play leading roles in public affairs. What lawyers were not, however, was especially well educated, certainly not to the degree that we now associate with being a legal professional. Why? Because American legal doctrine was still sketchy at best, because the supply of authoritative legal materials was still meager, and because in time English law was less applicable to the American colonial experience.

The Revolution was the turning point. It sealed the status of the American legal profession in large part because political discourse was to a considerable degree framed in legal language. Legal language was the language of the literate community. And legal language made sense because by then the Founders realized that the law was the foundation on which the American edifice was being built. "From that point on all the major issues of American political life would be cast in legal language and, accordingly, would receive their final shape from lawyers rather than from philosophers or political scientists."[39] The impact of the American Revolution on American law was, in a word, dramatic. The United States of America was now a separate legal entity, which soon led to another critical step in the professionalization of the law: providing a legal education in a university setting.

To be clear, even though lawyers on the American continent had long enjoyed relatively high status, until legal education in America implied higher education in America, the future of the law in what we now know as Western democracy was uncertain. It took a professional education, based on the principles and methods of legal analysis, to professionalize the law. Put another way, because law schools did not exist in colonial America (or even at the time in Britain), the law was still seen more as a vocation than as a profession. Men were trained to be lawyers primarily through some combination of reading law and practical experience—"akin to the training of a blacksmith's apprentice."[40] Not until late in the eighteenth century did a few universities establish a chair in law. And not until early in the nineteenth century did a few universities establish separate programs for the purposes of providing a legal education.

Harvard College was an example. In 1817, it established the Harvard Law School. Lectures were given, a small library was acquired, there were moot courts, and discussions and dissertations. However, students came and went largely as they pleased—many leaving before finishing their studies for apprenticeships in attorneys' offices.[41] There was no reason not to. For no law office required its lawyers to pass examinations or to have a law degree. In time, of course, this changed. Whereas in the early nineteenth century the emphasis was on the practice of law, in the late nineteenth century it was on the theory of law. In consequence, the process of becoming a lawyer became more difficult and demanding. Gradually, lawyers were required to be law school graduates. And gradually requirements for graduation from law school became more stringent. At Harvard, the laxity with which law degrees had been awarded came to an end. By the late 1800s, graduation from Harvard Law mandated one year of attendance and the successful completion of exams. Finally, in 1906, came a new requirement: that law school constitute a separate and distinct course of study that lasted fully three years. Put differently, by 1906, the law was fully professionalized, and law school graduates regarded themselves, and were regarded by others, as professionals.

So what do three years of study at law school look like now? It turns out that the process of getting a law degree is much like the process of getting a medical degree. Both are professional pedagogies. And both are professional pedagogies based on the proposition that instruction should comprise, in sequence, theory and practice, learning and doing. Consequently, both professional pedagogies advocate and indeed provide some combination of learning in the classrooms and learning in the field. It's as if the distant pedagogical past, during which practice and experience ruled (learning in an apprenticeship), was finally combined with the more recent pedagogical past, during which information and ideas ruled (learning in a classroom), to produce an amalgam now widely deemed optimal. In other words, in the first quarter of the twenty-first century law schools are like medical schools: they tend toward a teaching template that mandates professional education *and* professional training.

Again, the base is built first. And, again, the base is knowledge, basic knowledge. In 2016 Harvard Law School described its first year of study as just that—a year of study. In year one students receive "a solid intellectual foundation on which to build [a] legal education, covering foundational principles and concepts."[42] There are required courses in, for example, criminal law, contracts, civil procedure, torts, legislation and regulation, property, and problem-solving. And there is skill development: in their first year at Harvard Law students are required to acquire or further develop skills such as legal research, legal analysis, negotiation, and oral advocacy. However, after the first year, the nature of the pedagogical process changes dramatically. Then students "have a great deal of flexibility to craft their own curriculum." In fact, while "intellectual development" is required of students in their first year at Harvard Law, in their second year it is less emphasized. Years two and three are oriented toward practice, for example, in a clinical placement.

At Yale Law School the curriculum is similarly structured. During their first term students are required to master legal fundamentals in such courses as Constitutional Law, Contracts, Procedure, and Torts. Subsequently, they are free to choose from a range of elective courses. Again, most law schools are like most medical schools. Both assume that in the beginning, a professional education should consist of instruction tantamount to a core curriculum, a curriculum considered essential to becoming a professional, consisting of information and ideas with which all doctors should be familiar—and, respectively, all lawyers. It is assumed, in other words, even by those institutions that are the most highly ranked, that students planning to become professionals can to a considerable extent be left to their own devices, left to chart their own curricular course. But they should be permitted to do so only *after* they have mastered the fundamentals—only *after* they have mastered a critical body of knowledge or, if you prefer, a core curriculum consisting of materials that are basic and essential.

Finally, like the medical profession, the legal profession is committed to providing and in some cases mandating continuing education. Legal experts and educators have concluded that continuing legal education will enhance the competence of practicing lawyers, especially of those who graduated from law school years ago; that it will elevate the level of public trust in lawyers; and that it will provide lawyers with education and training that many have decided they need and want for their own professional edification and certification.[43] To be sure, there are some skeptics. Inevitably questions are raised about the quality of continuing legal education programs and about whether their benefits justify their costs. Still, there is no question that continuing education in the legal profession, as in the medical profession, is becoming the rule, not the exception. Whether voluntary or mandatory, increasingly being a lifelong legal learner is considered integral to being a lifelong legal professional.

In still another parallel to the medical profession, since 1878 the legal profession has been represented (and protected) by an association similar to the American Medical Association: the American Bar Association (ABA). The ABA's mission is to "serve equally our members, our profession and the public by defending liberty and delivering justice as the national representative of the legal profession." The "ABA Model Rules of Professional Conduct" serve as a template for most lawyers in most states, and they set the standards by which individual lawyers, and indeed the profession itself, are supposed to be judged. It's a detailed document, the first item of which, titled "A Lawyer's Responsibilities," sets the general tone: "A lawyer, as a member of the legal profession, is a representative of clients, an officer of the legal system and a public citizen having special responsibility for the quality of justice."[44]

Of course, notwithstanding its professed commitment to serving the public interest, the ABA resembles the AMA in that it is dedicated first and foremost to serving its own interests, that is, the interests of the legal profession and legal professionals. The ABA also resembles the AMA in that it is inordinately powerful. It is proximate to (though not directly involved in) the process by which law schools are or are not accredited. It is proximate to the process by which legal aspirants get schooled in the legal profession. And it is proximate to law school graduates' ability to practice law, because graduation from an ABA-accredited law school is almost always required before taking the bar exam.

In recent years, like every other professional association, the ABA has had no choice but to change in response to the changing times. Among its current concerns are legal education and everything that it entails, such as rising student debt, falling law school applications, and declines in the market for law school graduates. Still, the number of lawyers is far larger than it used to be. And, what-ever the inevitable concerns, lawyering remains every bit a profession, one as dis-tinct as distinctive, and as heavily involved in business and government as ever. It has, in addition to the national bar association, state and local bar associations, codes of ethics, and disciplinary procedures. Moreover, law schools and state bars require undergraduate degrees for admission. Law schools still generally consist of three years of study. And "bar examinations have become universal, written and difficult," with examiners insisting that prospective legal practition-ers possess American citizenship, state residence, and good character.[45]

But, legal professionals are like medical professionals. By and large they understand that in times like these—times in which change is as swift as certain—they have no choice but themselves to change. One of the legal profes-sion's major mantras is therefore familiar: that lifelong *education* and *training*, and continuing personal and professional *development*, are necessary not only to tackle the tasks at hand, but to protect lawyers' professional status.

Occupation to Profession

The word "profession" is somewhat fungible. It's difficult to say when exactly "groups can be said legitimately to have coalesced into professions."[46] Still, *Wikipedia* defines "professionalization" this way: a "social process by which any trade [vocation] or occupation transforms itself into a true 'profession of the highest integrity and competence.'" Professionalization "tends to result in establishing acceptable qualifications, and one or more professional associa-tions to recommend best practices and to oversee the conduct of members of the profession, and some degree of demarcation of the qualified from unqual-ified amateurs (that is, professional certification). It is also likely to create an 'occupational closure,' closing the profession to entry from outsiders, amateurs and the unqualified."[47]

However, professionalization presupposes even more than this. It also presup-poses a process that precedes the establishment of "acceptable qualifications": an extended, extensive process of education and training. I would argue, in fact, that extended, extensive education and training are essential to the professionalizing process—critical to achieving professional status. *Without* extended, extensive education and training, achieving professional status is impossible. *With* extended, extensive education and training, achieving professional status is possible.

These, then, are the markers associated with achieving professional status:

- Generally accepted system or body of knowledge
- Extended education

- Extended training
- Required continuing education and training
- Clear criteria for evaluation
- Clear criteria for certification
- Clear demarcation between those within the profession and those without
- Explicit commitment to the public interest
- Explicit commitment to a code of ethics
- Professional association or organization with the power and authority to monitor the status of the profession and the conduct of its members

So where does this leave leadership? A quick accounting, recounting, makes the point. Not only is leadership not a profession, it doesn't even come close. It remains an occupation with

- No generally accepted system or body of knowledge
- No extended education
- No extended training
- No required continuing education and training
- No clear criteria for evaluation
- No clear criteria for certification
- No clear demarcation between those within the profession and those without
- No explicit commitment to the public interest
- No explicit commitment to a code of ethics
- No professional association or organization with power and authority to monitor the status of the profession and the conduct of its members[48]

The most striking thing about these lists is not so much the evidence they provide of the failure of leadership to approximate the professions of medicine and law. It is how far short leadership falls of any professional ideal. It's not that the medical and legal professions are perfect. Not at all. Both, for example, mandate too high a degree of exclusivity and protectionism, neither of which is attractive or productive. But what they have signified in the past, and continue to signify in the present, is a striving toward excellence in every aspect: excellence in effectiveness, and excellence in ethics. It is this professional standard, these measures of professional performance, that leadership so sorely lacks. This makes it an outlier. By being so consistently resistant to the idea that they (we) should professionalize their (our) endeavors to even a modest degree, leadership experts and educators demean not only their work but themselves.

Ironically, these experts and educators resist reforming, regulating, and credentialing even now, when regulating and credentialing have become epidemic. In 2013 Arizona's Veterinary Medical Examining Board sent Grace Granatelli a cease-and-desist order, demanding that she close her animal massage business until she had in hand a degree in veterinary medicine. In Tennessee, "A license is required to shampoo hair; in Florida, to sell a yacht. In Montana, you need the state's approval to be an egg candler, in Utah, to repair upholstery; in Louisiana, to be a florist."[49] Things have got to the point where 30 percent of American workers need a license just to do their jobs—up from about 10 percent in the 1970s. "Why in the world," asked one politician railing against regulation, "do we regulate barbers?"[50]

Leaders, then, are *not* professionals—not remotely redolent of professional ideals or standards. They are casual purveyors of wares that we have come, during the forty-year history of the leadership industry, increasingly to dislike, diminish, demean, and distrust.

PART III

BECOMING A PROFESSIONAL

6

Inclusion

The leadership industry's leadership pedagogies are bedeviled by several issues—here I will focus on three.[1] First, most leadership pedagogies presume that followers—those who are other than leaders—are irrelevant or unimportant. Second, most leadership pedagogies presume that leadership is separate and distinct from the contexts within which it takes place. And third, most leadership pedagogies presume that good leadership matters, but that bad leadership does not. To put it directly, by and large the process of learning to lead is overwhelmingly leader-centric. It ignores the necessary other, the follower. And it ignores the situation within which all of the actors, leaders and followers, necessarily are situated. Further, the process of learning to lead is ceaselessly, exhaustingly, sunny. It is based on the aspirational assumptions that effective leadership can be taught and learned; that ethical leadership can be taught and learned; and that leadership that is ineffective, or unethical, or both, is not something with which either leadership teachers or leadership learners need to concern themselves. I'm reminded of the corporate colossus that is Facebook, which historically had a culture that accentuates the positive and eliminates the negative. In fact, Facebook's mission statement—"Give people the power to build community and bring the world together"—reflects the wildly optimistic assumption that people will use the power of social media only to good ends. But, as the company has learned, not all people are good all the time.

Overwhelmingly leadership pedagogy is exclusive rather than inclusive. The focus is narrow rather than broad, in part because the pedagogical process is short, not long, and in part because the pedagogical presumption is that focusing laser-like on single individuals will suffice. These single individuals, these "leaders," are rarely set in the larger world of other people—the single, occasional exception being the people with whom they work. And they are rarely set in context—the single, occasional exception being the organization within which they work. Instead these single individuals, these leaders, or would-be leaders, are, in effect, free-floating agents fixated largely if not entirely on themselves: on enhancing their experience and expertise, on developing their skill set, and on expanding their self-awareness, self-development, self-improvement, and, I would argue, self-importance.

The spectrum of leadership—from good to bad—is similarly constrained and constricted. By homing in on good leadership, we fail even to acknowledge the presence of, indeed the ubiquity of, bad leadership. This raises the question of how we can minimize that which we fail to recognize. How do we deal with bad leadership—decrease its frequency and diminish the baleful effects thereof—if we fail to take note of it? This raises another question: do leadership teachers and leadership learners have a moral—a professional—obligation to address bad leadership? To try to identify it? To try to rectify it? To try to reduce it? Or does it suffice for leadership teachers to convey to leadership learners—implicitly if not explicitly—that bad leadership is beside the point? For that matter, does it suffice for leadership learners to ignore everything other than their own education, training, and development? When we are dealing with power, and with authority, and with influence, does nothing other than individual enhancement matter? Or do traits and behaviors such as ineptitude, recklessness, stupidity, malfeasance, and even malevolence have a role to play in the theory of leadership and in the pedagogy of leadership—as they do in the practice of leadership?

Why, moreover, does any of this matter? Why does it matter if, for example, we confine our conceptions of leadership education, training, and development to our conceptions of leaders? It matters because it is unprofessional—because by confining our conceptions we are confining our aspirations. In other words, if leadership practice is ever to be based on leadership theory, that is, on a system of knowledge, and if leadership is ever to progress from being an occupation to being a profession, our conception of leadership must become more expansive and inclusive. It must come to include not only leaders but followers. It must come to include not only leaders and followers but contexts. It must come to include not only leaders and followers and contexts, but explorations and conversations about bad leadership as well as good leadership. Our ideas about leadership and about how we should teach leadership must come, in sum, more closely to resemble our ideas about medicine and law, and about how medicine and law ought to be taught.

Medicine would never be a profession if it educated, trained, and developed doctors in a vacuum—devoid of patients. Law would never be a profession if it educated, trained, and developed lawyers in a vacuum—devoid of clients. Nor would either one of them be a profession if their pedagogies were divorced from the contexts within which people practiced their professions. Similarly, can you imagine teaching how to be a doctor or how to be a lawyer while excluding from the discussion what happens when medicine or law are practiced badly? While excluding from the discussion the potentially disastrous consequences of doctors and lawyers who practice unethically or ineffectively, or both? I argue in this chapter that teaching how to lead reasonably and responsibly requires opening the conversation, expanding it for reasons that include, but are not limited to, professionalizing leadership.

Leadership Is a System

Leadership is not about individuals. More precisely, it is not *only* about individuals. Instead, leadership is, as already indicated, a *system*. It is a system in which each of these three parts—leaders, followers, contexts—is *equally* important and in which each of these three parts impinges *equally* on the other two. Leadership as a system is a somewhat more complicated construct than leadership as individual. But it is not rocket science. Getting leadership learners—those learning *about* leadership and those learning *how* to lead—to focus on three variables instead of just one is not a hurdle that's impossible to clear. To the contrary, this more expansive view of leadership explains as it enlightens.

I came fully to understand the importance of each of the three variables over a decade ago while writing the book *Bad Leadership*. In the process I became aware, viscerally as well as intellectually, that bad leadership without bad followership was impossible.[2] I became similarly aware that writing about bad leadership and bad followership without putting them in the petri dish within which they grew and, too often, thrived, was as misleading as misguided. This raises the question of why the leadership industry maintains a construct so constricted, so largely limited to single individuals.

Why, for example, are we so dismissive of followers? Why, if leadership is a relationship, a process that involves at least two people, one leader and one follower, do we continue to obsess about the one (the leader), while we continue to ignore the other (the follower)? We know that for various reasons—including hardwiring—we tend to look up, to focus on the person we perceive to be the leader. As biologist Robert Sapolsky put it, "Like other hierarchical species, [humans] have alpha individuals."[3] Moreover, as I earlier remarked, the 2016 American presidential campaign, with its fixation on the personas and personalities of Hillary Clinton and Donald Trump, was a vivid reminder of our relentless leader-centrism. But how does this explain *our* silence, the silence of nearly all leadership experts and educators—the silence of those in the leadership industry who know better but are mute about those who are not alpha individuals, those who are followers?

Mainly the answer is *money*. It is impossible to overestimate the degree to which money drives the leadership industry. While money is not the only motivator, it is the main motivator for leadership education and training, just as it is the main motivator for management education and training—for getting an

MBA degree. "By the time the 1980s were finished," writes Duff McDonald, "the majority of MBA degrees lacked any pretense to higher ideals and had become nothing more than a personal ad suggesting the graduate was a mercenary for hire." McDonald adds that this was precisely the time when salary levels for MBAs started "skyrocketing," while real wages for average American workers were in decline.[4] This more than anything else explains why leadership experts and educators have had it easy. It's been easy for them, for us, to keep it simple by focusing on, by fixating on, single individuals perceived to be leaders or future leaders—as opposed to complicating the conversation by including other variables that equally pertain.

This focus on the leader, in other words, on the self, is in keeping with recent developments in American culture, which Christopher Lasch famously named the "culture of narcissism." The culture of narcissism is related to our growing predilection for the virtues of individualism over those of communitarianism. (Note: the dawn of the culture of narcissism and of the leadership industry coincide. A coincidence?) It is related as well to the decline in social capital—instead of bowling together we now bowl alone.[5] The fact that in the late twentieth and early twenty-first centuries we have gone from teaching citizenship to teaching leadership, a trend that in recent years has only accelerated, is part of the same syndrome. Teaching people how to lead is, after all, to send a message. It is to say that the individual is more important than the commons. It is to say that you, you as a single individual, have the right and maybe even the obligation to stand out from the rest. It is to say that you deserve to think of yourself as separate from, and possibly even superior to, everyone else. And it is to say that teaching leadership in America—especially in American high schools and colleges—is better than (smarter? more virtuous?) what we used to do in America, which was to teach civics. As Nathan Heller pointed out in the New Yorker, "A guiding principle of today's liberal-arts education—the gold-filter admissions, the seminar discussions, the focus on 'leadership' . . . —is the cultivation of the individual."[6] Let's not, then, kid ourselves: the fierce focus on leadership and the divisiveness that it encourages is at the expense of the commonweal.

The evidence that money is the engine that drives the leadership industry is everywhere: in institutions and organizations, and at the level of the individual. Business got into the business of management (and, later, leadership) because of the growing assumption that professionalizing management—teaching how to manage to smart, ambitious individuals—was a way for corporate America to keep up, to get a leg up, ultimately to one-up. While the effort to professionalize management waned in the mid-twentieth century, the idea that management and, later, leadership, could be taught did not. To the contrary: during the last two decades of the last century and during the first two decades of this one, the business of teaching people how to lead burgeoned. For the last forty years, then, leadership education, training, and development—investing in single, presumably special individuals—have been viewed by American business as a way of trumping the competition, both domestic and foreign. In other words, the massive investment in teaching people how to lead has been seen by corporate America as a smart way to spend money to make money. Or, to put it differently, there has been no perceived need to focus on anyone or anything other than the leader, because the leader is the object not only of our collective attention, but our collective affection.

Schools, especially institutions of higher education, have profited handsomely from the extraordinarily high interest in learning to lead by people willing to pay for the privilege. Graduate and professional schools profit particularly handsomely from providing their various clients and customers, their various students, with the leadership programs they think they need. Think of it as a transactional arrangement from which both parties stand, or think they stand, to benefit. Would-be leaders (or their sponsors) are the buyers. Institutions and individuals, specifically leadership experts and educators, are the sellers. Given the nature of the arrangement and the perceived benefits to both sides, the single-minded focus on single individuals remains securely in place.

Do you doubt the level of interest in educating, training, and developing single individuals? Here some signs of how the leadership industry continues to grow. First, there are a thousand or more leadership degree programs in the United States alone. Second, US companies spend somewhere between $14 and $20 billion annually on leadership development.[7] Third, more than 57,000 books are listed (in 2015) on Amazon with the word "leadership" in the title. Fourth, the academic literature on leadership is by now is vast. (The British Library alone is estimated to hold over eighty thousand documents with the word "leadership" in the title.)[8] Fifth, countless leadership experts and educators, some with good credentials, many without, sell their pedagogical wares not only to buyers on the inside of the academy but to buyers on the outside, that is, to any individual, group, or organization willing to pay for what they have to sell.

Money as the reason for our fixation is equally apparent at the level of the organization, especially in business. Rakesh Khurana authored another book that here pertains, this one titled *Searching for a Corporate Savior: The Irrational Quest for the Charismatic CEO.*[9] Khurana claimed that corporate America was forever on the hunt for a savior, that is, for a single individual so superior that only he or, rarely, she was imagined capable of leading the firm to the promised land. Notwithstanding such searches, Khurana argued even in his subtitle that the quest for such a savior is "irrational."[10] The rise of "the more Darwinian system of investor capitalism," Khurana writes, led to the "greater focus on the individual CEO." The pressures brought to bear "by investors, via boards of directors, on CEOs—including demands for their dismissals—have been premised on the belief that CEOs can and should be held responsible for corporate performance, irrespective of . . . the many other factors that more decisively influence firm performance."[11] In other words, corporate America insists on seeing the leader, the CEO, as being all-important—never mind everyone else, never mind everything else. Never mind "the many other factors that more decisively influence firm performance"—the "many other factors" that, in my view, must be part of leadership pedagogy if leadership is to be professionalized.

Given the deep-seated and long-standing belief that highly placed people have a singularly strong impact, small wonder that though the cost of customized leadership programs at top business schools can run to more than $150,000 *per person*, some number of companies are ready, willing, able, and even eager to make the investment.[12] Consider the converse as well—the size of the investment in teaching leadership by an institution such as the University of Pennsylvania's Wharton School. In 2017, Wharton's website said that its executive education leadership programs were "designed to challenge . . . current perceptions about leadership and the values that shape it, encouraging you to think and lead differently."[13] The array of choices at Wharton is impressive: its many different leadership offerings divided into several groups such as Senior Leadership (for example, a two-day program, CEO Academy, and a five-day program, Global Executive Program) and Team & Individual Leadership (for example, a four-day program, Creating and Leading High-Performing Teams, and a four-day program, Leading and Managing People). Whatever the benefits of programs such as these—I never doubt that there are some—they are, in addition, major moneymakers.

Finally is the level of the individual. Why do we, we as individuals, invest so much time and so much money in learning how to lead, and nearly no time or money in the obvious obverse, in learning how to follow? After all, most of us, even those of us in leadership roles, follow most of the time—we do not most of the time lead. The overarching answer is, of course, that everyone wants to be, and wants to be perceived to be, a leader; no one wants to be, or to be perceived to be, a follower. This bias, for leaders and against followers, is by now endemic, epidemic, and it is deep-seated. For all our criticisms of leaders, in some vague, idealized way, they are still seen as being singularly smart, strong, and successful—as well as handsomely rewarded by both money and power. Followers, in contrast, are viewed as being ordinary at best, maybe even slightly weak and somewhat dim, certainly not, in any case, in any way outstanding.

Of course, there are other, more specific incentives for wanting to learn how to lead, incentives that depend on who, specifically, are the leadership learners and on what, specifically, is their circumstance. Are they young adults, in college, say, eager to be agents of change? Or are they middle-aged, driven above all to succeed professionally? Or are they perhaps older, in their sixties or seventies, persuaded that now is the time to create change for the common good? Similarly, are they driven by anger or ambition or by something else altogether? Are they American or Chinese? Are they situated in the US Army or in the Lutheran Church? Are they upper-level managers or community activists? It also depends on the nature of, and on the content of, the product. Is this a leadership course or program or book or workshop that equates leadership with self-improvement? Leadership with success? Leadership with personal and professional power and influence? Leadership with particular prowess or expertise? Leadership with public service? Leadership with public policy? Leadership with social activism? Leadership with upending the status quo?

The bottom line is that individuals have become extremely eager to learn how to lead, which is why we in the leadership industry have become extremely eager to teach how to lead. Those of us in the industry are not incentivized to teach how to follow or even about followership—there's no money in it, or nearly no money in it—and so by and large we do not. Similarly, those of us in the industry are not incentivized to teach about context—there's no money in it, or nearly no money in it—and so by and large we do not.

The leadership industry is, in short, like every other industry. It is driven to succeed. To be self-sustaining and profit-making—a moneymaking operation above all. Additionally, it is like every other industry in that it driven to succeed by giving its customers what they want. And what they want is to learn how to lead—preferably as quickly and easily as possible. Now you know why followers get left on the cutting room floor—not because they are not important, they are. But because they are not moneymakers. Now you know why contexts get left on the cutting room floor—not because they are not important, they are. But because they are not moneymakers. Ironically, by focusing so much on what their clients, customers, and consumers, including students, want, rather than on what they need, leadership experts and educators are undercutting themselves by undermining themselves. Imagine learning how to be a doctor or a lawyer so quickly and easily—as if the practice of medicine and law were so simple. It's inconceivable. Imagine learning how to be a doctor or a lawyer without taking the other—the patient, the client—into account. It's inconceivable. Imagine learning how to be a doctor or a lawyer without bringing into the equation the situation. It's inconceivable.

Leadership Is about Followership

Medicine as a profession is about the doctor—and it is, equally, about the patient. Optimally, it is about the doctor serving the patient, though doctors generally expect to be paid for their services. Law as a profession is about the lawyer—and it is, equally, about the client. Optimally, it is about the lawyer serving the client, though lawyers generally expect to be paid for their services. How curious it is, then, that most of those who teach leaders ignore followers—ignore whoever it is who must be brought along if leadership is to be exercised.

Let me be clear. I am hardly the first to argue that followers matter; this club is not confined to a single member. Though our numbers remain remarkably few, in fact the interest in followers, in those who are other than leaders, goes back decades, to, for instance the work of the previously mentioned Edwin Hollander. His 1978 book, *Leadership Dynamics,* was all about leadership as an influence process, between leaders and followers, each of whom was equally important, and each of whom was likely at some point to shift from being in one role (leader) to being in the other (follower). Hollander: "Leadership is a process of influence which involves an ongoing transaction between a leader and followers. The key to effective leadership is this relationship. Though most attention is given to the leader, leadership depends upon more than a single person to achieve group goals. Therefore, the followers as well as the leader are vital to understanding leadership as a process."[14] Though Hollander's work is recognized by leadership scholars as important, and though his findings are still echoed by experts—in 2016 two psychologists wrote in an article in *Daedalus* that leadership "involves leaders and followers motivating and influencing each other," and that leaders and followers are "bound together by being part of a single group"—followers remain widely ignored or even neglected entirely.[15]

There are some good reasons for this, in addition to those already mentioned, reasons that explain the omission, though they do not justify it. There is, for example, the problem of semantics. The word "follower" is weighed down by the presumption of weakness—followers thought of (erroneously) as being passive, not active. Additionally, there is the leader attribution error—we typically assume that leaders are of overweening importance and followers of little or no importance, even when this assumption is demonstrably false. Still, if leadership were a profession, as opposed to an occupation, followers would be part and parcel of the pertinent pedagogy.

When we omit from lessons on leadership conceptions of followership, the focus is, solely, on educating, training, and developing the leader, not the follower, the superior, not the subordinate. This is unfortunate—for there are good reasons for teaching followership to those ostensibly learning leadership. Among them is the fact that most leaders are followers most of the time. Among them is the fact that leadership can never be "all about me"—it must be "all about *we.*"[16] Among them is the fact that as soon as we expand the conversation from good leadership to bad leadership—as soon as we ditch our fixation on prescription and incorporate description—followers must become part of the picture. Among them is the fact that the way the world works now, in the first quarter of the twenty-first century, followers are much more important than they used to be and leaders much less. Among them is the fact that being a professional implies providing some sort of service—to the other. To the patient. To the client. To the follower.

Leadership studies plays, as we have seen, second banana to leadership development. You want to know why? Follow the money. Leadership development is where the money is. Leadership studies is, if you will, the poor stepsibling. Still, to break the leadership field into two groups—leadership studies is learning *about* leadership, leadership development is learning *how* to lead—is to provide a useful template for followership. I am arguing, then, that followership, like leadership, should be approached from two different pedagogical directions. The first is learning *about* followership; the second is learning *how* to follow—how to be a good follower. What might such a pedagogy look like? What might it look like to include the study of followership along with the study of leadership? And what might it look like to teach how to follow along with teaching how to lead?

Again, this is all about being inclusive, about including in our conception of leadership followership, so that instead of learning to lead being an exercise in narcissism, we open it up. We open leadership up to see it whole—to see leadership as a *system* with three parts, each of which is separate and distinct. I can confirm from my own experience that teaching followership is every bit as engaging and, arguably, more enlightening than teaching leadership, if only because it is so atypical, so new and different. More to the point, I am arguing that teaching followership is integral to teaching leadership, that teaching followership is part and parcel of a good leadership *education*—if only because it makes clear that leadership is a *process* that, by definition, is interactive. I am further arguing that teaching followership is part of good leadership *training* because it teaches a skill—along with how to be a good leader, how to be a good follower.

> Bottom line 1: Followership is a subject of study as leadership is a subject of study. Leadership without followership is an oxymoron.
> Bottom line 2: Followership is a practice as leadership is a practice. Good followership is as necessary to a good outcome as is good leadership.

What might a course or a workshop or a seminar on followership look like? Here are some ideas.

First is a focus on *concept*. Most leadership learners, whether young adults in college or older adults in the world of work, are so unfamiliar with the idea of "followership" that it takes some getting used to. It takes time to understand that followership is as important as leadership, and that to follow does not mean merely to submit or even to go along. Being a good follower can mean *not* to follow, can mean deliberately to refuse to play ball.

Second is a focus on *history*. The history of followership is, of course, simultaneously the history of leadership. The point is that followership, like leadership, changes over time. Followers in the present are different from followers in the past. Typically, these differences, the changes that take place over time, are in consequence of changes in the external environment, such as, for instance, the Enlightenment, the Industrial Revolution, and the information revolution. We know that in times long past leaders were everything and followers nothing. People thought in terms of heroes, princes, and philosopher-kings—the divine right of kings. But then the world changed. Power devolved, and so did our conception of who had the right to do what to whom. More recently, in the last half-century, changes in culture and technology have further accelerated—some would say exacerbated—this trend. Again, leaders, certainly democratic leaders, are weaker than before, and followers, those without obvious sources of power, authority, and influence, are stronger, especially in liberal democracies.

Third is a focus on *difference*, differences among followers. Only a few leadership experts have written in any serious way about followership. But among those who have, most have divided followers into several different groups or types.[17] The reasons for this were various, but clearly high on the list was conveying the conception that just as leaders are different one from the other, so are followers. Our tendency is to lump followers together—as in American voters, or Amazon customers. But of course followers no more mirror each other than do leaders, and so some of the experts, myself included, have made it a point to distinguish one type of follower from other types of follower. I, for example, chose to divide followers into five different groups based on only one criterion: their level of engagement. *Isolates* are followers who are completely detached—they know nothing and do nothing. *Bystanders* are followers who know something, but who decide, deliberately, to do nothing. *Participants* are followers who are in some way engaged. *Activists* are followers who feel strongly, pro or con, about their leaders and invest resources (such as time and money) accordingly. Finally, *diehards* are followers who are ready and willing to sacrifice whatever it takes for their cause, whether an individual, an idea, or both.[18]

Fourth is a focus on *relationships*, specifically on those between leaders and followers. How leaders and followers relate has been looked at through different disciplinary lenses, including philosophy, psychology, and political science. Here, for example, are several questions relating to relations between the leader, in this case Adolf Hitler, and his followers, in this case the German people during the twelve years the Nazis held power. Why did millions of ordinary Germans cheer a leader like Hitler, who threatened to become and then did a genocidal dictator? Why did tens of thousands do what he told them to do—incite mayhem and commit murder? Why were countless Germans bystanders, followers who stood by while atrocities were being committed and their country was being destroyed? Why does any political leader who flagrantly violates historical, political, and cultural norms appeal to followers, sometimes to many, many followers? And why in the workplace do subordinates obey superiors, even when the latter are manifestly ineffective or even unethical? Why do we lean so strongly toward obeying authority? And why, sometimes, do we choose, deliberately, to disobey authority?

Finally comes a focus on *values*. Values associated not with being a good leader, but with being a good follower. (Not that these, necessarily, are different. Indeed, many are the same.) Again, most of us spend most of our time not leading, but following. It behooves us, then—on the assumption that we value a good outcome, good as in effective *and* ethical—to pay attention not only to what it takes to be a good leader but also to what it takes to be a good follower. We might assume, for example, that if the leader is in most ways good, being a good follower means being supportive. Conversely, if the leader is in some significant way bad, being a good follower means *not* being supportive; it means withholding support. Of course, this holds true only at the most basic level. Life is often more complicated than this simple syllogism would seem to suggest. For example, in the workplace, subordinates typically are reluctant or even loathe to resist their superiors, or even in any way to object to them. Subordinates, employees, followers, are afraid of being professionally, maybe even personally, punished. A single case in point: there is evidence that the culture of misogyny and intimidation under CEO Roger Ailes at Fox News was so powerful that the more than twenty women who later claimed they had been sexually harassed at Fox chose for years to stay silent rather than to speak out. This is a vivid example of why leadership experts and educators who exclude from the discussion what Ira Chaleff calls "courageous" followership are, as I see it, remiss.[19]

While teaching *how* to be a good follower resembles teaching how to be a good leader, there is one big difference. Tens of thousands of teaching materials and structures (books, courses, workshops, programs, institutes, etc.) are available for the latter, instruction on how to be a good leader; but scarcely any to address the former, instruction on how to be a good follower. Why does this matter? Because, as Scottish philosopher David Hume put it, we should be appalled by the "implicit submission with which men resign their own sentiments and passions to those of their rulers."[20] Such "implicit submission" is everywhere in evidence: in the workplace, as in the commons. Our mission then, as leadership experts and educators, should be to work not only with those who have or likely will have power, authority, and influence, but also with those who do not and likely will not. We should teach them independent thinking and intrepid interceding and provide them with advice and admonitions, most intended to stiffen their spines, the spines of those typically too timorous to take on those more highly positioned than they. Of course, sometimes such instructions are followed by those in danger of being foolhardy. I am thinking especially of whistleblowers, who might be ready, willing, and able to take on those more powerful than they—but who usually do so at considerable risk to themselves. In other words, learning how to be a good follower is, among other things, learning when and how to speak truth to power without committing professional or political suicide.

Chaleff has spent most of his professional life teaching "courageous" followership. The courageousness to which he alludes is not meant necessarily to suggest that followers confront leaders, though sometimes they should. Rather it implies that followers, like leaders, should think of themselves as principals with their own roles to play in whatever the professional or political process. Chaleff: "The term *follower* conjures up images of docility, conformity, weakness, and failure to excel. Often, none of this is the least bit true. The sooner we move beyond these images and get comfortable with the idea of *powerful* followers supporting *powerful* leaders, the sooner we can fully develop and test models for dynamic, self-responsible, synergistic relationships in our organizations."[21] He goes on to explore the various ways in which followers should be courageous, such as taking responsibility, serving and supporting, and, when necessary, challenging and confronting. Whatever the specifics, as I see it, Chaleff's main contribution to the conversation is the idea that followers are important, not just leaders, and that those among us who are other than leaders, who are followers, ought to think long and hard about what it takes to follow wisely and well.

One more point about leaders and followers and language as the medium that mainstreams the message: The fashion now is to talk about shared leadership, and distributed leadership, and team leadership, and about how you too, indeed everyone everywhere, can be a leader. Heaven forefend that anyone admit to the truth! Heaven forefend that anyone admit to being a follower—even though, as I said, whatever our ostensible station, most of us spend our lives following, not leading. Precisely because there is such an onus on "follower," there are euphemisms for it, such as "constituents," "participants," and "stakeholders." I, however, remain persuaded that we should stick to the word "follower." It's the only obvious antonym of the word "leader." It's the professional equivalent of a patient or a client—that is, it is the person we are supposed, as leaders, to serve. And it sends the right message—that because leadership is a relationship, leadership and followership, leaders and followers, are inseparable, indivisible. It behooves us, then, those of us who are leadership experts and educators, to include the word in our lexicons. It behooves us as well to make clear that like the world "leader," the word "follower" is generally value free. A follower is not necessarily weak and submissive, any more than a leader is necessarily strong and decisive. Moreover, it is no better or more important to be a leader than to be a follower. For any group or organization or assemblage to be healthy and functional, as opposed to unhealthy and dysfunctional, everyone in it, not just those at the top, must have at least some sense of the different ways in which they can and should contribute to the whole.

Leadership Is about Context

I can somewhat understand why followers are excluded from most leadership conversations and curricula. But I cannot at all understand why most leadership conversations and curricula exclude the conception of context. Why is so little attention paid to the development of contextual consciousness (being aware of the importance of context), of contextual expertise (being familiar with the components of context), and of contextual intelligence (being strategic about context to attain designated goals)? Among other reasons is that, unlike followership, which is excluded from the leadership industry nearly entirely, context is not. Most experts and educators agree that context matters, which makes its marginalization difficult not only to understand, but to justify. Of course, part of the reason is practical. Since the leadership industry's highest priority is to teach people how to lead, and since it claims to get people to learn how to lead with ease and speed, everything that seems at all extraneous gets left on the cutting room floor.

Most professionals, in contrast, have no choice but to familiarize themselves with the contexts within which they practice their professions. For example, doctors learn not just about the human body but about medicine more generally—about medicine qua profession; about how medicine is practiced in a given location, in, say, the United States or in Canada, in the rural South or frozen North, in a small local hospital or a large urban medical center; about medicine as public policy; about medical technology and medical pharmacology; about the latest medical research, at least as it pertains to their specialties (cardiology, neurology, dermatology, and so on). Moreover, they must, absolutely must, know the contexts within which their patients are or were located. Is this patient in, or has this patient recently traveled to, China, Ghana, Argentina? Similarly, lawyers learn not just a body of law but about the law more generally—about law as a profession; about how the law is practiced in a given location, say in the United States or in Canada; in the state of Texas or Vermont; or in the city of Boise or Chicago; about the law as public policy; about the law as a regulatory system; about the courts, federal, state, and municipal; about new legal technologies; about legal norms; and about key legal actors such as judges both elected and appointed. Leaders, in contrast, are expected to lead in the dark. Unless they are learning to lead in a narrow context for a narrow purpose—for instance, learning to lead within Boeing for the benefit of Boeing—developing contextual consciousness, contextual expertise, and contextual intelligence is not considered essential or even, apparently, especially desirable.

In fairness, the importance of the contexts within which leaders and followers are located is not always so obvious. Among other reasons, these contexts number more than one. In other words, leaders and followers are located not just in a single context, but in several different ones, simultaneously. Some of these might have a major impact, others only a minor impact. Think of contexts as a series of concentric circles that, for the sake of this discussion, I will limit here to three: an inner circle, a middle circle, and an outer circle—each of which, to be a good leader, you should know like the back of your hand. Say you are a leader or upper-level manager at the Ford Motor Company. In this case, the inner circle, the context within which you are most immediately situated, likely consists of a small group or unit of some sort, such as a team or a committee. The next circle, the middle circle, is the organization within which the team or the committee is situated—in this case the organization is the firm that is Ford. Finally, there is an outer circle, here the car industry, the industry within which the firm that is Ford is located—the car industry with which anyone leading or managing in the car industry should be thoroughly familiar.

Here is just one quick example of the importance of context: the relationship between the United States and Israel. Since the inception of the state of Israel, in 1948, both countries deemed the alliance between them to be special not only for historical reasons, but for strategic ones. However, during the two terms of President Barack Obama, the long-standing tie between them frayed. As a report issued in 2016 by the Council on Foreign Relations put it, "The U.S.-Israel relationship is in trouble."[22] To most casual observers, and I include in this category most of the media, the primary reason for this deterioration was the lack of personal chemistry between the American president and his Israeli counterpart, Prime Minister Benjamin Netanyahu. By virtually every account they disliked and distrusted each other, which clearly did not help the relationship between the two states. But, as the authors of the report made clear, to personalize the reasons for the frayed relationship, to reduce what is a complex set of reasons to a single, simple reason is as mistaken as misguided.

There were several explanations for why the relationship between the United State and Israel had soured, most of which had nothing to do with the two men in question, and everything to do with the contexts within which they were situated. Among them were the growing differences between the two countries on policy issues. And among them were "significant demographic and political changes on both sides," which further drove the two countries apart and made it "harder for those who care deeply about the relationship . . . to maintain it."[23] On the Israeli side, the changes included constituents (followers) who were becoming "more religious, nationalistic, and conservative, exacerbating differences with Washington." And on the American side, the changes included constituents (followers), especially young people, who were "less sympathetic to Israel than their older counterparts."[24] The point of this aside is to make clear that no matter who are the leaders of the United States and Israel, managing the relationship between the two countries is bound to be more difficult now than it was in the past. Again, this is not to suggest that the leaders of the two countries, the president and the prime minister, and the relationship between them, are unimportant. Rather it is to say that along with this leader-centric explanation for recent events is another one, a systemic one, that includes players other than leaders, and that includes the circumstances, historical and contemporaneous, that leaders and followers share.

Again, some leadership scholars get it—get the importance of context. Professor Archie Brown (of Oxford) made the case from a political perspective: "Leadership must be placed in context if it is to be better understood. . . . What is appropriate or possible in one situation may be inappropriate or unattainable in another."[25] Professor Rakesh Khurana made the case from a corporate perspective: The "world changed during the 1970s and early 1980s. . . . The turn toward charismatic authority in business, while in part a reaction to a rapidly changing economic and business environment, was also reinforced by a changing cultural context."[26] I, meanwhile, wrote a book titled *Hard Times: Leadership in America*, in which I asked these questions: What is the context that constitutes the United States of America in the first quarter of the twenty-first century?[27] What are the components of context with which leaders in America should be familiar if they are to be effective? My interest in the book was not, in other words, in developing a certain trait or skill. It was in growing a body of knowledge about context that is country, and about the impact of this context on how leadership in America is exercised. My assumption was as it always is: that to become contextually conscious, contextually expert, and contextually intelligent is to become far better positioned to lead wisely and well.

I argued, for example, that leaders in America should know something about the *law* in America: "America's uniquely litigious culture is directly responsible for complicating and constraining the lives of leaders. . . . The enormous proliferation in recent years of compliance officers opens a window on how the law impinges on leaders. Say you're the chief executive officer of an organization of some size, a business, or a hospital, or a school. How to protect yourself against a lawsuit, frivolous or otherwise? . . . Bring on a compliance officer."[28] I also argued that leaders in America should know something about *class* in America: "The impact of growing class divisions on leadership and followership in America is, of course, impossible to assess precisely. But some surmising is in order. First, it seems reasonable to suppose that there is at least some correlation between the two. . . . Decades of increasing class distinctions (1970–2010) and a shrinking middle class coincide with decades of decreasing trust in leaders nearly across the board."[29] And I argued that leaders in America should know something about *media* in America: "Consider the impact of new media on leaders in business. In the past, companies could control the messages that went out and came in. . . . Now corporate leaders and managers are unable any longer to control the conversation. Now they have no choice but to listen, to learn from their customers and whichever other stakeholders choose to weigh in. . . . The bottom line is that no leader, anywhere, of any kind, without exception, now gets a pass."[30]

Can you be a leader in America without understanding something about how American history, ideology, religion, institutions, organizations, technology, culture, interests, law, class, and media (among other components of context) impinge on leadership in America? Yes, of course. But is it reasonable to assume that you would be a better leader in America if you better understood America? Yes, of course. For that matter, would you be a better leader in Greece if you better understood Greece? Or a better leader in Nigeria if you better understood Nigeria? Or, for that matter, a better leader at Macy's if a few years ago you better understood that the context within which retailers were situated was irrevocably changing? That shoppers were starting to ditch bricks-and-mortar stores in favor of buying online? Bloody likely the answer to all these questions is yes. Yes, of course. Can I prove this to be true? No, not conclusively, not scientifically. Nor can I prove conclusively, scientifically, that one leadership pedagogy is vastly superior to any other. What I can say is this: that leaders—like other professionals—should know something about the contexts within which they are situated seems simple common sense.

Leadership Is a Spectrum

What makes a doctor a bad doctor? What makes a lawyer a bad lawyer? What are the different ways of being bad, and how and why do professionals get bad? For that matter, why even ask about being bad? If the whole point of a professional education—say, a medical education or a legal education—is to generate good professionals, why bother to learn about bad professionals? Why learn about people who are doctors and lawyers, but whose performances in their professions are more bad than good?

Professionals can be bad in two basic ways: they can be unethical or they can be ineffective. Of course, some professionals are both, either sequentially or simultaneously. But for our purposes it is best simply to think of being bad as running along two different axes: one goes from ethical to unethical, the other from effective to ineffective. If a doctor or a lawyer is bad enough, sufficiently unethical or ineffective, he or she can reasonably be charged with malpractice—medical malpractice or legal malpractice. The prefix "mal" obviously has a strong negative connotation. Hence medical malpractice is generally defined as negligence by a medical professional, typically by a physician whose treatment of a patient was so substandard as to do serious harm. Similarly, legal malpractice is generally defined as negligence by a legal professional, typically an attorney whose treatment of a client was so substandard as to do serious harm.

The term "malpractice" does not necessarily cover all professional sins. It does not necessarily cover, for example, greed, that is, doctors or lawyers who overcharge. Still, the American context has become litigious, which explains why the number of malpractice suits has soared in recent decades, mostly in medicine but also in the law (and in other professions as well). Persons in the professions have been obliged to go on the defensive, and the professions themselves have been obliged to wrestle with what is expected of a good professional and what constitutes a bad professional—one who is so bad that he or she could be charged with malpractice. In consequence of this heightened awareness, medical and law students are often counseled about the risks of malpractice suits early on—while they are still in school. Most medical students learn about malpractice in medical school, while medical school faculty, in turn, have been conditioned to teach "considerable defensive medicine."[31] Similarly, most law students learn something about legal malpractice while they are still in school. In fact, some law schools offer courses on malpractice litigation. For example, the University of Georgia School of Law has a course titled Legal Malpractice, and the University of Minnesota Law School has a course to help "students recognize and avoid real life risks of legal malpractice exposure and liability."[32]

Because twenty-first-century America now constitutes so litigious a context, what used to be infrequent is now quite frequent—malpractice suits. That explains why both the medical and legal professions pay attention not only to keeping professionals from being bad, but to precluding suits against them for being bad. The reasons for this are both intrinsic and extrinsic. Overwhelmingly, professionals genuinely want to be good—reasonably effective and reasonably ethical. And, overwhelmingly, professionals who are pedagogues genuinely want to teach others to be good—ideally, effective and ethical. Their professed interest is to serve others—and to protect their professions as well as their own professional status. Professional associations such as the American Medical Association and the American Bar Association share this interest. Among their purposes is to protect reputations: of their members, of their professions, of their own associations.

Some have argued that the American disposition to litigiousness is, of itself, bad. Too costly. Too time consuming. Too much of a drain on the judicial system. It's an argument that in the last five, ten years has carried real weight, largely because it has come to be widely agreed that too many malpractice suits are being filed, and that too many of these are frivolous. However, one could argue that, whatever the disadvantages of this litigiousness, they are outweighed by the advantages. First, the idea that professionals can be guilty of malpractice reminds us of the converse: that we expect our professionals to adhere to high standards, to be both effective and ethical. Second, the idea that professionals can be guilty of malpractice reminds us that professionals are not on pedestals. They're only human, which means they too make grave mistakes and they too engage in egregious wrongdoing. Third, the idea that professionals can be guilty of malpractice reminds us that if someone has suffered seriously in consequence of professional malpractice, the victim, the aggrieved party, has the right to be compensated. Malpractice, the idea behind it, the threat of it, is, in other words, a way of leveling the playing field, of democratizing the system. It is a way of enabling those without power or authority to keep in check and hold accountable those with.

Here is my point: leadership has no analogous malpractice. There is such a thing as medical malpractice—because medicine is a profession. There is such a thing as legal malpractice—because law is a profession. *There is no such thing as leadership malpractice because leadership is not a profession—it is an occupation.* We can and generally do hold professionals accountable, bad doctors and bad lawyers, for example. But we generally do not hold leaders accountable, no matter how ineffectual or unethical.

Of course, to this general rule there are exceptions—the International Criminal Court, for example, does what it can to bring evil (political) leaders to justice. And in liberal democracies, followers, constituents, do have a vote that enables them to throw the rascals out. Moreover, in the corporate sector, CEOs are increasingly vulnerable to outsiders who want to oust them, especially shareholder activists. (In the first four months of 2017, activist investors deposed leaders of three high-profile S&P companies: AIG, CSX, and Arconic Inc.) But, in most cases, including cases in the workplace, followers (subordinates) have no obvious way to hold their leaders (superiors) to account, which explains why there is no punishment, or hardly ever any punishment to fit their fecklessness or even their crimes. The idea that a leader or manager might be guilty of malpractice escapes us because we have no widely shared standard for what constitutes good leadership, and we have no widely shared standard for what constitutes bad leadership. Moreover, in the leadership industry generally the subject is off the table. Bad leadership and bad followership are excluded from the discussion, as they are from the curriculum. This explains in good part why if you have a very bad doctor or a very bad lawyer, you can sue. But if you have a very bad boss, mostly there's nothing to be done other than to quit. Or, maybe, to blow the whistle. Or just to suck it up.

Let's face it: the leadership industry ignores the downside, the dark side, mainly because there's no money in it. People want to learn how to lead—they want to learn how to be "good" leaders. Most leadership experts and educators see no reason to research bad leadership or to teach it because they have no obvious incentive to do either. There's no benefit to it or, at least, no perceived benefit, certainly not, as they see it, any financial benefit, and not enough intellectual or pedagogical benefit. The fact that most leadership teachers ignore bad leadership is compounded by the fact that most leadership scholars do the same. In other words, although bad leadership is pernicious and ubiquitous, it's a subject that most leadership scholars ignore. There is a massive amount of material available on good leadership. But there is only a minimal amount of material available on bad leadership. By and large leadership scholars leave it to others— to, for example, biographers, philosophers, historians, political scientists, and journalists—to chronicle bad leadership, to research it, to dissect it, to analyze it, maybe, someday, to remediate it. Suffice to say here that while the catastrophic civil war in Syria dragged on for years, and while the calamitous consequences thereof extended far beyond the Syrian border, leadership scholars, like leadership teachers, do not consider Syria or its leader, Bashar al-Assad, their bailiwick. Why is it that we in the leadership industry have nothing to say about a disaster such as this one? Beats me.

All bad leadership is not the same. In *Bad Leadership* I identified seven different types:[33]

1. *Incompetent* leadership—the leader and at least some followers lack the will or skill (or both) to sustain effective action. In the face of at least one important leadership challenge, they do not create positive change.
2. *Rigid* leadership—the leader and at least some followers are stiff and unyielding. Although they may be competent, they are unable or unwilling to adapt to new ideas, new information, or changing times.
3. *Intemperate* leadership—the leader lacks self-control and is aided and abetted by followers who are unwilling or unable effectively to intervene.
4. *Callous* leadership—the leader and at least some followers are uncaring or unkind. Ignored or discounted are the needs, wants, and wishes of most members of the group or organization, especially subordinates.
5. *Corrupt* leadership—the leader and at least some followers lie, cheat, or steal. To a degree that exceeds the norm, they put self-interest ahead of the public interest.
6. *Insular* leadership—the leader and at least some followers minimize or disregard the health and welfare of "the other"—that is, of those outside the group or organization for which they are directly responsible.
7. *Evil* leadership—the leader and at least some followers commit atrocities. They use pain as an instrument of power. The harm done to men, women, and children is severe rather than slight. The harm can be physical, psychological, or both.[34]

These types are not etched in stone; nor are they intended to be codified or reified. They do, however, serve several purposes. They point to some of the obvious ways in which bad leadership manifests itself. They point to the impact of bad leadership, from minor to major, from stressful to lethal. And they point to the impact of bad followers—not just bad leaders. It is impossible to be a good leader without having at least one good follower. Similarly, it is impossible to be a bad leader without having at least one bad follower. Why do followers follow bad leaders? There are all sorts of reasons, ranging from fear of punishment to promise of reward. My point in any case is this: bad leaders are like good leaders. They cannot be divorced from their followers. Moreover, they cannot be considered separate and distinct from the contexts within which they are situated.

A final point about bad leadership—about leadership as a spectrum, from good to bad. Bad leadership was not always excluded from the conversation; on the contrary. Once upon a time, long, long ago, it was front and center: it was widely acknowledged that along with good leadership, bad leadership was endemic to the human condition. In fact, historically, the greatest political theorists were far more concerned with how to control the penchants of bad leaders than with how to promote the virtues of good ones.[35] Plato, for example, was as interested in tyrants as in philosopher-kings. "The point that we need to keep in mind . . . is that every one of us . . . harbors a fierce brood of savage and imperious appetites that reveal themselves most readily in dreams."[36] Machiavelli similarly was not only *not* resistant to the idea of bad leadership—he, like Plato, flat out *presumed* it. Machiavelli took it for granted that on occasion the leader, the prince, would have no choice but to inflict pain on his followers. This is precisely why he advised being bad, that is, inflicting pain, only if necessary, never gratuitously, only to maintain public order and preserve political power. "Cruelties can be called well used (if it is permissible to speak well of evil)," he advised, "that are done at a stroke, out of the necessity to secure oneself, and then are not persisted in but are turned to as much utility for the subjects as one can."[37]

Leadership as la-la land is not, in sum, of historical vintage. In fact, as America's founders would have attested, their primary concern was bad leadership—in particular a single individual (the president) accruing too much power. Hence the premium on curtailing leaders: on federalism, on the separation of powers, and on checks and balances. The notion of leadership as la-la land is, then, an artificial artifact of the profit-making operation that is the leadership industry. But if leadership is ever to be nudged from occupation to profession, this must change. Learning to lead must revert to what it was. It must be more difficult and demanding; more complex, complicated, and consuming; more far-seeing and far-reaching; and longer lasting. Fact is that learning how to lead is anything but simple and easy or short and sweet.

7

Evaluation

I began this book by pointing to the yawning gap between what the leadership industry claims to do and what it does. We know that the interest in corporate leadership remains sky-high. In 2015 a columnist for the *Financial Times* wrote, "Leadership is possibly the most written, lectured, TED-talked and blogged about topic in management."[1] We also know that the interest in political leadership remains sky-high—to wit America's obsession with Donald Trump, who single-handedly has dominated the news cycle since the beginning of his presidential campaign in June 2015. Finally, we know that the investment in leadership education, training, and development programs remains sky-high—that not only is the leadership industry not contracting, it is expanding.[2] Withal, disappointment is rampant. Never has public trust in leaders across the board been so low. And never has there been so much bitching and moaning about the failure of the leadership industry to deliver on its promise.

What can be done to alleviate and remediate the problem? What can be done to elevate leadership education, training, and development? What can be done—*should* be done—to professionalize the process? This chapter will explore what's not working—and what is. The next, the last chapter, will provide guidelines for transforming leadership from an occupation to a profession.

Failures

I earlier quoted Stanford University business professor Jeffrey Pfeffer, who concluded not only that the leadership industry had "failed" to develop better leaders, but that sometimes it made "things much worse."[3] His 2015 book, *Leadership BS*, amounts to a diatribe against the leadership industry, charging it, in effect, with false advertising. If Pfeffer were the only one with a litany of complaints, it would be one thing. But he is not. In the last few years a growing chorus of voices has insisted that something's amiss, that though the leadership industry continues to grow, there is no good, hard evidence that it does what it claims to do—develop better leaders.

Leadership programs have become ubiquitous, designed for adults of all ages and stages. To charge, therefore, that it's an empty vessel is to charge something serious. It is to say that the enormous investment in leadership learning is largely wasted, giving only meager evidence that it pays off. The problems are at several levels. At the most basic level are the most basic questions: Can how to lead be taught? Can how to lead be learned? If how to lead can be taught, who can teach it and how? And if how to lead can be learned, who can learn it and how? The answers to these questions remain elusive in part because the metrics remain elusive. I will have more to say about this below. Suffice it to say at this point that leadership is one of the few things that we teach without an obvious yardstick— a widely accepted yardstick to measure, to assess, what was learned.

The leadership industry faces a host of questions that raise legitimate concerns about how well we are educating, training, and developing leaders. Pfeffer, for example, charges it with prescribing instead of describing, with obsessing about what should be, at the expense of what is. He further charges it with being amateurish, pointing out, correctly, that the leadership industry has no barriers to entry and that no credentials are required to "pass oneself off as a leadership expert."[4] Further, Pfeffer charges, as do I, that the industry has too high a tolerance for disagreement and imprecision. He refers, for example, to "charismatic leadership" as a term that's often bandied about, though it's not clearly defined or even fully understood.

A piece published in 2014 by McKinsey titled "Why Leadership-Development Programs Fail" underscores the importance of leadership development programs to numberless institutions and organizations, including colleges and universities, which offer "hundreds of degree courses on leadership." Notwithstanding the ubiquity and popularity of such courses and leadership programs generally, the authors of the article identify four "common mistakes" that account for why satisfaction with leadership development initiatives remains low. First, though "context is a critical component of leadership" (sound familiar?), too many programs assume that "one size fits all and that the same group of skills or style of leadership is appropriate" in all situations. Second, though some off-site leadership programs have value, the evidence is that many ignore what we know about how adults learn, which is by doing, preferably on the front line. Third, though leaders may need to change their behaviors to become more effective, such change does not, of itself, usually suffice to make them better at what they do. Finally, leadership programs don't measure their results effectively. "Companies have no evidence to quantify the value of their investment." The usual way of evaluating leadership programs—obtaining participant feedback—has been found to be inadequate.[5]

An article from the *Harvard Business Review* I mentioned earlier has a title nearly identical to the report from McKinsey. It's "Why Leadership Training Fails—and What to Do about It." The article reiterates a familiar theme: that despite the enormous investment in the leadership industry, there is scant evidence that the investment is paying off. The authors also maintain that assessments that take place shortly after leadership programs are over are nearly worthless. They tend to skew positive at this point, whereas after some time has passed, they tend to skew significantly less positive. In fact, several years after most leadership development programs have ended, most managers think that they had little or no impact, "even though [they were] inspiring at the time." It seems that what happens over time is that disconnects become more apparent: the disconnect between happens off-site and what happens on the job; the disconnect between learning about the virtues of teamwork when workplace barriers include superiors (leaders, managers) who are heavy-handed and hierarchical; the disconnect between what takes place during the leadership program and what happens once the program is over.[6]

The truth is that while the leadership industry continues to grow, attacking the leadership industry has become a cottage industry. Another example is Tuck professor Sydney Finkelstein, who wrote a piece titled "Why We Loathe Leadership Training." Yet another example is consultant Deborah Rowland, who published "Why Leadership Development Isn't Developing Leaders."[7] While neither of these articles is as harsh as their titles imply, the titles reflect the moment, as does Duff McDonald's earlier mentioned 2017 book, *The Golden Passport: Harvard Business School, the Limits of Capitalism, and the Moral Failure of the MBA Elite*.[8] It's yet another example of an author taking direct aim, in this case at an eminent institution of the highest rank, that professes to "educate" leaders. Will critiques like these reach a tipping point? A point at which buyers of leadership programs will be more skeptical of sellers of leadership programs than they have been up to now? It's hard to tell. But they are signs that for the leadership industry the waters could get choppy.

In the past, it was a given that the best MBA program was the traditional two-year course of study, and that learning to lead was a top priority, *the* top priority. Harvard Business School (HBS) is among the foremost examples of this model. A student who graduated from HBS in 2006 remembered his experience this way: "The word *leadership* lurked in every corner of HBS. . . . Everyone at HBS, it seemed, could be a leader of one sort or another." The dean at the time, Kim Clark, was the messenger who sent the message. "He was focused and talked repeatedly about the HBS mission to educate leaders who would make a difference in the world."[9]

However, given the increasingly stiff competition, especially from one-year master in management programs, HBS dean (since 2010) Nitin Nohria now seems to think it necessary to defend his school's two-year course of study, to defend the proposition that investing so much time and money will eventually pay off. "In the last five years," said Nohria in 2016, "we have been very determined to double down in some ways on the MBA. Many of the investments we have made, they have been investments to strengthen and make even more compelling why you should spend two years in an MBA program."[10]

Every year the competition, even among top-ranked traditional business schools, is getting stiffer. In 2016 the *Wall Street Journal* reported that "though M.B.A.s still remains the most popular postgraduate business degree, a recent survey of 10,000 prospective students conducted by the Graduate Management Admission Council found that about 25 percent were considering one-years master's degrees, up from 15 percent in 2009."[11] In 2016 the *Financial Times* similarly reported that full-time two-year programs were losing ground to "cheaper and more flexible options."[12] Moreover, many of these "cheaper and more flexible options" were in Europe, not only saving American students time and money, but providing them with, as one put it, the opportunity to become "a more global citizen." Finally, in 2016 the *Financial Times* reported that applications for full-time, two-year MBA programs fell fully 53 percent in one year, while nearly three-quarters of business schools in Europe that offered shorter courses saw the number of their applications rise.[13]

Why does this matter to the matter at hand? Because of all the schools that profess to teach how to lead, business schools are at the top of the list. Though they are not what I would describe as professional leadership schools—they do not teach how to lead in accordance with professional standards—no other schools put such a high premium on educating, training, and developing leaders. That is precisely why the dramatic decline in applications to two-year MBA programs sends an important message to leadership experts and educators. The message reads something like this: If I, a prospective student, really and truly believed that in two years I could learn how to lead, I would invest the two years. But, it is not obvious to me that in two years I can be educated to lead, or trained to lead, or developed to lead. Moreover, it is not obvious to me that I can learn very much more about how to lead in two years than I can learn in one—which is to say that no business school has provided me with hard evidence or irrefutable data to this effect. Put differently, though "educating leaders who make a difference in the world" remains the top priority, the fact that the process of educating such leaders remains so poorly defined and weakly defended—so unprofessional—renders it suspect.

To be sure, in recent years medical schools and, especially, law schools have also suffered some slings and arrows. The latter have been criticized for being too much concerned with legal theory and too little concerned with legal practice, too little dedicated to teaching students the skills they need effectively to practice law. Nevertheless, notwithstanding the imperfections, by and large law schools are like medical schools: they do what they say they do. They teach people to become, to be, respectively, legal and medical professionals. In contrast, leadership schools, especially but not exclusively business schools, remain in this all-important sense untested and unproven. They have not demonstrated convincingly, not to speak of conclusively, that they teach people how to lead. To be sure, many business school graduates, like other professional school graduates, go on to enjoy splendid careers and to become splendid leaders. However, there is no strong evidence of a correlation between cause, learning how to lead in business school, and effect, leading after, generally long after, school is over.

This brings us to the matter of metrics. Scott DeRue, the dean of the University of Michigan's well-regarded Ross School of Business, seems interested in nothing so much as in developing leaders. Before becoming dean in 2016, he helped launch the Ross School's Sanger Leadership Center, which provides leadership training to each of the school's approximately 3,400 students. Additionally, under the rubric of the Sanger Center, a small number of students are selected for a yearlong, advanced leadership program that makes "leadership development a primary focus" of the Michigan experience. The program promises to engage students in a "powerful process" through which they will "deepen" their "self-awareness," "increase" their "personal influence," and "maximize" their "learning from daily experiences."[14]

Since DeRue became dean, he has continued to speak glowingly about the Ross School's commitment to the creation of "transformational leadership." DeRue: "We want to create transformational leadership development experiences for our students that demonstrate for them the power of business to create value for customers, create value for shareholders, create great places to work for employees and create value for our communities at large."[15] It should however be noted that, in addition to the school's traditional two-year master of business administration program, Ross now offers (since 2013) a one-year master of management program. Sounds swell on the surface—in fact DeRue sees this relatively new, one-year program as attracting a new student cohort, especially liberal arts students without extensive work experience.

However, the one-year program raises a question. On the one hand is the mission of the Ross School of Business, which remains the same: to "develop leaders who make a positive difference in the world." But on the other hand is the now unspoken assumption that Ross can "develop" such leaders as well in one year as in two. In fact, one of the four main selling points of the master of management program is "top-ranked leader development." In other words, if there is a distinction between how well each of these two programs, master of management and master of business administration, can accomplish what Ross wants and intends—to develop leaders who will "make a positive difference"—this distinction is not spelled out. It is not spelled out for the good and simple reason that it is impossible to spell out with conviction and precision. This is more evidence that leadership is an occupation—it is not a profession or even close to it—that gives those of us in the leadership industry license to make claims more casual than convincing.

To be sure, the Ross School of Business is only doing what the market will allow, and what the competition, especially but not exclusively in Europe, already provides: a one-year master's in management program. Ross offers students without extensive work experience an opportunity to earn a graduate degree in business leadership and management. Ross offers students who see no good reason to spend two years of their time and more of their money earning a graduate degree in business the opportunity to get a degree that seems to them to be similar in one year for less money. And Ross provides itself, the school, an opportunity to develop a new and almost certainly solid income stream at a time when income is not so easy to come by,

My comments are not targeted at any individual or institution—they are targeted at those of us in the leadership industry. At how vague is our approach to the work we do. At how casual is our use of language. At how reprehensible is our failure to spell out what we mean when we claim to educate leaders, train leaders, develop leaders. No one seems to raise an eyebrow when a highly ranked professional school maintains implicitly if not explicitly that it can accomplish its mission—developing leaders—as well in one year as in two. No one seems to question that leaders can be developed in a single year—or for that matter in two. No one seems to wonder how form fits function—how leadership curricula are cut to fit the fashion of learning to lead simply and swiftly.

Imagine an approximate analog. Imagine a medical school that offered a program that professed to accomplish its overarching mission in half the time. It would accept for admission a student cohort that would not earn an MD, but a similar degree that would certify that those who earned it were qualified to become clinicians, though in this case after only two years of education and training instead of the usual four. It's not unheard of. For example, the Yale School of Medicine offers a Physician Associate Program. Its graduates, like the school's MDs, will be certified to be clinicians. Still, the distinctions between the two programs are crystal clear. The goals of the MD program are manifestly more ambitious and rigorous than those of the PA program, which is not to say that one is better than the other, simply that the former is more demanding than the latter. The point is that medical schools teach medicine in ways that befit a profession, whereas business schools do not teach leadership in ways that befit a profession. Medicine is tight: tightly organized, tightly controlled, and tightly taught. Leadership is loose: loosely organized, loosely controlled, and loosely taught.

To be sure, in recent years there have been pressures to shorten medical education from four years to three. These pressures include a predicted physician shortage and the rising burdens of student debt. But, in contrast to the question of how long it takes to educate and train a good leader, the question of how long it takes to educate and train a good doctor has been "the subject of spirited debate in the peer-reviewed literature, the mainstream press, and online publications."[16] In other words, the discussion about a shorter period of medical education and training has been robust. Medical professionals have given every evidence of taking the matter extremely seriously, carefully weighing the merits and deficits of arguments for and against cutting the four-year medical school curriculum to three. This alone testifies to how carefully and deliberately we think about teaching how to be a doctor, in contrast to how carelessly and casually we think about teaching how to be a leader.

The matter of metrics—metrics that measure the success, or the lack thereof, of leadership programs—is critical to the conversation. For the lack of an obvious yardstick to assess leadership learnings and evaluate leadership programs is one of the reasons both are dealt with haphazardly. I already referenced the McKinsey report, which focuses on our failure to provide evidence that leadership programs work. The trouble is this failure increases the likelihood that whatever the "improvement initiatives" they will not be "taken seriously." Again, we run into the problem of feedback: the value of such feedback as is provided is diminished if not discounted. "The danger here," the authors maintain, is that "trainers learn to game the system and deliver a syllabus that is more pleasing than challenging to participants."[17] How to mitigate the problem? Suggestions include setting targets and monitoring achievement, requiring 360-degree feedback at the beginning of the program and then again six to twelve months later, and tracking participants' career development. Still, the problem of developing rigorous, reliable metrics to assess leadership programs is, if not intractable, resistant to a quick fix.

Many companies with their own in-house leadership programs have their own in-house metrics, their own ways of assessing their own leadership programs for their own pedagogical, practical, and political purposes. For example, in 2012, first among companies ranked "the cream of the crop" in leadership development was Proctor & Gamble. Bob McDonald, CEO at the time (he later became the eighth US secretary of veteran's affairs), personally oversaw P & G's leadership development initiatives, which emphasized recruiting leaders from within the organization. Because of this preference for internal succession, managers were measured by the number of their subordinates who were promoted. The higher the number, the better, for the higher the number of subordinates who were promoted, the better it reflected on their superiors. McDonald also trained many of the company's most promising executives and then, along with the board of directors, personally evaluated their performance.[18] Of course, when a company such as P & G has a leadership development program, it is primarily for the purpose of strengthening P & G. There is no larger social purpose—nor is one expected.

Predictably, General Electric also ranks high among firms considered the "cream of the crop" in leadership development. Its company-wide leadership development initiatives are among the most extensive—and expensive. GE reportedly spends over one billion dollars annually on its leadership programs, which aim to teach "leadership skills that everybody should have." GE's leadership programs engage some 50,000 to 60,000 persons a year digitally, and host some 9,000 executives at the company's fabled leadership development center on fifty-nine "leafy" acres in Crotonville, New York.[19] GE presumably has its own internal metrics, which have led the company to conclude over the years that its large investment in leadership development pays off. Unsurprisingly, not everyone is convinced that their meticulous methods continue to pay off. As one observer wrote in *Psychology of Management*, "GE is by no means the only company with a corporate college. . . . But is it really worth it to spend all this effort and cash on employee development . . . and to pluck managers away from their desks for weeks at a time to indulge in self-betterment in a sumptuous corporate compound? GE certainly thinks so. Even during the depths of the financial crisis . . . GE kept Crotonville running at full bore. . . . It's difficult [though] to quantify the precise value of an improved executive class."[20]

I'll say it's difficult. Fact is that notwithstanding its long-standing, legendary commitment to leadership development, GE fared poorly during the last financial crisis. The company was obliged to freeze its dividend, suspend its share buyback program, scale back its finance unit, and reduce its reliance on short-term borrowing. Things got so bad that before it was all over, GE became "one of the largest recipients of the federal government's lifelines."[21] In other words, whatever the returns on GE's enormous investment in leadership learning, during one of the most trying periods in the company's history there was scant evidence that the investment had paid off. By this obvious measure—the company's capacity to stay strong during a time of a crisis, not to speak of precluding a crisis in the first place—GE's costly and highly touted leadership programs had failed. It's also telling that during the sixteen years that Jeff Immelt was CEO (he was nudged out in 2017), GE's stock price fell 27 percent, while the Dow more than doubled. Moreover, immediately after his departure, GE stumbled still further.

Assessments and evaluations of leadership programs in institutions of higher education suffer from some of the same uncertainties, though there the problem is more transparent, more freely and openly debated and discussed. (The words "measurement," "assessment," and "evaluation" are sometimes used interchangeably. Here I generally use "assessment.") Most leadership teachers know that they should assess the effectiveness of what they do, which does not, however, mean that they know how precisely to proceed. Leadership educator Julie Owen writes that "there remains a level of confusion about . . . assessment instruments. . . . For leadership educators, especially, the task of assessment can be fraught with ambiguity, as most assessment processes depend on clearly definable and measurable constructs rather than on more abstract concepts like 'leadership.'"[22]

Since "leadership" is an "abstract concept," difficult to assess under any circumstance, especially if it aims to assess both ethics and effectiveness, it makes sense to construct some sort of template, some sort of model of what a leadership assessment initiative might look like. (I'm aware that ethics are notoriously difficult, if not impossible, to teach, to inculcate. Duff McDonald writes that "ethics surely holds the record for the most failed efforts to launch a sustained institutional commitment to a subject" at the Harvard Business School.)[23] For example:

Step 1: find out how similar leadership programs are being assessed.
Step 2: spell out your objectives.
Step 3: reach stakeholder agreement on the assessment process.
Step 4: clarify what is being assessed.
Step 5: employ some measures that are quantitative, and others that are qualitative.
Step 6: plan to implement at least one assessment measure several years after the program has ended.[24]

Of course, these are only suggestions. Every leadership program should have its own way of determining what was accomplished. We should not, in any case, let the perfect be the enemy of the good. Because leadership experts and educators have found it so difficult to develop a yardstick, they, we, have tended to throw in the towel, to pay assessment no more than lip service, treating it like an unpleasant and unnecessary afterthought, nothing to be taken too seriously. That is not good enough—it disrespects what is supposed to be a learning experience of consequence.

The failure of the leadership industry—of leadership experts and educators—to cooperate and collaborate on problems associated with evaluations and assessments is indicative. It reflects one of the reasons why leadership has stayed stuck—stayed an occupation. For the history of professionalization suggests that every occupation that becomes over time a profession requires that at some point in the process a critical mass of professionals or, if you will, preprofessionals, come together to work together. In this case this process would hammer out, regularize, and systemize how best to assess leadership programs. In other words, professionalization requires a measure of cooperation to further an endeavor about which people are passionate.

In the beginning such gatherings and assemblages tend to be small and insignificant. But over time they grow larger and more powerful. Over time people with an interest in professionalization join to form an interest group, or a guild, or a union, and, eventually, a professional association. They join to enhance the work they do. They join to expand the work they do. They join to protect the work they do. They join to promote the work they do. They join to provide pedagogical parameters. They join to raise the level of their individual professional status. They join to raise the level of their collective professional status. They join to have a voice that is more powerful and persuasive in concert than it could possibly be alone. They join to draw a distinction between those on the inside and those on the outside.

As we have seen, the American Medical Association and the American Bar Association are epitomes of such professional cooperation and collaboration. Whatever the fights and feuds that bedeviled their members at the start, and whatever the members' contests and conflicts over the last one hundred years, and whatever the disputations and disagreements that characterize their memberships even now, their willingness to put their shared interests ahead of their individual interests testifies to the enduring professional benefits of enduring professional association. As one expert on professionalization put it, "Other things being equal, the more strongly organized a profession is, the more effective" it is. The organized profession can "better mobilize its members, can better direct media support of its position, and above all, can better support the effective academic work that generates cultural legitimacy."[25]

There is a connection between the problems that plague the leadership industry—such as, for example, the lack of effective and widely accepted assessment techniques—and the lack of organization. Truth is that those of us in the leadership industry are almost as fractured a conglomerate now as we were when the industry was in its infancy. Of course, there are, as we have seen, groups and organizations, including professional leadership associations, that did not exist four decades ago. I am thinking, for example, of the International Leadership Association, described (in its mission statement) as "the global network for all those who practice, study, and teach leadership." The ILA has done modestly well over the years: in 2015, its Leadership Perspective webinars had more than fifteen hundred participants from forty-one different countries, and its annual conferences attract over a thousand attendees from all over the world.[26] Additionally, the ILA promotes leadership scholarship in various ways, for example, it affiliates with *Leadership Quarterly*, a solid academic journal that is published by Elsevier. But, for all the accomplishments of the ILA, and for all the accomplishments of other leadership groups, organizations, and affiliations, the fact that leadership as an area of intellectual inquiry and practice lacks a single, strong, reasonably cohesive national professional association hinders leadership from becoming a profession.

Had management taken a different trajectory, had it been professionalized, the American Management Association (AMA) might have evolved into the large umbrella organization to which I here refer—it might have been the logical professional repository not only for those with an interest in management, but for those with an interest in leadership, including, I might add, political leadership.[27] But, as it turned out, the American Management Association does not now and never did meet the needs of most leadership researchers, teachers, and practitioners, which is one of the reasons why cleavages of all kinds continue to bedevil leadership experts and educators. Nor are they trivial: cleavages between those who practice leadership and those who teach leadership; between those whose primary interest is in leadership studies and those whose primary interest is in leadership development; between those in highly ranked institutions and organizations and those in institutions and organizations that are ranked lower; between those more concerned with leadership and those more concerned with management; between those teaching how to lead in institutions of higher education and those teaching how to lead elsewhere, in the Boy Scouts, for example, or at IBM; between those teaching leadership to young adults, in college, and those teaching leadership to older adults, already in the workplace; between those teaching how to lead in for-profit organizations and those teaching how to lead in nonprofit organizations; between those teaching how to lead in China and those teaching how to lead in Canada; between those teaching how to lead men and women in the army and those teaching how to lead to men and women in the clergy—I could go on.

My own institution, Harvard, is not immune to the problem. Harvard obsesses about teaching people how to lead, especially in its professional schools, including but not limited to the Business School and the Kennedy School. To take just some examples, the mission statement of the Harvard Law School reads in part, "to educate *leaders* who contribute to the development of justice and the well-being of society." The mission statement of the Harvard Medical School reads in part, "to create and nurture a diverse community of the best people committed to *leadership* in alleviating suffering." The mission statement of the Harvard Divinity School reads in part, "to educate scholars, teachers, ministers and other professionals for *leadership* and service."[28] But each of these leadership ambitions and initiatives sits, in effect, in its own silo. Learning to lead at the Harvard Medical School has little or no connection to learning to lead at the Harvard Divinity School, which has little or no connection to learning to lead at the Harvard Kennedy School. There is no center or institute or logical or obvious academic home to which everyone at the University with an interest in the study of leadership, and in the exercise of leadership, students and scholars alike, naturally gravitates. In other words, learning leadership at Harvard is like learning leadership most everywhere else: no clear, consistent definition; no organizing principles; no shared language; no core curriculum; and no obvious commonalities or communities. No wonder the leadership industry is no closer to achieving professional status now than it was when the industry was in its infancy.

Successes

There are some—not many, but some—groups and organizations that have their act together. In general, they are in the enviable position of having had considerable resources to spend—institutional, intellectual, pedagogical, fiscal, temporal—to develop, hone, and refine over time their leadership programs. One example is the aforementioned University of Richmond's Jepson School of Leadership Studies. But the Jepson School constitutes its own small, special universe—it cannot and does not constitute a template for what could or should happen on other campuses. There is, however, a single American institution from which any of us with any interest in leadership have a great deal to learn. It's the only major American institution that can legitimately claim to get from the American people a high rate of approval. It's the only major American institution that can legitimately claim to take leadership teaching and leadership learning seriously—very seriously. It's the only major American institution that can legitimately claim to teach *about* leadership—and to teach *how* to lead. It's is the only major American institution that can legitimately claim to treat leadership as a *profession*. I refer to an institution that enables leadership learning every which way—by insisting on leadership *education*, by providing leadership *training*, and by encouraging leadership *development*. I refer to an institution in which leadership learners are taught by leadership experts—either because they have the academic chops legitimately to fill their designated roles, and, or, because they have done the deed, they have led. I refer of course to the American military.

I am not comparing learning how to lead in the American military with learning how to lead anywhere else in America. There is an intensity to learning how to lead in the military, a sense of heightened urgency, that simply does not exist anyplace else. One of the reasons is obvious: leading wisely and well in the military can make the difference between life and death. The army and the marine corps are the most striking examples of this singular situation. They are the only services where, upon being commissioned, a twenty-two-year-old second lieutenant is immediately given 24/7 responsibility for the mission, welfare, and lives of a forty-person platoon.[29]

So I am not suggesting that other groups, organizations, or institutions should follow the military model. That would in any case be impossible—people in the military constitute very particular populations and are in very particular positions. Nor do I claim that American military leaders are without fault. Hardly.[30] The so-called Fat Leonard corruption scandal, which has bedeviled the US Navy in recent years, is a vivid reminder that members of the military are not angels—as are online sexual harassment and brutal hazing scandals that have embarrassed the marines. This does not, however, militate against the proposition that American civilians have a lot to learn from the American military, from the only American institution that has taken learning to lead to heart since the inception of the Republic. For the US Military Academy has roots that go all the way back to 1801, "when President Thomas Jefferson directed, shortly after his inauguration, that plans be drawn for the establishment of the United Sates Military Academy at West Point."[31] Put differently, the army, navy, and marine corps are, in this significant sense, *not* a part of the leadership industry. The leadership industry is less than a half-century old. In contrast, learning to lead in the army, the navy, and the marine corps has a long and storied history that goes all the way back to the American Revolution.

I am not the first to suggest that leaders generally have something to learn from military leaders specifically. Books with titles such as *Leadership Lessons from West Point* and *Building Leaders the West Point Way* have been on the market for years.[32] And articles with titles such as "How to Apply Marine Leadership Traits to Business" similarly abound.[33] Moreover, to reiterate, the military is the only American institution that has effectively resisted the dramatic decline in trust in America's leadership class more broadly. Americans' confidence in the military is not only higher than in any other American institution, but strikingly higher. Fully 73 percent of Americans have either a "great deal" or "quite a lot" of confidence in the military. Contrast this with the level of our confidence in Congress, which stands at 7 percent (total), or in newspapers, which stands at 20 percent (total), or even in the Supreme Court, which stands at 36 percent (total)—and you get a strong sense of how atypically high is the level of esteem in which Americans hold their military.[34] Military leaders have, moreover, a singularly strong track record in Washington. They have, in other words, developed the capacity to lead not only in wartime, but in peacetime as well.

Under President Donald Trump no fewer than four senior military officers took on dominant roles: retired marine corps general John Kelly, the president's chief of staff; retired marine general James Mattis, secretary of defense; army lieutenant general H. R. McMaster, national security advisor; and marine general Joseph Dunford, chairman of the Joint Chiefs of Staff. But even in other administrations, the power and influence of military leaders has, in recent decades, observably increased. They more than anyone else are responsible for the "gradual seeping in of military perspectives and priorities into the broader foreign policy and national security strategies and policies of the United States." They more than anyone else are responsible for policymakers' increasing reliance "on military instruments as they shape, decide on, and implement foreign policy and national security policy choices."[35] Finally, military leaders—think, for instance, of Ulysses S. Grant and Dwight David Eisenhower—historically have played outsized roles not only in the armed services, but in business and government, government especially. A remarkable recent example is four-star army general Colin Powell. He had a brilliantly successful military career during which he served as national security advisor (under President Ronald Reagan), commander of the US Army Forces Command, and chairman of the Joint Chiefs of Staff. He then went on to become a statesman, serving as secretary of state under President George W. Bush. Subsequently he pursued a career as a writer and public speaker—who focused on leadership. Though most of his "rules of leadership" are more common sense than they are anything else, they continue even now, ten years after he left public service, to have currency, largely because of the esteem in which Powell still is held.[36]

What is it about the American military that makes it special—that enables its leaders to stand out even now, during a time of distrust and disgust? First, the American military is special because it assumes that leadership is a profession: it educates, trains, and develops leaders in accordance with high professional standards. To be a military professional, especially but not exclusively a military officer, is like being a medical professional, a doctor, or a legal professional, a lawyer. Second, the American military is special because it educates, trains, and develops leaders in a professional manner, to be professionals, which explains why military leaders seem to us superior to leaders in other sectors. The reason for their superiority is obvious: they are far better prepared over a much longer time to assume positions of leadership and indeed to lead, wherever they are positioned. Third, the American military is special because it assumes that no one ever would or should take on a leadership role without being properly educated, trained, and developed. In politics, it is demonstrably possible to ascend to the nation's highest office—the presidency—without any relevant experience or expertise whatsoever. In the military, such an ascension would be impossible—inconceivable. Finally, the American military is special because it regularly reminds military personnel of the importance of character—of old-fashioned virtues such as integrity, inclusivity, responsibility, accountability, moral courage, and service.[37] While it is impossible precisely to measure the impact of such a consistent, continuing emphasis on having good character, on having high ethical standards, it is unlikely it has no impact at all.

Though the following discussion will focus mainly on the army, it's important I reiterate that every one of the armed services considers leadership a profession—not an occupation or even a vocation—for which men and women must be educated, trained, and developed. Arguably the air force, the newest of the services (it was established only after the Second World War, in 1947), takes education especially seriously. This is not, I hasten to add, "education" as narrowly defined. Rather it is education as broadly defined. To wit, an article aptly titled "Commitment to Liberal Education at the United States Air Force Academy" (USAFA), which describes educating, training, and inspiring men and women to become "officers of character motivated to *lead* the United States Air Force in service to our nation."[38] To this end, from its inception (in 1954) to this day, the USAFA has remained committed to providing its cadets with a comprehensive and rigorous liberal education, including the humanities, engineering, the social sciences and basic sciences, to prepare graduates "for the unknown challenges of military service anywhere in the world."[39] I should add that the USAFA regularly evaluates its curriculum, to confirm it continues to correspond to its strategic vision.

The US Naval Academy is somewhat similar. It is in any case also committed to providing its students with a liberal education. It has a core curriculum consisting of required courses in humanities and mathematics, in science and engineering, and in "leadership rooted in the behavioral sciences." The purpose is to ensure that the Naval Academy's "core learning outcomes" further its mission, which in this case is to "develop midshipmen morally, mentally, and physically and to imbue them with the highest ideals of duty, honor and loyalty in order to graduate *leaders* who are dedicated to a career of naval service."[40] The Naval Academy's undergraduate education is further intended to, among other things, enable students to "recognize moral dilemmas and use ethical frameworks and principles to generate solutions that embody the highest moral standards."

Each of America's armed services emphasizes morals and ethics in its leadership teachings and trainings. Among the "Marine Corps Leadership Principles and Traits," for example, are integrity, loyalty, unselfishness, and courage.[41] Arguably, though, the USAFA takes the responsibility of developing leaders "of character" to a new level. On its campus in Colorado Springs is a striking new building that houses the previously mentioned (in chapter 2) Center for Character and Leadership Development. The center serves as an education and research hub in support of its mission: "to integrate character and leadership development into all aspects of the Cadet experience while also serving as a think tank for leadership and character development initiatives nationwide."[42] A leader of character lives honorably, lifts others, and elevates performance to a "common and noble purpose." Note that the USAFA presumes that character is malleable, not static, that it can change, get better and stronger over time. It presumes, in other words, that character is like leadership: it can be *developed*. The air force has several "guiding principles of purposeful development," one of which was earlier suggested: that leadership *development* is different from, distinguishable from, leadership *education* and leadership *training*. Development requires "purposeful engagement"—involving, among other things, the resolve, both by the individual and by the institution to act in alignment with shared "commitments, values, and beliefs."[43]

One more thing about the air force. The USAFA does not simply include the concept of followership in its conversation about leadership. It is explicitly committed to developing *followers* of good character, along with leaders of good character. Among their other virtues, followers of good character demonstrate loyalty to air force values, to the air force's mission, and to the chain of command. Followers of good character operate and comply with the intent of air force policies and directives, and they "hone followership abilities."[44] It's a reminder of how foolish is the fixation on leadership among civilians. So while the air force explicitly *includes* followers in its cadet curricula, civilian institutions seeking to enroll undergraduate analogues explicitly *exclude* them. Harvard's application informs students that its mission is to "educate our students to be citizens and citizen-leaders." Yale advises applicants that it seeks "the leaders of their generation." Even Wesleyan, "known for its artistic culture, was found by one study to evaluate applicants based on leadership potential."[45]

The mission of the Military Academy at West Point is to "educate, train, and inspire the Corps of Cadets so that each graduate is a commissioned *leader* of character committed to the values of Duty, Honor Country." A West Point publication titled *Building Capacity to Lead: The West Point System for Leader Development* delves into the process in detail. Here some highlights.

- West Point provides a rigorous, broadly based leadership *education.* "The intellectual development of cadets remains paramount to realizing the Military Academy's mission."
- West Point requires different types of leadership *training,* such as, for example, for physical fitness. "Leaders must be physically ready and capable of leading from the front at all times. . . . [They must] develop and maintain high levels of . . . physical fitness: muscular strength and endurance, cardiovascular endurance, flexibility, and body composition."
- West Point emphasizes leadership *development.* "Framing leader development is a necessary condition for the design and implementation of a curriculum capable of developing cadets into leaders of character."
- West Point is conscious of context. It recognizes that components of context, such as, for instance, "globalization and interconnectedness," have an impact on the exercise of leadership.

- West Point assumes assessment. Assessment is conducted annually "through systematic mechanisms for gathering, analyzing, and reporting on evidence in order to implement change as necessary."
- West Point prioritizes character. "A leader of character is one who seeks to discover the truth, decide what is right, and demonstrate the courage to act accordingly"
- West Point presumes that learning to lead is a process—a process that *must* be comprehensive. "A combination of education, training, and development is required to produce leaders of character. Although training, education and development are not synonymous with one another, the capacity of training and educational experiences to influence development is contingent upon how each is structured and implemented."[46]

So far, I have emphasized learning to lead at the Air Force Academy in Colorado Springs, Colorado; at the Naval Academy in Annapolis, Maryland; and at the Military Academy at West Point, New York. So far, then this discussion has focused on leadership learners in the American military who are young adults, something of an elite cadre between the approximate ages of eighteen and twenty-two, who, moreover, constitute an essentially captive audience for a four-year period. However, the military's universe of leadership learners is far larger than this emphasis would seem to suggest. Each of the military branches teaches leadership not only to young adults, but to older adults. And each of the military branches teaches leadership not only to officers, more of whom now go on to get PhD degrees, but to others, including non-commissioned officers. While officers may constitute the military's most visible leadership learners, they do not constitute the military's only leadership learners.

The United States Army War College (USAWC) is one of the three senior service colleges—the navy and the air force also have war colleges—under the rubric of the Department of Defense. USAWC, located on a five-hundred-acre campus in Carlisle, Pennsylvania, is a graduate school for senior leaders in the US Army. Its mission is to "prepare selected military, civilian, and international *leaders* for the responsibilities of strategic *leadership*; educate current and future *leaders* on the development and employment of landpower in a joint, multinational and interagency environment; [and to] conduct research and publish on national security and military strategy."[47] It is, in brief, an education and training ground, especially but not exclusively for colonels and lieutenant colonels, who show promise for promotion to positions of increased responsibility in the US Army. It is also a degree-granting institution (master of strategic studies), and a research center. (The Strategic Studies Institute, located in the USAWC, conducts strategic and security research.) Finally, it is yet another army repository dedicated to leadership. The USAWC has a Center for Strategic Leadership that focuses specifically on developing senior leaders by providing them with opportunities for experiential learning and by conducting research that supports the work of senior army leaders.

The USAWC is a graduate institution primarily for army leaders in middle adulthood who show potential for leadership positions more senior than the ones that they already hold and who, therefore, have been selected for admission by their superiors. (The USAWC does not accept applications from individuals.) The Center for Army Leadership (CAL), in contrast, which is located in Fort Leavenworth, Kansas, is dedicated to leadership across the board, at every level. It conducts research on leadership. It assesses and evaluates various leadership programs. It provides the army with different products and services, including leadership development doctrine. And it manages the Army Leader Development Program. In 2011 CAL published a Survey of Army Leadership that found that 64 percent of all army leaders (including noncommissioned officers) were considered effective. However, at the same time it found that one in five army leaders judged their immediate superiors to have demonstrated behaviors that were "toxic."[48]

Clearly, then, the military, in this case the army, is not, for all its leadership development efforts, without its flaws. Why, otherwise, would 20 percent of army leaders claim that their immediate superiors demonstrated behaviors that were toxic? "Toxic" is a strong word—and one-fifth of all army leaders is not a small number. However, whatever the army's failings, it's not for lack of trying. It is impossible not to be struck by the magnitude of the army's effort to get it right—to get leadership education, training, and development right for army personnel at virtually every level.

Two more army publications drive home the point. The first, titled "Army Leadership Development Strategy," is from 2013. Again, it distinguishes among leadership education, training, and, here, "experience." The most striking thing about the document is its insistence that whatever the process of leadership development, it is continuous, ongoing. It does not begin at any preordained point; nor does it end at any preordained point. To the contrary: to be a military professional is to learn to lead lifelong. Period. Experience "begins before the individual joins the Army and continues after separation. Experience includes war and peace; the personal and the professional; the private and the public; leading and following; training and education. Career-long learners reflect on all experiences."[49]

The second publication to which I again draw attention is titled, simply, *Army Leadership*. (I refer to it also in chapter 2.) It's a smart, solid discussion of leadership and leadership development in the context of the American army. Leadership is defined—"it is the process of influencing people by providing purpose, direction, and motivation to accomplish the mission and improve the organization"—and leadership is analyzed. There is discussion about the distinction between formal and informal leadership; about core leadership competencies; about various leadership roles and levels of leadership; about what, ideally, characterizes an army leader; about the importance of "intellect"; about traits such as mental agility, sound judgement, and expertise; about what constitutes influence and how to exercise it; about leaders' responsibilities to develop others, to "prepare talented Soldiers and Army Civilians to assume positions with greater leadership responsibility"; and about what it means to be a military *professional*.

The final section of *Army Leadership* is about "strategic leadership," about leadership at the highest level of the US Army. Strategic army leaders are "keenly aware of the complexities of the national and international security environment." Strategic army leaders represent a "finely balanced combination of high-level thinkers, accomplished warfighters, and geopolitical military experts." Above all, strategic army leaders swear to uphold the Constitution. "This oath subordinates the military leader to the laws of the nation and its elected and appointed leaders, creating a distinct civil-military relationship. A critical element of this relationship is the trust that civilian leaders have in their military leaders to represent the military and provide *professional* advice."[50]

The leadership industry has a double-edged problem: the perception that in the first quarter of the twenty-first century, *leaders* are inadequate to the task at hand; and the perception that in the first quarter of the twenty-first century, leadership *programs* are inadequate to the task at hand. The only significant American exception to this confounding correlation is outside the leadership industry—it is the military. Whatever the concerns—after all, military leaders, like other leaders, are imperfect—a large majority of the American people have a high level of confidence in them. Americans perceive the military generally, and military leaders specifically, to be *effective* and they perceive them to be *ethical*. This means that they perceive military leaders as superior to leaders in other sectors. This suggests, in turn, that whatever their flaws, military leadership programs are in general superior to civilian leadership programs. To be sure, as indicated, the contexts within which military leadership programs take place are very different from the contexts within which civilian leadership programs take place. Withal, the evidence suggests that the military does a demonstrably better job of teaching people how to lead than do its countless civilian counterparts.

Of course, the military has no magic formula. Some of the problems that bedevil leadership learning generally—say, leadership as a "vast and sprawling field with no clear contours or boundaries"—bedevil leadership learning in the military as well. Moreover, military leadership learners are likely to be no better or smarter at addressing some of the big questions—such as, do leaders much matter?—than civilian leadership learners. *But what the military does that distinguishes it from every other American institution is to presume that leadership is a profession. To presume that being a leader is being a professional. To presume that being a professional requires education, training, and development befitting a professional. And to presume that being professionally educated, trained, and developed requires educators, trainers, and developers who are experts.*

- Leadership in the military is defined.
- Leadership in the military is not confused or conflated with management.
- Leadership programs in the military mandate leadership education.
- Leadership programs in the military mandate leadership training.
- Leadership programs in the military mandate leadership development.
- Leadership programs in the military contain a common curriculum.
- Leadership programs in the military presume a connection between leadership development and adult development.
- Leadership programs in the military equate leadership development with character development.
- Leadership programs in the military assume the importance of followership.
- Leadership programs in the military assume the importance of context.
- Leadership programs in the military are assessed, regularly and rigorously.
- Leadership programs in the military demand proof of competence.
- Leadership programs in the military require commitment to a code of ethics.
- Leadership programs in the military involve a vow to uphold military standards.
- Leadership programs in the military are ongoing, continuous.
- Leadership programs in the military have gravitas—they are central to what the military does, not marginal.
- Leadership in the military is considered a public service.
- Leadership in the military presumes professional status.

I recognize that these are strong statements—shorn of complexities and ambiguities. I also recognize that there are differences among the different services. Leadership in the army, for instance, is preached and practiced at least somewhat differently from leadership in the air force. Further, I recognize that what constitutes a core leadership curriculum in one branch of the American military differs somewhat from what constitutes a core leadership curriculum in another. Finally, I recognize how far short learning to lead falls from any imagined ideal, if only because leadership remains, ultimately, something of a "mystery."

Withal, the gap between how the American military teaches how to lead and how every other American institution teaches how to lead is enormous. This gap raises several questions. Is there anything to be learned by, for example, civilian undergraduate institutions from military undergraduate institutions? Is there anything to be learned by, for example, professional schools such as schools of business and government from military academies or war colleges? Is there anything to be learned by, for example, civilian in-house leadership programs from military in-house leadership programs? Is there anything to be learned by, for example, some nonprofit leadership programs such as the countless ones in education and religion, from other nonprofit leadership programs, such as the countless ones in the American military? Is there anything to be learned by, for example, civilian leadership educators from military leadership educators? Is it possible, in short, to borrow from the very good to make the not so good better? Is it possible to change learning how to lead in the leadership industry so that it more closely resembles learning how to lead in the American military? Is it possible to adopt and adapt, to transform leadership from what it is now, an occupation, into something different, a profession?

8

Professionalization

This book is predicated on three fundamental assumptions. The first is that the leadership industry does not take sufficiently seriously its responsibility for teaching people how to lead. The second is that the leadership industry has the human and fiscal capital to prime the pedagogical pump, to enhance and elevate the pedagogical process—if it can muster the political will. The third is that leadership experts and educators must lead the charge. They, we, must change our conception of leadership, our perception of leadership, from occupation to profession if it is to be preached and practiced more ethically and effectively.

This is not just idle intellectual chatter—it's a practical issue of the utmost consequence. For professionalism is how we "institutionalize expertise in industrialized societies."[1] Therefore, so long as leadership experts and educators shun professionalism, so long will leadership stay stuck: an occupation of dubious repute instead of a profession of serious repute. Leadership cannot be taught or learned quickly and easily. Leadership cannot simply be summarized and codified.[2] Leadership cannot be mastered overnight and on the job. We cannot for instance expect someone who is politically uninformed and inexperienced—wholly uninformed and entirely inexperienced—to from one day to the next exercise presidential leadership with competence and grace.

Most of history's master leadership teachers had core beliefs in common. Above all they shared a deep seriousness of purpose. They believed that to lead was the most significant, most urgent, of all human endeavors. They believed that leadership could be learned, and that it could be taught. But they thought that it ought to be taught only *by* those who were supremely well qualified *to* those who were supremely well qualified. They further believed that it took time to learn how to lead—a long time. Boys and later men could learn how to lead only by dedicating their lives to the process for years and even decades. Similarly, they believed that learning to lead was hard, not only long but difficult, requiring great dedication to different areas of mental and physical endeavor. Moreover, they conceived of leadership broadly as opposed to narrowly. They were as occupied with bad leaders and bad leadership as with good leaders and good leadership. The notion that good leaders were supremely important, but that bad leaders were unimportant, was inconceivable. Finally, master leadership teachers shared the belief that leaders were of the utmost importance—as were followers. Once upon a time there was no such thing as thinking about leadership without thinking about followership.

For a constellation of reasons, today none of these beliefs are at the heart of how leadership is conceived or perceived. In fact, most have been junked by the leadership industry, which ignores them. We do not bestow on leadership a deep seriousness of purpose—except as lip service. We do not share the belief that leadership should be taught only by a select few to a select few. To the contrary—we believe just the opposite. We have democratized leadership. We think of it as something that can be taught by the relatively uninitiated to the entirely uninitiated. And we believe, or we profess to believe, that everyone can lead. As one leadership textbook put it, "Leadership is not something possessed by only a select few. . . . We are all involved in the leadership process, and we are all capable of being effective leaders."[3] Further, the leadership industry is not predicated on the presumption that learning to lead takes years or even decades. Or on the presumption that learning to lead is hard because learning to lead is a process as profound as prolonged. Finally, the leadership industry has little or no interest in bad leaders—either in theory (how does bad leadership come to pass?) or in practice (how to stop bad leaders or, at least, slow them?). And it has little or no interest in followers, or even in their relations with leaders, notwithstanding they're symbiotic.

I obviously am something of a throwback. I believe that some, indeed most, of the ideas held by the great ancient leadership teachers are as important now, as pertinent now, as they were hundreds and even thousands of years ago. After all, human nature stays the same, which is why most of what held true about power and authority in ancient China or Greece holds true today. What has changed are the contexts within which leadership is exercised. And what has changed are our ideas about what is right and good and true. We cannot, in other words, simply clone Confucius and Plato and apply what they proselytized to the here and now. This does not, however, mean that we should reject or even ignore them, as if they were no longer in any way relevant.

Here is what we *might* take from the past and apply to the present: the idea that learning how to lead is learning theory and practice of supreme importance; the idea that learning how to lead ethically and effectively includes learning about its ubiquitous, obvious, obverse, leading that is unethical and ineffective; the idea that learning how to lead includes learning how to follow; and the idea that learning how to lead is a process that is continuous. Here is what we *must* take from the past and apply to the present—lest the leadership industry stall or even ultimately fail: *the idea that leadership is not an occupation—it is a profession.* Lao-tzu,

Confucius, Plato, Plutarch, and Machiavelli all thought that learning to be a leader was learning to be someone of great consequence. It was not, they thought, something that a man could casually learn or easily do. Instead, becoming a leader required the utmost seriousness of purpose, and the utmost perseverance and dedication. It was, in this important sense, analogous to becoming in our own time a doctor or a lawyer. That is, learning how to lead was thought about then as it is not now: to require a rigorous education, to require extensive training, and to require a continuing commitment to development in adulthood.

Let me be clear. I do not expect that this book or anything else, for that matter, will transform the leadership industry overnight, or that the industry will in the short term look dramatically different from the way it looks now. Nor do I anticipate that leadership experts and educators will immediately become converts, that from one day to the next they will rethink how leadership should be conceived. What I do hope to do is to start a discussion, to get those involved in the industry to think about what we do and how we do it in a way that is markedly different from what it has been up to now. It should be markedly more deliberate, markedly more determined, markedly more disciplined—and markedly more collaborative. To this end, in this last chapter, I provide guidelines or principles for individuals, groups, organizations, and institutions ambitious to improve the quality of their leadership programs; ambitious to acquire information and ideas that could in time translate into leaders who are better educated and trained, and who continue to develop lifelong; ambitious to transform leadership, if only gradually, from occupation to profession. Such a transformation would have two clear virtues: first, better leaders—leaders who lead more wisely and well, and second, better followers—followers who follow more wisely and well, which would mean among other things, clearly and consistently holding their leaders to high standards.

This is a road, I hasten to add, that has long been paved with good intentions. I am hardly the first to try to improve the quality of leadership programs—of leadership education, training, and development. Earlier in this book I described how Mary Parker Follett attempted almost a century ago, and failed, to professionalize management. Moreover, as we have also seen, some of my colleagues, notably Rakesh Khurana and Nitin Nohria, have spoken to the issue of bringing to the study of leadership and management greater rigor, and to the practice of leadership and management greater moral purpose. Even the Harvard Kennedy School's Center for Public Leadership, with which I have been affiliated since its inception in 2000, took a crack early on at crafting a rigorous model for leadership development. It consisted of "seven distinct competencies":

1. Catalytic—identifying challenges and mobilizing others to address them
2. Contextual—understanding the different contexts within which leaders and followers are situated

3. Interpersonal—modulating our behaviors to interact effectively
4. Theoretical—understanding fundamental leadership concepts
5. Organizational—planning and implementing collective action
6. Personal—becoming and remaining self-aware
7. Social—analyzing social and political systems.[4]

But this model for leadership development, like others that preceded and succeeded it, turned out nothing more than a thought experiment. For various reasons, not long after it was developed, it was abandoned.

Of course, some individuals, groups, organizations, and institutions have seeded and sustained models of leadership education, training, and development that they have found effective. I am thinking of the American military particularly, which has long poured enormous resources into learning to lead. But, by and large, even the most successful of these efforts have remained siloed. They have remained contained, as opposed to becoming over time a template, or a model that others found fit to emulate. Again, the reasons for this are multiple, and they are complex. They are personal and professional and political, and they are also fiscal and organizational. What we can say in any case is this. One of the reasons why leadership remains, with exception of leadership in the military, an occupation, is because there is no single, widely recognized, generally accepted professional leadership association that assembles leadership experts and educators, practitioners and pedagogues, and provides them with personal, political, and professional connection and protection. Not only is there no leadership analogue to the American Medical Association, there is no leadership analogue to the American Political Science Association.

Similarly, there is no single institution that is known as a great center of leadership learning, of leadership teaching, of leadership education, training, and development. There are several institutions that appear regularly in the top ten rankings of medical schools and the top ten rankings of law schools. They are known worldwide for being superlative centers of medical and legal research, and superlative centers of medical and legal teaching and training. Names such as Yale University, Stanford University, and Columbia University regularly appear at the top of such lists. But, is there any analog for leadership? For leadership research and for leadership teaching and training? There is none, not one. To be sure, Yale, Stanford, and Columbia all have excellent schools of business. And, as I earlier observed, schools of business are the probably the closest analogs to schools of leadership. But they are not one and the same—not by a long shot.

What, then, is to be done? The principles provided below are supposed to be a start. They are supposed to begin the transition from thinking about leadership as an occupation to thinking about leadership as a profession. I recognize of course that not every individual or institution has the same energy or capacity.

What I offer resembles a set of guidelines or, perhaps better, principles, which are intended to be adoptable and adaptable by different people in different places in different ways. There is no reason, of course, to presume that they will apply in the same way to leadership programs at General Electric as to leadership programs at Westminster College. Still, there are some overarching themes that are cross-cutting. That are important to everyone with an interest in leadership as a serious exercise with a proper sense of purpose.

Learning How to Lead

I will discuss leadership education, training, and development in turn, after these more general comments.

First, some comments about leadership students and teachers, and the contexts within which learning to lead is presumed to take place. Leadership learners are in the main adults, albeit of different ages and at different stages. They are distinct in other ways as well. They have different histories and cultures; different mindsets and motivations; different personalities and professions; different concerns and capacities; different intelligences and incentives; different experiences and expertise. While leadership learners are, by definition, learning how to lead, the differences between and among them should be, insofar as is reasonable, acknowledged and addressed. But to this general rule there is an exception. There is one part of the pedagogical process that should be consistent—equally applicable to all leadership learners: socialization.

I earlier discussed the importance of socialization to professionalization. Each of the professions socializes those within it early on, to inform them about, attune them to, and engage them in the professional culture within which, as fully credentialed professionals, they will eventually be embedded. For example, in chapter 5, I wrote that medical professionals are socialized in medical school, which itself constitutes "a rite of passage during which neophytes are structurally separated from their former environments." This socializing to professional status cannot, however, take place unless those who are doing the socializing—in this case leadership educators, experts, practitioners, pedagogues—convey that what they are doing is of utmost consequence. They must convey that leadership is a profession, not merely an occupation. For whatever the nature of leadership learners and whatever the differences between and among them, none can conceive of leadership as a profession unless their leadership teachers are themselves so persuaded. If we in the leadership industry fail to bestow on leadership professional status, and if we in the leadership industry fail to communicate to clients, customers, consumers, and students that leaders should be professionals, we can never convey that becoming a leader is becoming someone of whom much is expected.

The contexts within which leadership teachers teach, and leadership learners learn, are also of consequence. As always, there are immediate contexts: for example, some leadership educators stress the value of "learning communities," and others of "educationally purposeful leadership learning environments." Additionally are contexts more distant. It cannot in any case be emphasized enough that the larger, global context within which leadership now takes place is daunting: the amount of uncertainty, the level of complexity, the pervasive sense of threat, and, above all, the rapidity of change. Futurist Ray Kurzweil says we are in an age of acceleration. "Because of the explosive power of exponential growth, the twenty-first century will be equivalent to 20,000 years of progress at today's rate." No wonder organizations will have no choice but to "redefine themselves at a faster and faster pace."[5] Context, then, matters in two related though somewhat different ways. It matters because leaders cannot distance themselves from the circumstance within which they situated.[6] And it matters because leaders' levels of contextual consciousness, contextual expertise, and contextual intelligence will determine to a degree the level of their accomplishment.

Second, some comments, one final time, about the distinction, or lack thereof, between learning to lead and learning to manage. I chronicled their historical trajectories, especially from the early preference for "management" to the more recent preference for "leadership." And I chronicled the contemporaneous confusions, specifically the fungibility between leadership and management; the lack of specificity about both the former and the latter; and the dubious distinctions between them, such as the one (usually the leader) being valued more highly than the other (usually the manager). Most organizations and institutions have simply thrown in the towel on this one. They no longer take the time or trouble to define the two words, or to distinguish between them, or to use them in ways that are clear and consistent. This, I argue, has got to stop. If we—we in the leadership industry, we leadership experts and educators—are unable or unwilling to use the words "leadership" and "management" so that they are clear and consistent, how can we expect others to do differently?

I admit that it's a problem. It's a problem because both words have a long history of being confounding. Still, I maintain that if we are serious about professionalizing leadership, there is one meaning or component of the word "leadership" that must become integral, certainly when we distinguish between teaching leadership and teaching management. "Leadership" can and sometimes does imply service—"management" mostly does not. "Leadership" can and sometimes does imply commitment to the public interest—management mostly does not. Leadership can and sometimes does imply adherence to a code of ethics—"management" mostly does not. In this all-important sense, then, "leadership" is closer to medicine and law than is "management." In other words, learning to be a doctor or learning to be a lawyer is to receive, among other messages, a message about morality. Learning to lead should be the same. Leadership teachers should convey to leadership learners that they too will provide a *professional service*: a service rendered by leaders who are presumed ethical as well as effective because they were professionally educated, trained, and developed.

Here is an example of how leadership and service get conflated. Leadership is defined by consultant Mike Myatt as "the professed desire and commitment to serve others by subordinating personal interests to the needs of those being led."[7] Myatt's conception of leadership is in keeping with others', both ancient and contemporaneous, with, for example, Robert Greenleaf's—it was Greenleaf who conceived of servant leadership. Myatt also meshes with James MacGregor Burns's conception of leadership —it was Burns who conceived of transformational leadership. Greenleaf wrote that the "servant-leader is servant first. . . . It begins with the natural feeling that one wants to serve, to serve first."[8] Burns wrote that transforming leadership occurs "when one or more persons engage with others in such a way that leaders and followers raise one another to higher levels of motivation and morality."[9] While Greenleaf and Burns place all-important adjectives in front of the word leadership—"servant" and "transforming" respectively—what Myatt, Greenleaf, and Burns have in common is the idea that leadership is akin to a calling, a calling to a way of life that is in the service of others.

I am mindful of the continuing confusions. I am mindful, for example, that earlier in this book I mentioned that Nohria and Khurana wrote not about leadership as a profession, but about "management as a profession." Their criteria for achieving professional status included both a "commitment to use specialized knowledge for the public good" and "a code of ethics." In other words, I recognize that by suggesting that once and for all we distinguish teaching leadership from teaching management by ascribing to the former an ethical or service component that we do not ascribe to the latter, I am distancing myself from some of my colleagues.

Still, to refuse to settle on a distinction is to continue to be vague. It is to continue tacitly to approve of the countless organizations and institutions that think distinguishing leadership from management is neither necessary nor important. It is to continue to confuse consumers to whom we ostensibly provide a service. And it is to continue to shrink from the task before us—to professionalize the process of learning to be a leader so that it, like the process of learning to be a doctor or a lawyer, implies service and a code of conduct. Conversely, to claim that leadership should be a calling is no more than, and no less than, a return to the distant past, when great leaders were what Aristotle called "great souled," or what later was termed "magnanimous." Leadership scholar Haig Patapan has described magnanimous leaders as longing "for great deeds and achievements requiring personal sacrifice." Such leaders take on such tasks without aggrandizing themselves: they are leaders "of a specific moral disposition, with a profound sense of public service or duty, and willingness to sacrifice for a greater cause."[10]

The implications of semantic rigor are, potentially, significant. After all, the enormous sums of money being poured into the leadership industry are expended in good part by publicly held companies with an interest in getting their high-level executives to learn how to "lead"—not to learn how to "manage." Moreover, they invest in getting their high-level executives to learn how to lead for their benefit, that is, for the benefit of the company that foots the bill, as opposed to the benefit of others. So while a line such as "leadership for the public good" might not be alien to, say, Southwest Airlines, its leadership development programs, like other such corporate programs, are not intended to educate, train, or develop leaders in the interest of the public good. They are intended instead to educate, train, and develop leaders in the interest of Southwest, which, of course, is perfectly reasonable. What is not perfectly reasonable is that leadership programs such as these—run by organizations solely for their own benefit—should have the same nomenclature as leadership programs that consider service to be integral, such as, to take an obvious example, those at the Robert K. Greenleaf Center for Servant Leadership. What I am arguing then is that a company like Southwest should change the name of its Emerging Leader Development Program (ELDP) to Emerging Manager Development Program (EMDP). Failing this, a company like Southwest should change the content of its management program to include a service component—which, then, would make it a leadership program. More to the point perhaps, or, at least, more realistically, I would charge all institutions of higher education particularly with settling this issue once and for all—with distinguishing leadership from management by including in the meaning of the former, but not of the latter, a clear and unambiguous commitment to public service.

Third, some comments about providing people learning to be professionals with professional learning environments. If you want to see how striking the comparison between a first-rate professional program—that is, a program that educates, trains, and develops first-rate professionals—and other professional, not to speak of occupational, programs, look at the website of the Yale School of Medicine. At Yale you can study to be a physician and obtain an MD degree, and you can obtain other degrees as well. But notwithstanding the considerable differences among the School of Medicine's various degree programs, *all* students are expected not only to *become* professionals, but to *be* professionals. They are expected to behave, even during their time at Yale, in a professional manner. Yale has a formal statement, "Medical School Professionalism," that spells out how exactly it expects its students to act as *professionals*. Again, service is key: "Professionalism implies that students serve the interests of patients above self-interest. Professionalism includes honesty, respect for colleagues, faculty, staff and peers and behavior in public that is not embarrassing to the ideal of the physician. Continual self-reflection about one's attitudes and behaviors must occur as one strives to be a better physician."[11] The statement goes on to describe various "components" of *professional* behavior, including integrity, confidentiality, conscientiousness, demeanor, behavior toward colleagues, and commitment to lifelong learning. My point, of course, is less about the specifics of the statement than it is about the statement itself. The statement represents the work of an expert or an educator, or of a group of experts and, or educators, committed to conveying to students the importance of being *professionals,* and of comporting themselves accordingly. It is, if you will, a statement that *socializes* Yale's students to become graduates of the Yale School of Medicine—graduates who have attained *professional* status.

Of course, Yale's School of Medicine is not perfect. But it is a model of what a school that aspires to professionalism should look like. It is a model of how a school with a clearly defined mission and purpose, and a high standard of professional excellence, chooses to present itself. There is no confusion of terms. There is no ambiguity about professionalism, or uncertainty about what the school requires of its students to achieve professional status. There is no doubt about the level of its ambition. And there is no lack of clarity about the school's overarching purpose: to graduate physicians and others, including physician assistants, who are professionals, and who have been educated, trained, developed, *and* socialized to this end.

The Yale School of Medicine is, then, an exemplar of a professional school. It is also an illustration by implication: of how much time and trouble it takes to get from inception to implementation, from occupation to profession. No wonder leadership has had no parallel. Because for all its recent ascendency and popularity, leadership, excepting in the military, has had no community of experts and educators who have been completely committed to cooperating, collaborating, and compromising to get the work done.

If just one major institution or organization would set itself apart, would have the vision, ambition, and determination to enlist a cadre of leadership experts and educators to develop a curriculum and culture that clearly are professional, it would establish a template. It would be a leader in leadership education, training, and development and, thereby, elevate in its entirety the leadership industry. What likely will be required to get this ball rolling is the involvement and commitment of a top-flight institution of higher education such as Harvard or Stanford that is ready, willing, and able to take on a reform such as this one. Such an institution would have what it will take, including educators and experts, pedagogues and practitioners. It would, moreover, have license to be imaginative and innovative. It could, for example, develop a four-year course of leadership education, training, and development: two years at the undergraduate level, and two years (or more) at the professional level. Two years of *educating* for leadership through the arts and sciences. Two more years of *training* for leadership through exposure to and experience in, for example, business, government, education, medicine, or law. Four years and counting of *developing* leaders.

Graduates of a professional leadership program such as this one would be analogous to graduates of other professional programs such as medicine and law. They would have been educated, trained, and, to a degree at least, developed over time. They would have been tested and assessed throughout their four-year course of study. They would have committed themselves to public service and sworn faithfully to adhere to a code of ethics. And they would have concluded their course of learning how to lead with a degree that legitimately testified to their professional status.

Finally, some comments about the act itself—about learning how to lead. Once upon a time, long, long ago, when I was a child, so far as I knew there was no such thing as learning how to lead. In fact, what I learned in school was not how to lead, but how to follow. Or, better, how not to focus on myself but to focus instead on something larger than myself. What I learned in school was not, in other words, leadership: it was civics. Civics suggested a commonweal to which everyone was supposed to contribute. Civics suggested a community to which everyone was supposed to belong. Civics suggested a civilization (Western civilization) that joined Americans together. And civics suggested cooperation and collaboration rather than individuality or superiority or, to use an earlier word, aggrandizement. It was a time during which the word "public" still had resonance and respect—as in public schools, public parks, and public deliberations. *New York Times* columnist Thomas Friedman recalled that when he was a child, "public spaces were both a product of and an engine of trust, pluralism, and social capital generally."[12] Thus, the idea that as a child or adolescent or even young adult I would learn how to lead was inconceivable. In elementary schools, in high schools, even in colleges and universities as well as in other organizations or institutions, there scarcely was such a thing as a leadership program or a leadership curriculum. And if, and when, there was, such as in the army, or in a school of business, or, occasionally, in a school of public administration, it was limited in its intention. Leadership instruction then was targeted at a specific population as opposed to being, as it is now, targeted at everyone and anyone. Leadership instruction has gone from being infrequent and exclusive to being frequent and inclusive.

This is testimony, obviously, to the moneymaking machine that is the leadership industry and to the fickleness of fashion. For there is something about "leadership" that is fashion. Come to think of it, leadership is not exactly fashion, it is more a fad. A fashion is a popular trend. A fad, in contrast, is "an intense and widely shared enthusiasm for something," especially if it is an enthusiasm that is "without basis in the object's qualities." Learning to lead in America fits this description—it is an enthusiasm as ubiquitous as intense. Withal, the enthusiasm for learning to lead is largely "without basis." Or, at least, it is, as the low levels of satisfaction with leadership programs testify, without sufficient basis to justify the enthusiasm.

Teaching How to Lead

Given that we are not disposed to bite the hand that feeds us—in this case the leadership industry—where does this leave us? In other words, given the state of the leadership industry in the here and now, as opposed to down the line, what can be done by leadership teachers for the benefit of leadership learners, so that what the former are selling is worth the latter buying?

Before turning to specifics, let me reiterate a general statement. Every leadership program (as opposed to every management program), no matter who the target audience, should have a service component or, at least, send a service message—send a message that states clearly and unambiguously that leaders are expected to serve others, not only themselves. Among the purposes of this service component would the following:

1. Distinguish leadership from management.
2. Make apparent that leadership is not about individual aggrandizement.
3. Connect leaders to followers, not only implicitly, but explicitly.
4. Join leadership learners in the private sector to leadership learners in the public and nonprofit sectors.
5. Connect those learning to lead to those learning to practice other professions, such as medicine and law.
6. Bestow on leadership programs a greater measure of dignity and respectability.
7. Restore to leadership a measure of the esteem that was presumed in the past.
8. Elevate leadership in the eyes of the public, which, in the United States as elsewhere in the world, has grown distrustful of the leadership class.

Note, though, this distinction: I am not arguing that the word "leadership" should be *defined* as having a service component. Rather I am arguing that leadership education, training, and development programs—programs that profess to teach how to lead—have a service component, one that is made explicit.

I should stress that when service is integral to how we think about learning to lead, the gap between leaders and followers effectively closes. Leaders and followers become joined, inseparable, the relationship between them explicitly, not just implicitly, symbiotic. Just as professionalism in medicine implies that "doctors put the interests of patients above self-interest," so professionalism in leadership should imply that leaders put the interests of followers above self-interest (think Greenleaf and Burns). This reaffirms the earlier point that learning how to lead wisely and well should presume learning how to follow wisely and well. Since changes in cultures and technologies are giving "people more power to destabilize ... than ever before," thinking about leadership without thinking about followership has become patently absurd.[13]

Professor Danielle Allen has written about education as an engine of equality. She is interested in developing in every student what she calls "participatory readiness." Participatory readiness is as it sounds: the readiness to participate actively in civic and political life. "The idea that all students should be educated for political participation—and not merely a select few prepared for political leadership as suggested in Plato—is already an egalitarian feature of the humanistic baseline education."[14] It seems to me that participatory readiness is not very different from what I and a handful of others describe as the readiness to be a good follower. For example, Ira Chaleff teaches followers to be active, not passive, to engage and, if necessary, to resist, to decline to do something unethical or illegal even if ordered by a superior to do so. My point is that when we teach how to follow along with how to lead, democratizing learning leadership makes sense. It makes sense to teach many different people in many different places— say, undergraduates, military personnel, middle managers—how to lead so long as it is coupled with teaching how to follow. Among other reasons, it deprives learning leading of the implication that leaders are somehow superior to, or more successful than, followers. In this sense, teaching how to be a good leader along with how to be a good follower is more like teaching civics than teaching leadership. For it is more about the whole than a part, more about what can be accomplished together than alone.

Finally, I return to the distinctions among leadership education, training, and development and assert the importance of each. I wrote earlier that leadership development can reasonably be said to incorporate or even subsume leadership education and training, a statement from which I do not now deviate. But for the purposes of providing principles to put us on the path to professionalizing leadership, it remains useful to distinguish among them.

Of course, all leadership programs are not equal. Some leadership programs are small; others are large. Some leadership programs are poorly funded; others are richly endowed. Some leadership programs are in the private sector; others are in the public or nonprofit sector. Some leadership programs are in institutions of higher education; others are in religious institutions or in military institutions or in government institutions. Some leadership programs are targeted at the poor and badly organized; others at the rich and well organized.

Some leadership programs are targeted at those at the top, others at those close to the top, and still others at those in the middle or at the grass roots. Some leadership programs are designed to be broad, others to be narrow, such as, for example, those intended for school superintendents or systems engineers. (NASA, America's space agency, has SELDP, the Systems Engineers Leadership Development Program.) Some leadership programs are (relatively) long, a year; others are short, a week, a weekend, a day at a time. Some leadership programs are led by single individuals, others by a large cadre of faculty or other leadership experts or educators. Some leadership programs consist primarily of classroom learning; others consist primarily of experiential learning. I could go on.

Because there are many differences among the many thousands of leadership development programs, the principles that I propose below are not specific—they are, as I said, general, applicable to anyone responsible for planning, developing, implementing, maintaining, and monitoring a leadership program. For the purposes of this discussion, the assumption is the intention to transform leadership from an occupation with an ignoble reputation to a profession with a noble one—or, at least, one that approximates that of medicine and law.

- Leadership programs should be led by a small, collaborative group of leadership experts and educators, who are open and fair-minded, and deeply dedicated to teaching how to lead.
- Leadership programs should make explicit the connection between leadership studies and leadership development, that is, between leadership theory and leadership practice.
- Leadership programs should constitute a clear and coherent whole by having an obvious beginning and end, and a logical pedagogical sequence between.
- Leadership programs should have a cognitive component. More specifically, they should have a common curriculum that provides at least brief exposure to the liberal arts, the social sciences, and the hard sciences.
- Leadership programs should encourage and enable skill development and improvement.
- Leadership programs should incorporate experiential learning.
- Leadership programs should be followership programs.
- Leadership programs should aim to develop leaders who are ethical and effective—while acknowledging and addressing the challenges presented by leaders who are unethical and, or, ineffective.
- Leadership programs should spend at least as much time on developing contextual awareness as on self-awareness.
- Leadership programs should focus on contextual expertise as well as technical expertise.

- Leadership programs should develop contextual intelligence as well as emotional intelligence.
- Leadership programs should have a service component or, at least, send a service message.
- Leadership programs should consistently adhere to a consensually crafted code of ethics.
- Leadership programs should establish policies and procedures for self-assessment.
- Leadership programs should establish policies and procedures for assessments by their participants. At least one of these assessments should be longitudinal.
- Leadership programs should be regularly reviewed and, as necessary, revised.
- Leadership programs should provide clear criteria for the evaluation of their participants.
- Leadership programs should provide certification of competence on completion of the program—but only if a rigorous standard of competence has demonstrably been met.
- Leadership programs should support development—adult development and leadership development—by incorporating continuous learning, that is, learning that continues well after the program has ended.
- Leadership programs should be professional—they should every day in every way convey an exemplary professional standard.

The above list might seem daunting—but it is not. While each of these principles is essential to professionalism, each can be scaled up or down depending on the nature of the program, on those who participate, and on the level of the available human, fiscal, and temporal resources. It is true that one of the things that I rail against in this book is the brevity of twenty-first-century leadership programs—other than those in the military. As will be obvious by now, it strikes me as ridiculous that it takes four years of medical school—not to speak of subsequent internships and residencies—to learn how to practice medicine, but in some cases not even four days to learn how to exercise leadership. Still, I'm a pragmatist. Each of the aforementioned principles is, therefore, to an extent at least adoptable or adaptable by virtually all leadership programs.

Finally, some comments about the components: education, training, and development.

Education. What should leaders learn? More specifically, what should be the cognitive content of leadership programs? Is there an intellectual foundation, a certain body of knowledge, on which the edifice of experience should be built?

Let me be clear. The nature of the content, the content of the content, is less important than the thing itself. That is, learning *how* to lead (leadership development) should necessarily, automatically, imply learning *about* leadership (leadership studies), learning that leadership is, among other things, an objective area of intellectual inquiry and that leadership can be approached from various disciplinary perspectives, including history, economics, psychology, biology, politics, business, technology, and philosophy. Similarly, leadership programs should impart the idea that leadership is about power, authority, and influence, and that learning about leadership implies learning about followership. The point is that *all* leadership programs should devote some of their human and other resources to leadership *education*, to the cognitive component of learning to lead. After all, every professional pedagogy is based on the time-honored presumption that learning to practice begins with learning the basics. Or, to put it more technically, "In most professions [practice] is tied directly to a system of knowledge that formalizes the skills on which [practice] proceeds."[15] In other words, to become a doctor, you must absolutely study anatomy—early on. To become a lawyer, you must absolutely study civil procedure—early on. In fact, to become a hairdresser you must learn, early on, about the nature and texture of hair. And to become a truck driver you must learn, early on, the rules of the road.

Of course, even if we agree that learning about leadership is important, the discussion about what exactly this learning should consist of can become contentious. I know—been there, done that. It's one of the reasons why I recommend that every leadership program be led by a "small, collaborative group" that is, among its other virtues, politically savvy. For the issue of governance—how leadership programs are led and managed—is not trivial. It is also why, for the sake of this discussion, I am providing no more than a general set of principles, guidelines, each of which is fungible, adaptable as necessary to the circumstance.

I will presume agreement that every student of leadership should have at least some early exposure to leadership studies. Depending on the circumstances— the students, the teachers, the resources, the learning environment, the purposes of the leadership program, the length and depth of the program, the pedagogy of the program—exposure to, say, the liberal arts, could take several terms to complete, or several months, or several weeks, or even several days. It does not, in other words, take a lot of time to teach adult learners at least something about how the liberal arts apply to leadership. They might learn a bit about, to take a few examples, the history of leadership, the philosophy of leadership, the literature of leadership, or, for that matter, Beethoven's "Eroica" (his Third Symphony, originally written in celebration of Napoleon), or Picasso's *Guernica* (his ferocious response to the Spanish Civil War).

Adult learners are remarkably open to liberal learning. And, to return to one of my favorite themes, they are remarkably open to the idea that leadership is a system. They can easily grasp that leadership is not only about them: that it is also about others, followers, and about the various contexts within which leaders and followers interact. Once adults get that learning to lead is about more, much more, than learning about themselves, they get that you cannot be a leader in the twenty-first century, should not be a leader in the twenty-first century, without having some understanding of other people in other places, of other cultures in other countries. Similarly, you cannot be a leader in your workplace, should not be a leader in your workplace, without knowing something about the organization within which you work. As an article in the *Harvard Business Review* put it, "Organizations are *systems of interacting elements*" that include, among other things, roles and responsibilities, policies and practices.[16] It's why the success of leadership development programs depends not only on how clever and committed the various participants, but, additionally, on whether the circumstance to which they return is amenable to change.

I would argue, in fact, that one of the primary purposes of leadership education is precisely to point out to leadership learners that their capacity to lead will depend on their capacity to read—to read the handwriting on the wall (for example, regarding the import of artificial intelligence), and even, pardon my pushing the metaphor, the wall itself. Here is Tony Mayo, who in the early 2000s was responsible for something called the Great American Business Leaders Database: "Contextual intelligence is the ability to understand the macro-level factors that are at play during a given period of time.... A business leader's ability to make sense of his or her contextual framework... often made the difference between success and failure."[17]

Of course, the question of what leaders should learn can and perhaps should be subsumed under the larger question of what any of us should learn. What is the purpose of an education in first quarter of the twenty-first century? What should we aspire to become in consequence of being educated? These are knotty questions, particularly during a time in which even so fundamental an issue as the function of a liberal arts education is hotly debated. On the one side are those who argue for the continuing virtues of a liberal education; on the other side are those who believe that the purpose of education is to prepare to earn a living. Though there are some basics—for example, no one, I repeat no one, should be considered educated to lead without understanding that leadership is relational—by and large there are few obvious answers to the question of what exactly leaders should learn. This does not, however, preclude this simple proposition: that learning something *about* leadership is, or it should be, essential to learning *how* to lead. Essential to the pedagogical process. Essential to being socialized to being a professional. Essential to becoming or, for that matter, to being a leader. Providing some semblance of a serious education is providing some sense that leadership is serious business, and that someone who is completely uneducated about leadership is unprepared to assume a leadership role.

Training. The line between education and training is not always clear. That is precisely why the 2013 US Army leadership manual titled "Army Leader

Development Strategy" made a point of distinguishing between them. (This publication is also referred to in chapter 7.) Education was described as "the process of imparting knowledge and developing the competencies and attributes Army professionals need to accomplish any mission the future may present. Education contributes to . . . leader competencies." Training, in contrast, was described as "an organized, structured, continuous, and progressive process based on sound principles of learning designed to increase the capability of individuals, units, and organizations to perform specified tasks or skills. The object of training is to increase the ability of leaders to competently perform."[18] In sum, though the distinction between the two remains imprecise, in the army education is generally associated with acquiring "knowledge," and training is generally associated with acquiring "skills."

Education, in any case, is more associated with knowing; and training is more associated with doing. Thus, the distinction between the missions of the Harvard Business School and the Harvard Kennedy School would suggest that the former is more about imparting knowledge, since it professes to "educate" leaders, and the latter is more about developing skills, since it professes to "train" leaders. In truth, though, most leadership programs are much more about developing skills (training) than they are about imparting knowledge (education). The different types of trainings include, first, experiential learning, such as applied learning, learning in the workplace, learning in the field, and learning as a member of a group; second, skill learning, skills such as communicating, persuading, organizing, negotiating, decision-making, and strategizing; and, third, active learning, such as giving presentations, engaging in role playing, and participating in simulations.

In the book titled *How Learning Works* is an excellent section on developing skills, on what the authors call "mastery." Mastery involves four separate steps: (1) recognizing the skills that you do not have but should; (2) acquiring these skills; (3) practicing these skills; and (4) applying these skills to the right situations at the right time. One of the difficulties students face is that some seemingly simple skills involve a complex combination of skills. For example, the ability to analyze a case "requires component skills such as the capacity to identify the central question or dilemma of the case, articulate the perspectives of key actors, enumerate constraints, delineate possible courses of action, and recommend and justify a solution."[19] In other words, getting good leadership training is, like getting a good leadership education, neither simple nor swift. Mastering skills takes time—we get better at using our skills the more we use them. Similarly, knowing when to apply a certain skill is itself a skill that takes time to acquire. It takes time because unless our skills are applied in situations with which we're familiar, the challenges of "transfer" can be daunting.

Development. There is no leadership development, can be no leadership development, without time in which to develop. Arguably you can be educated to lead, at least to a minimal degree, in a week or a month. Arguably you can be trained to lead, at least to a minimal degree, in a week or a month. But there is no way that you can develop as a leader in a week or a month. Development—adult development, leadership development—takes time. It takes years. It takes years because development implies change and growth, neither of which take place in haste. On this point let me again quote General Fred Franks: "The longest developmental process we have in the United States Army is the development of a commander. . . . [Leaders] must continue to grow and to learn and to study."

Given that development remains at least somewhat elusive, difficult for the most part to assess, here I make just three points. First, leadership "development" is especially important precisely because it conveys or it should, as Franks made clear, that learning to lead takes time. The very idea that leaders "develop" therefore sends an essential message: you cannot become a leader or even a significantly better leader than you already are by any single thing you do, such as enrolling in a leadership program, or hiring an executive coach, or securing a leadership mentor or sponsor. This is not to say that these have no value. It is simply to say that we inflate their value. We think they will make a big difference over the long term when the best they usually do is to make a small difference over the short term. What does make a big difference over the long term is just what General Franks said, continuous learning, learning that cumulates precisely because it continues.

What else continues? We continue to age. As we have seen, lifespan theories of adult development make clear that most of us are at least somewhat different at fifty from what we were at thirty, and at least somewhat different again at seventy from what we were at fifty. The differences in age are themselves significant; they can, though they do not necessarily, relate to how we lead, for example, making us markedly more generative (Erik Erikson's term) later in life than we were earlier on. We continue as well to accumulate experiences, experiences that are personal, interpersonal, and professional, experiences that we seek out or that are imposed on us by someone or something. Experiences matter. If we process them productively they contribute to, cumulate to the benefit of, development, adult development and leadership development.

Which brings me to my second point. Some of us—leaders and followers alike—develop because of the circumstances within which we find ourselves. Most of the time these circumstances are happenstance. We happen to find ourselves in situations or in contexts that are more, or less, conducive to development. But some of the time we find ourselves in situations or in contexts that were deliberately designed to support and sustain development. As earlier mentioned, there is in fact a small literature now on "deliberately developmental" organizations, organizations that intentionally encourage everyone, from top to bottom, to develop, to change, to grow. "Imagine," Robert Kegan and Lisa Lahey write, "so valuing the importance of developing people's capabilities that you design a culture that itself immersively sweeps every member of the organization into an ongoing developmental journey in the course of working every day."[20] How is such a culture designed? Not obviously or easily, though words and terms like "meritocracy," "transparency," "holding on," and "letting go" recur. But, again, the specifics do not here concern us. What does concern us is the overarching point: there is evidence to support the proposition that workplaces, for instance, can be consciously and creatively constructed to encourage development. The process is not, though, again, either swift or simple. To the contrary. Development is a "lifelong activity."[21]

My third point is really a reminder: with regard to development there is only so much that those of us in the leadership industry, experts, educators, practitioners, and pedagogues, can do for our clients, customers, consumers, and students. We can instruct with insight and intelligence. We can provide support. We can establish learning communities and holding environments and deliberately developmental organizations. But, in the end, development is not something that we can do for others or to others. Rather it is something, work of a sort, that we do ourselves, to ourselves and for ourselves. In other words, in the end it is up to leaders to develop themselves, just as it is up to leaders to educate and train themselves. Put differently, leadership programs, leadership experts and educators, leadership practitioners and pedagogues, all have a role to play. In fact, this book is all about how they—we, those of us in the leadership industry—can do a better job of teaching how to lead in the future than we have in the recent past. But it is leaders who've got to see that their likelihood of being good—of being ethical and effective—is far higher if they're the ones doing the heavy lifting.

Finally, under the rubric of "development" I put the acquisition of self-awareness or self-knowledge, which in my view plays an outsized role in many if not most leadership programs. I'm not against increasing self-awareness or acquiring self-knowledge. What I am against is the amount of time devoted to it, which, necessarily, is at the expense of other information and ideas that get left on the cutting room floor. Participants in leadership programs are frequently asked to get 360-degree feedback; to assess their leadership styles; to pose self-reflective questions, such as what their purpose is as a leader and how their leadership affects others; and to work on developing what Bill George (former CEO of Medtronic and on the Harvard Business School faculty) has called "authentic" leadership. George's course on authentic leadership is designed for executives "who want to develop their leadership and are prepared to participate openly in discussing their leadership journeys, their crucibles, and the challenges they face."[22] A staple of the curriculum at the University of Chicago's Booth

School of Business is similar. The course is called Leadership Effectiveness and Development (LEAD); its intention is to "enhance self-awareness and to teach students how to learn the 'right' lessons from experience." More specifically, LEAD students engage "in a variety of hands-on exercises designed to provide them with an accurate view of their strengths and developmental needs, and guiding them to accurate process feedback from various sources."[23] Without speculating here on why in recent years leadership programs have focused so heavily on developing self-awareness, let's at least be clear that this emphasis on leaders per se means precious time away from every*one* else (think followers) and every*thing* else (think context).

Coda

Too much of the leadership literature is cluttered with stuff on how to go from good to great. On how to become not only a good leader, but a great leader, one who is a paragon of virtue, an apotheosis of what a leader should look like: competent and committed, intelligent and insightful, strategic and systematic, honest and decent, determined and disciplined, involved and invested, experienced and expert, motivated and motivational, collaborative and communicative, efficient and effective, ingratiating and inspiring, prescient and perceptive. You get the idea.

But this book is not about that. It is not about greatness or exceptionalism. It is not about heroes or heroines or leaders who are legends. Rather it is about being good: about exercising good leadership by being ethical and effective. It is about educating, training, and developing cadres of leaders who are like cadres of doctors and lawyers. Most doctors and lawyers are not standouts. But because they have been well prepared, well educated and trained, most are good at what they do, and some become over time very good or even great. Most, in any case, are good enough, good enough for us generally to depend on them to perform as professionals and to act in a professional manner.

Professionalizing leadership is not rocket science. But it does require that we reconceive leadership. It does require that we stop thinking of leadership as an occupation and start thinking of it as a profession entailing proper preparation and unremitting dedication. Once we take that leap, the rest is easy. Or it's easier, not to speak of better, far better than stomaching leaders who regularly are denigrated for being too greedy for money or hungry for power; too inaccessible or intemperate; too ignorant or inept; too self-interested or self-involved; too corrosive, coarse, callous, or corrupt. It is time—past time—to set our sights higher.

NOTES

Introduction

1. Barbara Kellerman, *The End of Leadership* (New York: HarperCollins, 2012), p. xii.
2. Simon Caulkin, "Leading Myths," *FT.COM Business Education*, December 6, 2015.
3. Deborah Rowland, "Why Leadership Development Isn't Developing Leaders," *Harvard Business Review*, October 14, 2016.
4. Gillian Pillans, "Leadership Development—Is It Fit for Purpose?," Corporate Research Forum, May 2015, section 1. The McKinsey finding is from Jeffrey Pfeffer, *Leadership BS: Fixing Workplaces and Careers One Truth at a Time* (New York: HarperCollins, 2015), p. 16.
5. Duff McDonald, *The Golden Passport: Harvard Business School, the Limits of Capitalism, and the Moral Failure of the MBA Elite* (New York: HarperCollins, 2017), p. 314.
6. Pew Research Center, "Beyond Distrust: How American View Their Government," November 2015. All quotes in this paragraph are from this same study.
7. Pfeffer, *Leadership BS*, p. 6.
8. Pfeffer, *Leadership BS*, p. 5.
9. Scott Snook, Nitin Nohria, and Rakesh Khurana, eds., *The Handbook for Teaching Leadership: Knowing, Doing, Being* (Thousand Oaks, CA: Sage, 2012), p. xiii.
10. David Benoit, "Activist Investors Step Up Efforts to Throw Out CEOs," *Wall Street Journal*, May 17, 2017.
11. Pfeffer, *Leadership BS*, p. 10.
12. Pillans, "Leadership Development," p.8.
13. Michael Beer, Magnus Finnström, and Derek Schrader, "Why Leadership Training Fails—and What to Do about It," *Harvard Business Review*, October 10, 2016.
14. Joseph Rost, *Leadership for the Twenty-First Century* (New York: Praeger, 1991), p. 6.
15. Bernard Bass's tome on leadership (most recently with Ruth Bass) remains a worthy acquisition for any leadership library. It is titled *The Bass Handbook of Leadership: Theory, Research, Managerial Applications*, 4th ed. (New York: Free Press, 2008).
16. John Antonakis, Anna Cianciolo, and Robert Sternberg, eds., *The Nature of Leadership* (Thousand Oaks, CA: Sage, 2004), p. 5.
17. Warren G. Bennis, *On Becoming a Leader*, rev. ed. (Cambridge, MA: Perseus, 2003), pp. 39, 40.

Chapter 1

1. Steve Coutino, *An Introduction to Daoist Philosophies* (New York: Columbia University Press, 2014), p. 71.
2. For a more detailed discussion of this see Coutino, *Introduction to Daoist Philosophies*, who writes that, to the question of how we as social beings live in greatest harmony with the

natural way, there are two opposing answers in the Tao. "There is a utopian strand that ideal-izes small-scale social groups and another strand that advocates ruling a large state by a para-doxical method of not ruling" (p. 71).

3. Quoted in Barbara Kellerman, *The End of Leadership* (New York: HarperCollins, 2012), p. 8.
4. Meher McArthur, *Confucius: A Throneless King* (New York: Pegasus, 2011), p. 16.
5. R. A. W. Rhodes and Paul 't Hart, eds., *The Oxford Handbook of Political Leadership* (New York: Oxford University Press, 2014), p. 69.
6. Rhodes and 't Hart, *Oxford Handbook of Political Leadership*, p. 61.
7. In Barbara Kellerman, ed., *Leadership: Essential Selections on Power, Authority, and Influence* (New York: McGraw-Hill, 2010), pp. 9–13.
8. In Kellerman, *Leadership: Essential Selections*, p. 16.
9. Mostafa Rejai and Kay Phillips, *Concepts of Leadership in Western Political Thought* (New York: Praeger, 2002), p. 13.
10. In Kellerman, *Leadership: Essential Selections*, p. 17.
11. The quote, this paragraph, and the preceding one are based on Rejai and Phillips, *Concepts of Leadership*, pp. 13, 14.
12. Nannerl O. Keohane, "Western Political Thought," in Rhodes and 't Hart, *Oxford Handbook of Political Leadership*, pp. 27, 28.
13. In Kellerman, *Leadership: Essential Selections*, p. 32.
14. John Dillon, "Dion and Brutus: Philosopher Kings Adrift in a Hostile World," in Noreen Humble, ed., *Plutarch's Lives: Parallelism and Purpose* (Swansea: Classic Press of Wales, 2010), p. 92.
15. In Dillon, "Dion and Brutus," p. 92.
16. Dillon, "Dion and Brutus," p. 97.
17. Keohane, "Western Political Thought," p. 30.
18. Maurizio Viroli, *Redeeming "The Prince": The Meaning of Machiavelli's Masterpiece* (Princeton, NJ: Princeton University Press, 2014), p. 10.
19. Erica Benner, *Machiavelli's "Prince": A New Reading* (New York: Oxford University Press, 2013), p. xxx.
20. In Kellerman, *Leadership: Essential Selections*, p. 35.
21. Charles Murphy, "Isocrates and Education for Political Leadership," *Classical Bulletin*, January 1, 1944.
22. John Humphreys, Wallace Williams, Russel Clayton, and Milorad Novicevic, "Towards the Augmenting Role of Authenticity: Xenophon as Leadership Theorist," *Management & Organizational History* 6, no. 2 (2011), p. 193.
23. Nathan Laufer, *The Genesis of Leadership: What the Bible Teaches Us about Vision, Values and Leading Change* (Woodstock, VT: Jewish Lights, 2006), p. 16.
24. Lee Whittington, *Biblical Perspectives on Leadership and Organization* (New York: Palgrave, 2015), p. 81.
25. Bruce Winston and Paula Tucker, "The Beatitudes as Leadership Virtues," *Journal of Virtues & Leadership* 2, no. 1 (2011), p. 15.
26. Deirdre McClosky, *Bourgeois Equality: How Ideas, Not Capital or Institutions, Enriched the World* (Chicago: University of Chicago Press, 2016), pp. xxxi, xxxiii.
27. Joseph Rost, *Leadership in the Twenty-First Century* (New York: Praeger, 1991), p. 44. Rost once combed through no fewer than 587 books, chapters, and articles published between 1900 and 1990 and found no fewer than 221 definitions of "leadership."
28. John Locke, *Second Treatise of Government*, in Kellerman, *Leadership: Essential Selections*, pp. 50, 51.
29. This paragraph is based on Kellerman, *Leadership: Essential Selections*, p. 123.
30. In Kellerman, *Leadership: Essential Selections*, pp. 120, 121.
31. In Kellerman, *Leadership: Essential Selections*, p. 126.
32. Kellerman, *The End of Leadership*, p. 14.
33. Samuel Huntington: *American Politics: The Promise of Disharmony* (Cambridge, MA: Harvard University Press, 1981), p. 33.
34. Kellerman, *Leadership: Essential Selections*, p. 238.
35. Kellerman, *Leadership: Essential Selections*, p. 267.

36. Kellerman, *The End of Leadership*, p. 20.

37. Rakesh Khurana, *From Higher Aims to Hired Hands: The Social Transformation of American Business Schools and the Unfulfilled Promise of Management as a Profession* (Princeton, NJ: Princeton University Press, 2007).

38. Khurana, *Higher Aims*, p. 40.

39. The quotes in this paragraph are from Khurana, *Higher Aims*, pp. 88, 105, 106.

40. For my further analysis of the relationship between leadership studies and leadership development see *The End of Leadership*, pp. 153ff.

41. Khurana, *Higher Aims*, p. 158.

42. Khurana, *Higher Aims*, p. 192.

43. Daniel Wren and Ronald Greenwood, *Management Innovators: The People and Ideas That Shaped Modern Business* (New York: Oxford University Press, 1998), p. 197.

44. Chester Barnard, *The Functions of the Executive* (Cambridge, MA: Harvard University Press, 1968), pp. 282, 283.

45. Nan Stone in her introduction to Peter Drucker, *Peter Drucker on the Profession of Management* (Boston: Harvard Business Review, 2005), p. xiii.

46. Drucker, *Profession of Management*, pp. 19, 20. From "The Effective Decision," *Harvard Business Review*, January–February 1967.

47. Drucker, *Profession of Management*, pp. 38, 39. From "How to Make People Decisions," *Harvard Business Review*, July–August 1985.

48. Drucker, *Profession of Management*, p. 157. From "Management and the World's Work," *Harvard Business Review*, September–October 1988.

49. Khurana, *Higher Aims*, p. 291.

Chapter 2

1. James MacGregor Burns, *Leadership* (New York: Harper & Row, 1978).

2. The quote is from Rakesh Khurana, *From Higher Aims to Hired Hands: The Social Transformation of American Business Schools and the Unfulfilled Promise of Management as a Profession* (Princeton, NJ: Princeton University Press, 2007), p. 297. For more on the inception of the leadership industry and its early years see Barbara Kellerman, *Reinventing Leadership: Making the Connection between Politics and Business* (Albany: State University of New York Press, 1999), and Joseph Rost, *Leadership for the Twenty-First Century* (New York: Praeger, 1991).

3. Khurana, *Higher Aims*, p. 294.

4. Khurana, *Higher Aims*, p. 297.

5. Rost, *Leadership*, p. 93.

6. This and the previous quote are from Khurana, *Leadership*, p. 353.

7. Khurana, *Higher Aims*, p. 355.

8. Khurana, *Higher Aims*, p. 353.

9. Jay Conger and Beth Benjamin, *Building Leaders: How Successful Companies Develop the Next Generation* (San Francisco: Jossey-Bass, 1999), p. 5.

10. Deborah Rowland, "Why Leadership Development Isn't Developing Leaders," *Harvard Business Review*, October 14, 2016.

11. The mismatch quote is from Rowland, "Leadership Development." For some figures on the investment in leadership learning see Gilliam Pillans, "Leadership Development: Is It Fit for Purpose?," Corporate Research Forum, 2015, executive summary.

12. Michael Beer, Magnus Finnström, and Derek Schrader, "Why Leadership Training Fails— and What to Do about It," *Harvard Business Review*, October 2016.

13. Pillans, "Leadership Development," section 1.

14. See "Collaborative Priorities and Critical Considerations for Leadership Education," published by the Inter-association Leadership Education Collaborative, 2016, https://acui.org/docs/default-source/default-document-library/ilec_final.pdf?sfvrsn=b49a885f_2.

15. The leadership programs described in this chapter are not a scientific sample. They were chosen for inclusion because they are various—some small, some large; some in the eastern United States, some in the West; some older, some younger—and because they clearly are indicative of the trends to which I refer.

16. John Dugan, "Research on College Student Leadership Development," in Susan Komives et al., *The Handbook for Student Leadership Development*, 2nd ed. (San Francisco: Jossey-Bass, 2011), p. 61.

17. Susan Komives, Nance Lucas, and Timothy McMahon, *Exploring Leadership: For College Students Who Want to Make a Difference* (San Francisco: Jossey-Bass, 2013).

18. From the preface to Komives et al., *Handbook for Student Leadership Development*, p. xvi.

19. Julie Owen, "Considerations of Student Learning in Leadership," in Komives et al., *Handbook for Student Leadership Development*, p. 109.

20. "Jump Start Leader," Ithaca College, https://www.ithaca.edu/sacl/osema/opportunities/jsleader/.

21. "University of Texas Leadership and Ethics Institute," http://deanofstudents.utexas.edu/lei/ and "ProjectLEAD," http://deanofstudents.utexas.edu/lei/projectlead.php.

22. "Leadership Studies," Williams College, http://leadership-studies.williams.edu/.

23. Dennis Roberts, "Transitions and Transformations in Leadership," in Susan Komives and Wendy Wagner, eds., *Leadership for a Better World: Understanding the Social Change Model of Leadership Development* (San Francisco: Jossey-Bass, 2017), p. 5. I am grateful to Craig Stack for his further information on the model. Stack is the director of the National Clearinghouse for Leadership Programs.

24. The definition is from the preface of Komives and Wagner, *Leadership for a Better World*, p. xiii.

25. Kristan Cilente Skendall, "An Overview of the Social Change Model of Leadership Development," in Komives and Wagner, *Leadership for a Better World*, p. 19.

26. "The Social Change Model of Leadership Development," Pomona College, http://www.pomona.edu/administration/campus-center/services-programs/leadership.

27. "Social Change Model of Leadership Development," Reed College, https://www.reed.edu/leadership/social_change_model.html.

28. "President's Leadership Fellows," University of Tampa, http://www.ut.edu/leadership/presidentfellows/.

29. "Master of Arts in Leadership Studies," University of San Diego, https://www.sandiego.edu/soles/academics/ma-leadership-studies/.

30. "Doctor of Education Leadership," Harvard Graduate School of Education, https://www.gse.harvard.edu/doctorate/doctor-education-leadership.

31. The curriculum of this program is based on the "2011 National Standards for Teacher Leadership," https://education.uw.edu/programs/leadership/mil.

32. Global Executive Doctor of Education (EdD) Program 2016 brochure, Rossier School of Education, University of Southern California.

33. "Master of Arts in Community Leadership," Westminster College, https://www.westminster-college.edu/macl/.

34. "Leadership & Management," University of Minnesota, https://www.hhh.umn.edu/areas-expertise/leadership-management. The materials on the Humphrey School are from various school websites.

35. "Leadership Programs," Division of Policy Translation and Leadership Development, T.H. Chan School of Public Health, Harvard University, http://www.hsph.harvard.edu/policy-translation-leadership-development/leadership-programs/.

36. "Not All Who Wander Are Lost," School of Medicine, Creighton University, http://med-school.creighton.edu/leadership/.

37. "Lawyers and Leadership," Stanford Law School, https://law.stanford.edu/courses/law-leadership-and-social-change/.

38. "Law School Introduces Keystone Professionalism & Leadership Program for Students," University of Chicago Law School, https://www.law.uchicago.edu/news/law-school-introduces-keystone-professionalism-leadership-program-students.

39. "Riding High," *FT Business Education: Master's in Management Ranking*, September 14, 2015.

40. MiM program rankings are in *FT Business Education*,

41. http://www.unisg.ch/en/studium/master/cems, p. 58.

42. In Della Bradshaw, "Elite Pulls Away from the Pack," *FT.Com Business Education*, January 24, 2016.

43. Kaye Wiggins, "Women Balk at Opportunity Cost of MBA Study," *Financial Times*, March 6, 2017. The article notes that for the last five years the proportion of female MBA applicants worldwide has been "stuck at an average of 38 percent."

44. "Master in Business Administration," INSEAD, http://mba.insead.edu/home/.

45. "Forge Your Future with a Tulane Master of Business Administration (MBA) Degree," Freeman School of Business, Tulane University, http://freeman.tulane.edu/programs/graduate/full-time-mba.

46. "Forge Your Future."

47. All quotes in this paragraph are from "Leadership Development," Booth School of Business, University of Chicago, http://www.chicagobooth.edu/programs/evening/academics/effective-leadership

48. "Leadership Development," Emory Goizueta Business School, http://goizueta.emory.edu/degree/two_year_mba/curriculum/leadership_development.html.

49. "Leadership," Stanford Business, https://www.gsb.stanford.edu/stanford-gsb-experience/academic/leadership.

50. "Stanford Launches Knight-Hennessy Scholars Program," *Stanford News*, February 23, 2016, http://news.stanford.edu/2016/02/23/scholars-program-announce-022316/.

51. "Leadership," INSEAD, http://executive-education.insead.edu/leadership-education-training/.

52. Wharton Executive Education, https://executiveeducation.wharton.upenn.edu.

53. "State Street's SHE: Investing in Women Leaders," Harvard Business School, http://www.hbs.edu/Pages/default.aspx.

54. Barbara Kellerman, *The End of Leadership* (New York: HarperCollins, 2012), p. 185.

55. Boris Groysberg and Scott Snook, "The Pine Street Initiative at Goldman Sachs," Harvard Business School Case 407053, November 2006.

56. "I Work Where My Ideas Are Brought to Life," IBM General Management Leadership Program, http://www-03.ibm.com/employment/gmldp.

57. "Leadership Development," *2012 Corporate Responsibility Report*, IBM, http://www.ibm.com/ibm/responsibility/2012/the-ibmer/leadership-development.html.

58. "Boeing Leadership Center," http://www.boeing.com/careers/life-at-boeing/building-leaders.page#/boeing-leadership-center.

59. "What Sustainability Means to Us," *Sustainability Report 2016/17*, Ford, http://corporate.ford.com/microsites/sustainability-report-2013-14/people-workplace-employees-leadership.html.

60. "Pearson Students," http://www.pearsonstudents.com/get-involved/leadership-developemnt-program/.

61. http://us.whirlpoolcareers.com/STUDENTS/General-Manager-Development-Program.aspx, accessed December 16, 2015.

62. "How Bank of America Develops Global Leaders," *Human Resources*, March 27, 2015, http://www.humanresourcesonline.net/events/bank-america-develops-leadership-talent-around-world/.

63. "Candidate Development Programs," Senior Executive Service, Office of Personal and Management, https://leadership.opm.gov. All the quotes in this section are taken from the website.

64. "Candidate Development Programs," Senior Executive Service, Office of Personal and Management, https://www.opm.gov/policy-data-oversight/senior-executive-service/candidate-development-programs/.

65. "NIH Executive Leadership Program," Office of Human Resources, National Institutes of Health, https://trainingcenter.nih.gov/exlp/.

66. J.W. Fanning Institute for Leadership Development, University of Georgia, http://www.fanning.uga.edu/.

67. "Redefine Leadership," Kansas Leadership Center, http://kansasleadershipcenter.org.

68. "About PICO," PICO National Network, http://www.piconetwork.org/about.

69. "Leadership," Marshall Goldsmith Group, http://www.marshallgoldsmithgroup.com/leadership.

70. "Open-Enrollment Programs," Center for Creative Leadership, http://www.ccl.org/leadership/programs/index.aspx.
71. For a critical look at the connection between McKinsey and leadership see John Gapper, "McKinsey's Fingerprints Are All Over Valeant," *Financial Times*, March 23, 2016.
72. "Unlocking Leadership Potential," McKinsey Institute, McKinsey & Company, http://mld.mckinsey.com/programs/bower-forum#.Vih.WHLRVikp.
73. "Unlocking Leadership Potential."
74. "Unlocking Leadership Potential."
75. "United States Air Force Academy Officer Development System," September 2013, section A. Italics mine.
76. United States Military Academy, West Point, http://www.usma.edu/wplc/Sitepages/Home.aspx.
77. Bruce E. Keith et al., eds., *Building Capacity to Lead: The West Point System for Leader Development* (West Point, NY: United States Military Academy, 2009), introduction by F. L. Hagenback, Lieutenant General, US Army Superintendent.
78. In *Army Leadership* (Washington, DC: Headquarters, Department of the Army, August 2012).
79. "LEAD Division," Division of Leadership Education and Development, United States Naval Academy, http://www.usna.edu/LEAD/.
80. "About," U.S. Naval War College, https://www.usnwc.edu/About.aspx.
81. http://www.marines.com/being-a-marine/leadership-principles.
82. Barbara Kellerman, "Leadership—It's a System, Not a Person!," *Daedalus*, Summer 2016, pp. 83–84.
83. United States Air Force Academy, "Officer Development System," September 2013.
84. "Confidence in Institutions," Gallup, http://www.gallup.com/poll/1597/confidence-institutions.aspx.

Chapter 3

1. Robert M. McManus and Gama Perruci, *Understanding Leadership: An Arts and Humanities Perspective* (New York: Routledge, 2015), p. 1.
2. Gardner's quote is from 1990. It is in McManus and Perruci, *Understanding Leadership*, p. 3.
3. "Mission - About Us," Harvard Business School, http://www.hbs.edu/about/Pages/mission.aspx.
4. "The Leadership," Stanford Graduate School of Business, www.gsb.stanford.edu/stanford-gsb-experience/leadership.
5. Wendy Wagner, "Considerations of Student Development in Leadership," in Susan Komives et al., *The Handbook of Student Leadership Development* (San Francisco: Jossey-Bass, 2011), p. 86.
6. In Robert M. Sapolsky, *Behave: The Biology of Humans at Our Best and Worst* (New York: Penguin, 2017), p. 182.
7. Robert Kegan, *The Evolving Self: Problem and Process in Human Development* (Cambridge, MA: Harvard University Press, 1982), pp. 50ff. It should be noted that psychologist Carol Gilligan took issue with Kohlberg, specifically for what she considered his bias against women. In her 1982 book, *In a Different Voice*, Gilligan argued forcefully that women approached moral problems differently than men. They approached them more with an "ethic of care" than an "ethic of justice."
8. Cynthia McCauley, Wilfred Drath, Charles Palus, Patricia O'Connor, and Becca Baker, "The Use of Constructive-Developmental Theory to Advance the Understanding of Leadership," *Leadership Quarterly* 17 (2006), p. 635. My writing in this section on development draws from this article.
9. Kegan, *The Evolving Self*.
10. Robert Kegan, *In over Our Heads: The Mental Demands of Modern Life* (Cambridge, MA: Harvard University Press, 1994).
11. Robert Kegan and Lisa Laskow Lahey, *An Everyone Culture: Becoming a Deliberately Developmental Organization* (Boston: Harvard Business Review Press, 2016), p. 60.
12. McCauley et al., "Constructive-Developmental Theory," p. 643.
13. Kegan and Lahey, *An Everyone Culture*, pp. 63, 74, 75.

14. Wagner, "Considerations of Student Development," p. 86.
15. Erik H. Erikson, *Young Man Luther: A Study in Psychoanalysis and History* (New York: Norton, 1958) and *Gandhi's Truth: On the Origins of Militant Nonviolence* (New York: Norton, 1993).
16. Daniel Levinson with Charlotte Darrow, Edward Klein, Maria Levinson, and Braxton McKee, *The Seasons of a Man's Life* (New York: Knopf, 1978), p. ix.
17. Levinson et al., *Seasons*, p. 41.
18. Craig Lambert, "The Talent for Aging Well," *Harvard Magazine*, March 1, 2001, http://harvardmagazine.com/2001/03/the-talent-for-aging-wel-html.
19. Herminia Ibarra, Scott Snook, and Laura Guillen Ramo, "Identity-Based Leader Development," in Nitin Nohria and Rakesh Khurana, eds., *Handbook of Leadership Theory and Practice* (Boston: Harvard Business Press, 2010), p. 658.
20. Wagner, "Considerations of Student Development," p. 97.
21. Bruce E. Keith et al., eds., *Building Capacity to Lead: The West Point System for Leader Development* (West Point, NY: United States Military Academy, 2009), p. 16.
22. John Rybash, William Hoyer, and Paul Roodin, *Adult Cognition and Aging: Developmental Changes in Processing, Knowing and Thinking* (New York: Pergamon Press, 1986), p. 18.
23. Mark Tennant and Philip Pogson, *Learning and Change in the Adult Years: A Developmental Perspective* (San Francisco: Jossey-Bass, 1995), p. 3.
24. Rybash, Hoyer, and Rudin, *Adult Cognition and Aging*, p. 36.
25. Frances Stage, Patricia Muller, Jillian Kinzie, and Ada Simmons, *Creating Learning Centered Classrooms* (Washington, DC: Graduate School of Education and Human Development, George Washington University, 1999).
26. Patricia Alexander, P. Karen Murphy, and Jonna Kulikowich, "Expertise and the Adult Learner: A Historical, Psychological, and Methodological Exploration," in M. Cecil Smith, ed., *Handbook of Research on Adult Learning and Development* (New York: Routledge, 2009), p. 486.
27. Discussion in this paragraph is based in part on Tennant and Pogson, *Learning and Change*, pp. 33, 35.
28. This paragraph and the one immediately preceding it are based in part on a discussion in Alexander, Murphy, and Kulikowich, "Expertise," pp. 488ff.
29. Pierre Gurdjian, Thomas Halbeisen, and Kevin Lane, "Why Leadership Development Programs Fail," *McKinsey Quarterly*, January 2014, http://www.mckinsey.com.global-themes/leadership/why-leadership-development-programs-fail.
30. Jay Conger and Beth Benjamin, *Building Leaders: How Successful Companies Develop the Next Generation* (San Francisco: Jossey-Bass, 1999), p. 213.
31. Conger and Benjamin, *Building Leaders*, p. 254.
32. Helen Barrett, "Let the Games Begin," *FT Business Education*, May 15, 2007.
33. Jonathan Moules, "Disruptive Influence," *FT Business Education*, May 15, 2007.
34. Jonathan Moules, "How to Reinvent Yourself as a Business Academic," *Financial Times*, March 13, 2017.
35. Lindsay Gellman, "A New Push for Real-World Lessons at B-Schools," *Wall Street Journal*, April 7, 2016.
36. Susan Jones and Ana Gasiorski, "Service-Learning, Civic and Community Participation: Contributions to Adult Development," in Smith, *Handbook of Research on Adult Learning and Development*, pp. 648–649.
37. Keith et al., *Building Capacity to Lead*, p. 16.
38. Max Klau, "City Year: Developing Idealistic Leaders through National Service," in Scott Snook, Nitin Nohria, and Rakesh Khurana, eds., *The Handbook for Teaching Leadership: Knowing, Doing, and Being* (Thousand Oaks, CA: Sage, 2012), pp. 409–431.
39. Rob Goffee and Gareth Jones, "Teaching Executives to Be Themselves—More—with Skill: A Sociological Perspective on a Personal Question," in Snook, Nohria, and Khurana, *Handbook for Teaching Leadership*, pp. 151–162.
40. Quoted in Conger and Benjamin, *Building Leaders*, p. 239.
41. Gillian Pillans, "Leadership Development—Is It Fit for Purpose?," Corporate Research Forum, May 2015. For a list of her suggestions for improving leader learning, see section 2. For information on the "deliberately developmental organization, see Kegan and Lahey, *An Everyone Culture*.

42. Wagner, "Considerations of Student Development," pp. 87, 88.
43. The phrase is in Pillans, "Leadership Development," section 2.
44. Julie Owen, "Considerations of Student Learning in Leadership," in Susan Komives et al., *The Handbook for Student Leadership Development*, 2nd ed. (San Francisco: Jossey-Bass, 2011), p. 109. Additionally, in my book, *The End of Leadership*, I pointed out that, for example, nearly all of Harvard graduate and professional schools have the words "leader" or "leadership" in their mission statements. But, do I, should I, care if my brain surgeon or divorce lawyer is a "leader"?

Chapter 4

1. The discussion on the distinction between an occupation and a profession is based on the following: Surbhi S., "Difference between Occupation and Profession," Key Differences, October 31, 2015, http://keydifferences.com/difference-between-occupation-and-profession.html.
2. Andrew Abbott, *The System of Professions: An Essay on the Division of Expert Labor* (Chicago: University of Chicago Press, 1988), p. 318.
3. Jay Conger's book on this general subject, *Learning to Lead: The Art of Transforming Mangers into Leaders* (San Francisco: Jossey-Bass, 1992), while in some ways dated, in other ways still pertains. Though he did not name it "the leadership industry," Conger was on to it before most of his academic colleagues.
4. Nitin Nohria and Rakesh Khurana, eds., *Handbook of Leadership Theory and Practice* (Boston: Harvard Business Press, 2010).
5. Nitin Nohria and Rakesh Khurana, "Advancing Leadership Theory and Practice," in Nohria and Khurana, *Handbook of Leadership Theory and Practice*, pp. 3, 4.
6. Nohria and Khurana, "Advancing Leadership Theory and Practice," p. 6.
7. Richard Hackman, "What Is This Thing Called Leadership?," in Nohria and Khurana, *Handbook of Leadership Theory and Practice*, p. 107.
8. Hackman, "What Is This Thing," p. 115.
9. For a brief discussion of leadership as meaning-making, see Joel Podolny, Rakesh Khurana, and Marya Besharov, "Revisiting the Meaning of Leadership," in Nohria and Khurana, *Handbook of Leadership Theory and Practice*, pp. 69ff.
10. Barbara Kellerman, ed., *Leadership: Essential Selections on Power, Authority, and Influence* (New York: McGraw-Hill, 2010). Carlyle's quote is on p. 57 and Spencer's is on p. 59.
11. Nohria and Khurana, "Advancing Leadership Theory and Practice," p. 8.
12. Nohria and Khurana, "Advancing Leadership Theory and Practice," p. 9.
13. Sonja M. Hunt. "The Role of Leadership in the Construction of Reality," in Barbara Kellerman, ed., *Leadership: Multidisciplinary Perspectives* (New York: Prentice-Hall, 1984), p. 171.
14. For more on transformational and transactional leadership, see James MacGregor Burns's book *Leadership* (New York: Harper & Row, 1978). Burns is also one of the very few leadership scholars to make a connection between biography and leadership theory. He did precisely this, all the way back in the mid-1950s, in volume 1 of his biography of Franklin Delano Roosevelt, *The Lion and the Fox* (New York: Harcourt, Brace, 1956). The book is now available in print and also on Kindle.
15. See, for example, Joseph Nye, *The Powers to Lead* (New York: Oxford University Press, 2008) p. 27ff.
16. Alice Eagly and Linda Carli, *Through the Labyrinth: The Truth about How Women Become Leaders* (Boston: Harvard Business School Press, 2007), p. ix.
17. Deborah L. Rhode, "Introduction: Where Is the Leadership in Moral Leadership," in Rhode, ed., *Moral Leadership: The Theory and Practice of Power, Judgment, and Policy* (San Francisco: Jossey-Bass, 2006), p. 3.
18. Lee Iacocca, *Iacocca: An Autobiography* (New York: Bantam, 1986), and also *Where Have All the Leaders Gone?* (New York: Scribner, 2008); Pat Riley, *The Winner Within: A Life Plan for Team Players* (New York: Berkley, 1994); Rudolph Giuliani, *Leadership* (New York: Hyperion, 2002); Colin Powell, *It Worked for Me: In Life and Leadership* (New York: Harper Perennial, 2014); Stanley McChrystal, *Team of Teams: New Rules of Engagement for a Complex World*

(New York: Portfolio/Penguin, 2015); Robert Gates, *A Passion for Leadership: Lessons on Change and Reform from Fifty Years of Public Service* (New York: Knopf, 2016).

19. Herminia Ibarra, *Act Like a Leader, Think Like a Leader* (Boston: Harvard Business Review Press, 2015), p. 3.

20. Ibarra, *Act Like a Leader*, p. 5.

21. Sydney Finkelstein, *Superbosses: How Exceptional Leaders Master the Flow of Talent* (New York: Portfolio, 2016), p. 3.

22. "History of the Jepson School of Leadership Studies," Jepson School of Leadership Studies, University of Richmond, http://jepson.richmond.edu/about/history/index.html.

23. "Major & Minor: Course of Study," http://jepson.richmond.edu/major-minor/.

24. "Why Study Leadership?," http://jepson.richmond.edu/about/index.html.

25. Scott Snook, Nitin Nohria, and Rakesh Khurana, eds., *The Handbook for Teaching Leadership: Knowing, Doing, and Being* (Thousand Oaks, CA: Sage, 2012).

26. Scott Snook, Nitin Nohria, and Rakesh Khurana, "Teaching Leadership: Advancing the Field," in Snook et al., *Handbook for Teaching Leadership*, p. xiii.

27. The course led to a book on the subject, an anthology that I edited titled *Leadership: Essential Selections on Power, Authority, and Influence* (New York: McGraw-Hill, 2010).

28. Deborah Ancona, "Sensemaking: Framing and Acting in the Unknown," in Snook et al., *Handbook for Teaching Leadership*, p. 4.

29. Michael Useem, "The Leadership Template," in Snook et al., *Handbook for Teaching Leadership*, p. 115.

30. Max Klau, "City Year: Developing Idealistic Leaders through National Service," in Snook et al., *Handbook for Teaching Leadership*, p. 410.

31. Louis Csoka, "Being a Leader: Mental Strength for Leadership," in Snook et al., *Handbook for Teaching Leadership*, p. 226.

32. Manfred F. R Kets de Vries and Konstantin Korotov, "Transformational Leadership Development Programs: Creating Long-Term Sustainable Change," in Snook et al., *Handbook for Teaching Leadership*, p. 263.

33. Susan Komives, Nance Lucas, and Timothy McMahon, *Exploring Leadership: For College Students Who Want to Make a Difference* (San Francisco: Jossey-Bass, 2013).

34. There is a chapter in Snook et al., *Handbook for Teaching Leadership*, about the leadership program at Goldman Sachs. It is by Shoma Chatterjee, Cary Friedman, and Keith Yardley and is titled "Leadership Acceleration at Goldman Sachs," pp. 453–465.

Chapter 5

1. Quoted in Duff McDonald, *The Golden Passport: Harvard Business School, the Limits of Capitalism, and the Moral Failure of the MBA Elite* (New York: HarperCollins, 2017), p. 98.

2. Abraham Flexner, quoted in John T. Samaras, *Management Applications: Exercises, Cases, and Readings* (New York: Prentice-Hall, 1989), p. 12.

3. Mary Parker Follett, "Management as a Profession," reprinted in Samaras, *Management Applications*, p. 18.

4. Rakesh Khurana, Nitin Nohria, and Daniel Penrice, "Management as a Profession," working paper, Center for Public Leadership, Harvard Kennedy School, 2004, p. 4. https://dspace.mit.edu/bitstream/handle/1721.1/55923/CPL_WP_04_01_KhuranaNohriaPenrice.pdf. This was the basis for a working paper that was being prepared for the American Academy of Arts and Sciences on the state of the American professions.

5. Khurana et al., "Management as a Profession," p. 4.

6. Khurana et al., "Management as a Profession," p. 10.

7. Rakesh Khurana and Nitin Nohria, "It's Time to Make Management a True Profession," *Harvard Business Review*, October 2008.

8. Khurana and Nohria, "Time to Make Management," p. 72.

9. Khurana and Nohria, "Time to Make Management," p. 73.

10. Khurana and Nohria, "Time to Make Management," p. 74.

11. Khurana and Nohria, "Time to Make Management," p. 77.

12. "MBA Oath," *Wikipedia*, last edited September 4, 2017, at 06:11, https://en.wikipedia.org/wiki/MBA_Oath.

13. Peter Tyson, "The Hippocratic Oath Today," *Nova*, March 27, 2001, http://www.pbs.org/wgbh/nova/body/hippocratic-oath-today.html. In 1924 just 24 percent of all US medical schools administered the oath; now this number is nearly 100 percent.

14. Lawrence I. Conrad, Michael Neve, Vivian Nutton, Roy Porter, and Andrew Wear, *The Western Medical Tradition: 800 BC to AD 1800* (New York: Cambridge University Press, 1995), p. 385.

15. Lisa Rosner, "The Growth of Medical Education and the Medical Profession," in Irvine Loudon, ed., *Western Medicine* (New York: Oxford University Press, 1997), p. 148. This section also drew on Conrad et al., *Western Medical Tradition*.

16. Rosner, "Growth of Medical Education," p. 149.

17. Conrad et al., *Western Medical Tradition*, p. 384.

18. Rosner, "Growth of Medical Education," p. 152.

19. James Surowieki, "Doctors Orders," *New Yorker*, December 19 and 26, 2016.

20. Andrew Abbott, *The System of Professions: An Essay on the Division of Expert Labor* (Chicago: University of Chicago Press, 1988), p. 21.

21. "About Us," American Medical Association, http://www.ama-assn.org/ama/pub/about-ama.page?.

22. Colin Walsh and Herbert Abelson, "Medical Professionalism: Crossing a Generational Divide," *Perspectives in Biology and Medicine* 51, no. 4 (Autumn 2008), p. 556.

23. Brandon Vaidyanathan, "Professional Socialization in Medicine," *AMA Journal of Ethics*, February 2015, http://journalofethics.ama-assn.org/2015/02/msoc1-1502.html.

24. Melissa Bailey, "Female Professors Are Woefully Outnumbered at Med Schools Nationwide," *STAT*, https://www.statnews.com/2016/01/12/women-medical-school-faculty/.

25. David Hirsh, Barbara Ogur, George Thibault, and Malcolm Cox, "'Continuity' as an Organizing Principle for Clinical Education Reform," *New England Journal of Medicine*, February 22, 2007, p. 858.

26. Hirsh et al., "Continuity," p. 858.

27. Hirsh et al., "Continuity," p. 859.

28. David Hirsh and Paul Worley, "Better Learning, Better Doctors, Better Community: How Transforming Clinical Education Can Help Repair Society," *Medical Education* 47, no. 9 (2013), p. 942.

29. Hirsh et al., "Continuity," p. 864.

30. Alex Stagnaro-Green, "Applying Adult Learning Principles to Medical Education in the United States," *Medical Teacher* 26, no. 1 (2004), p. 79.

31. "10-Year and C-MOC Programs," American Board of Psychiatry and Neurology, Inc., http://www.abpn.com/maintain-certification/maintenance-of-certification-program/moc-programs/.

32. James Brundage, *The Medieval Origins of the Legal Profession: Canonists, Civilians, and Courts* (Chicago: University of Chicago Press, 2008), p. 2.

33. Brundage, *Medieval Origins*, pp. 1, 2.

34. Brundage, *Medieval Origins*, p. 4.

35. Brundage, *Medieval Origins*, p. 282.

36. For reasons I do not understand, when Brundage makes this general point, he does not reference the medical profession or the Hippocratic oath. See *Medieval Origins*, p. 284.

37. Anton-Hermann Chroust, *The Rise of the Legal Profession in America*, vol. 1, *The Colonial Experience* (Norman: University of Oklahoma Press, 1965), p. 17. The discussion in this section is based on Chroust.

38. Chroust, *The Colonial Experience*, p. 1.

39. Chroust, *The Colonial Experience*, p. 54. This paragraph is based on Chroust.

40. Ralph Michael Stein, "The Path of Legal Education from Edward I to Langdell: A History of Insular Reaction," January 1, 1981, Pace University, DigitalCommons@Pace, http://digitalcommons.pace.edu/lawfaculty/228/.

41. Stein, "Path of Legal Education," p. 446.

42. "Curriculum," Harvard Law School, http://hls.harvard.edu/dept/jdadmissions/why-harvard/academics-scholarship/curriculum/.

43. Deborah Rhode and Lucy Buford Rice, "Revisiting MCLE: Is Compulsory Passive Learning Building Better Lawyers?," *Professional Lawyer* 22, no. 2 (2014), http://www.americanbar.org/content/dam/aba/administrative/professional_responsibility/tpl_22__2_2014.auth-checkdam.pdf.

44. "Model Rules of Professional Conduct: Preamble & Scope," American Bar Association," http://www.americanbar.org/groups/professional_responsibility/publications/model_rules_of_professional_conduct/model_rules_of_professional_conduct_preamble_scope.html.

45. Richard Abel, "The Transformation of the American Legal Profession," *Law and Society Review* 20, no. 1 (1986), p. 9, http://www.jstor.org/stable/3053410.

46. Abbott, *System of Professions*, p. 315.

47. "Professionalization," *Wikipedia*, last updated September 8, 2017, at 14:41, https://en.wikipedia.org/wiki/Professionalization.

48. Not the American Management Association, or the Academy of Management, or the International Leadership Association, or any of the other associations of management and leadership can remotely begin to rival either the American Medical Association or the American Bar Association or, for that matter, several other professional associations.

49. Patricia Cohen, "Horse Rub? Where's Your License?," *New York Times*, June 18, 2016.

50. Cohen, "Horse Rub."

Chapter 6

1. See, for example, my book, *The End of Leadership* (New York: HarperCollins, 2012).

2. I first came to recognize that leadership was a system when I wrote a book about bad leadership. Impossible, I learned, to have bad leaders without bad followers. Impossible, I equally learned, to understand either bad leaders or bad followers without situating them in context. See *Bad Leadership: What It Is, How It Happens, Why It Matters* (Boston: Harvard Business School Press, 2004).

3. Robert M. Sapolsky, *Behave: The Biology of Humans at Our Best and Worst* (New York: Penguin, 2017), p. 425.

4. Duff McDonald, *The Golden Passport: Harvard Business School, the Limits of Capitalism, and the Moral Failure of the MBA Elite* (New York: HarperCollins, 2017), p. 382.

5. The phrase "bowling alone" is Robert Putnam's. See his book *Bowling Alone: The Collapse and Revival of American Community* (New York: Simon and Schuster, 2001).

6. Nathan Heller, "The Big Uneasy," *New Yorker*, May 30, 2016.

7. Pierre Gurdjian, Thomas Halbeisen, and Keven Lane, "Why Leadership-Development Programs Fail," *McKinsey Quarterly*, January 2014. Also see Kristi Hedges, "If You Think Leadership Development Is a Waste of Time You May Be Right," *Forbes*, September 23, 2014, http://www.forbes.com/sites/work-in-progress/2014/09/23/if-you-think-leadership-development-is-a-waste-of-time-you-may-be-right/#d3f93175dccc.

8. S. Alexander Haslam and Stephen D. Reicher, "Rethinking the Psychology of Leadership: From Personal Identity to Social Identity," *Daedalus*, Summer 2016, p. 22.

9. Rakesh Khurana, *Searching for a Corporate Savior: The Irrational Quest for the Charismatic CEO* (Princeton, NJ: Princeton University Press, 2002).

10. Khurana in *Searching for a Corporate Savior* argues that the quest for a corporate savior goes back to the early 1980s. I would be remiss not to point out that this overlaps precisely with the rise of the leadership industry.

11. Khurana, *Searching for a Corporate Savior*, p. 67.

12. Gurdjian, Halbeisen, and Lane, "Why Leadership-Development Programs Fail."

13. "Leadership Programs," Aresty Institute of Executive Education, Wharton School, University of Pennsylvania, http://executiveeducation.wharton.upenn.edu/for-individuals/program-topics/leadership.

14. Edwin Hollander, *Leadership Dynamics: A Practical Guide to Effective Relationships* (New York: Free Press, 1978), p. 16.

15. Haslam and Reicher, "Rethinking the Psychology of Leadership," p. 27.

16. Haslam and Reicher, "Rethinking the Psychology of Leadership," p. 22.

17. See, for example, Abraham Zaleznik, "The Dynamics of Subordinacy," *Harvard Business Review*, May–June 1965; Robert Kelley, *The Power of Followership* (New York: Doubleday, 1992); and Ira Chaleff, *The Courageous Follower: Standing Up to and for Our Leaders* (San Francisco: Berrett-Koehler, 2009).

18. For more on these five different types, see Barbara Kellerman, *Followership: How Followers Create Change and Change Leaders* (Boston: Harvard Business Press, 2008).

19. Chaleff, *The Courageous Follower*.

20. Kellerman, *Followership*, p. 257.

21. Chaleff, *The Courageous Follower*, p. 3. Chaleff's more recent book, on a particular aspect of good followership, is *Intelligent Disobedience: Doing Right When What You're Told to Do Is Wrong* (San Francisco: Berrett-Koehler, 2015).

22. Robert D. Blackwill and Philip H. Gordon, *Repairing the U.S.-Israel Relationship*, Council Special Report No. 76, Council on Foreign Relations, November 2016, http://wwwcfr.org/israel/repariing-us-israel-relatioship/p38484.

23. Blackwill and Gordon, *Repairing the U.S.-Israel Relationship*, p. 1.

24. Blackwill and Gordon, *Repairing the U.S.-Israel Relationship*, p. 15.

25. Archie Brown, *The Myth of the Strong Leader: Political Leadership in the Modern Age* (New York: Basic Books, 2014), p. 25.

26. Khurana, *Searching for a Corporate Savior*, pp. 68, 69.

27. Barbara Kellerman, *Hard Times: Leadership in America* (Stanford, CA: Stanford University Press, 2015).

28. Kellerman, *Hard Times*, p. 96.

29. Kellerman, *Hard Times*, p. 185.

30. Kellerman, *Hard Times*, pp. 139–141.

31. William F. Johnston, Robert M. Rodriguez, David Suarez, and Jonathan Fortman, "Study of Medical Students' Malpractice Fear and Defensive Medicine: A 'Hidden Curriculum?,'" *Western Journal of Emergency Medicine* 15, no. 3 (2014), pp. 293–298, http://www.ncbi.nlm.nih.gov/pmc/articles/PMC4025526/.

32. "Legal Malpractice—6212," University of Minnesota Law School, https://www.law.umn.edu/course/6212/legal-malpractice.

33. Kellerman, *Bad Leadership*. See chapter 3 for a summary of the different types, pp. 29–48.

34. Kellerman, *Bad Leadership*.

35. Kellerman, *Bad Leadership*, p. 5.

36. In Barbara Kellerman, ed., *Leadership: Essential Selections on Power, Authority, and Influence* (New York: McGraw-Hill, 2010), p. 21.

37. In Kellerman, *Bad Leadership*, p. 5.

Chapter 7

1. Simon Caulkin, "Have We Created an Unachievable Myth of Leadership?," *Financial Times*, December 6, 2015.

2. The figures relating to the size of the investment in leadership learning vary. These are from Caulkin, "Unachievable Myth of Leadership."

3. Jeffrey Pfeffer, *Leadership BS: Fixing Workplaces and Careers One Truth at a Time* (New York: HarperCollins, 2015), pp. 5, 6.

4. Pfeffer, *Leadership BS*, p. 24.

5. Pierre Gurdjian, Thomas Halbeisen, and Kevin Lane, "Why Leadership-Development Programs Fail," *McKinsey Quarterly*, January 2014, http://www.mckinsey.com/global-themes/leadership/why-leadership-development-programs-fail.

6. Michael Beer, Magnus Finnström, and Derek Schrader, "Why Leadership Training Fails—and What to Do about It," *Harvard Business Review*, October 10, 2016.

7. Sidney Finkelstein, "Why We Loathe Leadership Training," BBC, July 20, 2016, http://www.bbc.com/capital/story/20160719-why-we-loathe-leadership-training; and Deborah

Rowland, "Why Leadership Development Isn't Developing Leaders," *Harvard Business Review*, October 14, 2016.

8. Duff McDonald, *The Golden Passport: Harvard Business School, the Limits of Capitalism, and the Moral Failure of the MBA Elite* (New York: HarperCollins, 2017).

9. Philip Delves Broughton, *What They Teach You at Harvard Business School* (New York: Penguin, 2008), pp. 84, 85.

10. Quoted in Adam Jones, "Harvard Business School's Bricks-and-Clicks Spending Spree," *Financial Times*, July 18, 2016.

11. Dahlia Bazzaz, "Taking a Fast Track to Global Business," *Wall Street Journal*, September 2, 2016.

12. Jonathan Moules, "Europe's Shorter Courses Dent US MBA Applications," *Financial Times*, September 26, 2016.

13. Jonathan Moules, "FT Big Read: Education," *Financial Times*, October 21, 2016.

14. "Sanger Leadership Center," Ross School of Business, University of Michigan, http://michiganross.umich.edu/sanger.

15. Jonathan Moules, "Meet the Dean—Scott DeRue," *FT Business Education*, September 12, 2016.

16. John Raymond, Joseph Kerschner, William Hueston, and Cheryl Maurana, "The Merits and Challenges of Three-Year Medical School Curricula: Time for an Evidence-Based Discussion," *Academic Medicine* 90, no. 10 (2015), pp. 1318–1323, https://www.ncbi.nlm.nih.gov/pmc/articles/PMC4585483/.

17. All the quotes in this paragraph are from Gurdjian, Halbeisen, and Lane, "Why Leadership-Development Programs Fail."

18. J. P. Donlon, "40 Best Companies for Leaders 2012: How Top Companies Excel in Leadership Development," *Chief Executive*, January 12, 2012, http://chiefexecutive.net/40-best-companies-for-leaders-2012-how-top-companies-excel-in-leadership-development.

19. Donlon, "40 Best Companies."

20. Seth Stevenson, "How Do You Make Better Managers?," *Psychology of Management*, June 9, 2014.

21. Maureen Farrell, "A Look at GE's Slim-Down since the Financial Crisis," *Wall Street Journal*, June 9, 2015.

22. Julie Owen, "Assessment and Evaluation," in Susan Komives et al., *The Handbook for Student Leadership Development* (San Francisco: Jossey-Bass, 2011), p. 177.

23. McDonald, *Golden Passport*, p. 429.

24. These steps are based on the assessment literature. For more on assessing leadership programs, see Owen, "Assessment and Evaluation."

25. Andrew Abbott, *The System of Professions: An Essay on the Division of Expert Labor* (Chicago: University of Chicago Press, 1988), p. 82.

26. *ILA 2015 Annual Report*, pp. 2, 3.

27. American Management Association, *International Directory of Company Histories*, 2008.

28. Italics all mine. These and other various Harvard University mission statements are in Barbara Kellerman, *The End of Leadership* (New York: HarperCollins, 2012), p. 156. The mission statement of the Harvard Divinity School has changed slightly since that book went to print. Accordingly, this version has been updated. http://hds.harvard.edu/about/history-and-mission.

29. I am grateful to General Dana Born for making this point explicit.

30. For a book that explores mistakes made by military leaders during the war in Vietnam, see H. R. McMaster, *Dereliction of Duty: Lyndon Johnson, Robert McNamara, the Joint Chiefs of Staff and the Lies That Led to Vietnam* (New York: HarperCollins, 1997).

31. "United States Military Academy," *Wikipedia*, last edited September 4, 2017, at 18:18, https://en.wikipedia.org/wiki/United_States_Military_Academy#Curriculum.

32. Doug Crandall, *Leadership Lessons from West Point* (San Francisco: Jossey-Bass, 2006); and Joseph P. Franklin, *Building Leaders the West Point Way: Ten Principles from the Nation's Most Powerful Leadership Lab* (Nashville, TN: Thomas Nelson, 2007).

33. Mario L. Mangiameli, "How to Apply Marine Leadership Traits to Business," *Task & Purpose*, October 21, 2014, http://taskandpurpose.com/14-marine-leadership-traits-apply-business/.

34. Gallup, "Confidence in Institutions," June 15, 2015 and June 13 2016.

35. Gordon Adams and Shoon Murray, eds., *Mission Creep: The Militarization of US Foreign Policy?* (Washington, DC: Georgetown University Press, 2014), pp. 13, 14.

36. Robert Tanner, "Revisiting Colin Powell's 13 Rules of Leadership," *Management Is a Journey*, last updated January 2, 2017, https://managementisajourney.com/revisiting-colin-powells-13-rules-of-leadership/.

37. See, for example, Dana H. Born, Andrew T. Phillips, and Timothy E. Trainor, "America's Service Academies, Your Service Academies," *Liberal Education* 98, no. 1 (Winter 2012).

38. Rolf Enger, Steven Jones, and Dana H. Born, "Commitment to Liberal Education at the United States Air Force Academy," *Liberal Education* 96, no. 2 (Spring 2010). Italics mine.

39. The quotes in this paragraph are from Enger et al., "Commitment to Liberal Education."

40. The United States Naval Academy Core Learning Outcomes. https://www.usna.edu/Academics/Academic-Dean/Assessment/. Italics mine.

41. "Marine Corps Leadership Principles and Traits," http://www.tcsnc.org/cms/lib010/NC01910389/Centricity/Domain/592/Leadership%20Principles%20and%20Traits.pdf.

42. "U.S. Air Force Academy Center for Character & Leadership Development / SOM," http://www.archdaily.com/789740/us-air-force-academy-center-for-character-and-leadership-development-som.

43. Center for Character and Leadership Development, "Developing Leaders of Character at the United States Air Force Academy: A Conceptual Framework," foreword by Brigadier General Richard Clark, US Air Force Academy, 2011.

44. *The Officer Development System: Developing Officers of Character*, HQ United States Air Force Academy, Pamphlet 36-3527, September 24, 2013.

45. Susan Cain, "Followers Wanted," *New York Times*, March 26, 2007.

46. All quotes in this paragraph are from Bruce E. Keith et al., eds., *Building Capacity to Lead: The West Point System for Leader Development* (West Point, NY: United States Military Academy, 2009). Also see United States Military Academy, "West Point Leader Development System Handbook," which draws on US Army, "ALDS: Army Leader Development Strategy, 2013." Also see "Educating Future Army Officers for a Changing World," which came out of the Office of the Dean of the United States Military Academy in 2007.

47. "United States Army War College," *Wikipedia*, last updated August 6, 2017, at 00:48, https://en.wikipedia.org/wiki/United_States_Army_War_College. Italics mine.

48. 2010 Center for Army Leadership, "Annual Survey of Army Leadership (CASL)," volume 1, Executive Summary, May 2011.

49. All the information in the paragraph and the quotes are in US Army, "ALDS: Army Leader Development Strategy, 2013," with a foreword by, among others, then-army chief of staff General Raymond Odierno.

50. Italics mine. All the information in this paragraph and the quotes are in *Army Leadership* (Washington, DC: Headquarters, Department of the Army, August 2012).

Chapter 8

1. Andrew Abbott, *The System of Professions: An Essay on the Division of Expert Labor* (Chicago: University of Chicago Press, 1988), p. 323.

2. Elena Botehho et al., "What Sets Successful CEOs Apart," is an example of an article that in my view reduces leadership, in this case of chief executive officers, to far too simple an algorithm—in this case to "four specific behaviors that prove critical to their performance." *Harvard Business Review*, May–June 2017.

3. Susan Komives, Nance Lucas, and Timothy McMahon, *Exploring Leadership: For College Students Who Want to Make a Difference* (San Francisco: Jossey-Bass, 2013), p. viii.

4. Todd Pittinsky, "How to Develop Public Leaders," *Kennedy School Bulletin*, Summer 2006, p. 13.

5. Quoted in Thomas Friedman, *Thank You for Being Late: An Optimist's Guide to Thriving in the Age of Accelerations* (New York: Farrar, Straus, and Giroux, 2016), p. 189.

6. For more on the impact of country and culture on leadership, see my book *Hard Times: Leadership in America* (Stanford, CA: Stanford University Press, 2014).

7. Myatt is a leadership coach and consultant. Mike Myatt, "A Leadership Job Description," *Forbes*, September 5, 2012, at 13:29, http://www.forbes.com/sites/mikemyatt/2012/09/05/a-leadership-job-description/#1ee047687e33.

8. "What Is Servant Leadership?," Robert R. Greenleaf Center for Servant Leadership, https://www.greenleaf.org/what-is-servant-leadership/.

9. James MacGregor Burns, *Leadership* (New York: Harper & Row, 1978), p. 20.

10. Haig Patapan, "Magnanimous Leadership: Edmund Barton and the Australian Founding," *Leadership and the Humanities* 4, no 1 (2016), pp. 1, 2.

11. Yale University School of Medicine Policy, "Medical Student Professionalism," https://medicine.yale.edu/education/ppgg/Professionalism%20Policy-Feb2016_281932_284_5.pdf.

12. Friedman, *Thank You for Being Late*, p. 388.

13. Anne-Marie Slaughter, "How to Succeed in the Networked World," *Foreign Affairs*, November–December 2016, p. 89. Also, for more on the sea change in leader-follower relations in consequence of the changes in culture and technology, see my book *The End of Leadership* (New York: HarperCollins, 2012).

14. Danielle Allen, *Education and Equality* (Chicago: University of Chicago Press, 2016), p. 28.

15. Abbott, *System of Professions*, p. 52.

16. Michael Beer, Magnus Finnström, and Derek Schrader, "Why Leadership Training Fails—and What to Do about It," *Harvard Business Review*, October 10, 2016.

17. Sean Silverthorne, "What Great American Leaders Teach Us," *Working Knowledge*, April 12, 2004, http://hbswk.hbs.edu/item/what-great-american-leaders-teach-us.

18. US Army, "ALDS: Army Leader Development Strategy, 2013," p. 11.

19. Susan Ambrose, Michael Bridges, Michele DiPietro, Marsha Lovett, and Marie Norman, *How Learning Works: Seven Research-Based Principles for Smart Teaching* (San Francisco: Jossey-Bass, 2010), p. 99.

20. Robert Kegan and Lisa Laskow Lahey, *An Everyone Culture: Becoming a Deliberately Developmental Organization* (Boston: Harvard Business School Press, 2016), p. 5.

21. Kegan and Lahey, *An Everyone Culture*, p. 281.

22. Bill George, "Authentic Leadership Development' for Executives," September 13, 2010, http://www.billgeorge.org/page/authentic-leadership-development-for-executives.

23. Jeffrey Anderson and Stacey Kole, "Leadership Effectiveness and Development: Building Self-Awareness and Insight Skills," in Scott Snook, Nitin Nohria, and Rakesh Khurana, eds., *The Handbook for Teaching Leadership: Knowing, Doing, Being* (Thousand Oaks, CA: Sage, 2012), pp. 182, 184.

INDEX